The Communist Party
in Power

About the Book

Karel Kaplan spent eighteen years of his professional life in the Communist Party of Czechoslovakia, in which he held positions at all echelons of the party hierarchy. His extensive experience and his access to the party's official archives form the basis for this unique account of the internal life and functioning of the Communist party.

Although the CPCz has broken from Moscow's direct influence, Kaplan's description of party structure and function resemble those found in other parties under Communist rule. All are based on a monopoly of power, have a common social role and similar internal organization, and draw upon Soviet and Leninist principles of party construction.

Focusing upon the actual working structure that exists behind the party's formal facade, Kaplan maintains that the party is able to function as the backbone of the power monopoly in Communist societies because all of its members are bound to it by ideological, power, social, and existential ties. These ties may vary in substance and effectiveness, but they operate at all levels and in all domains of the party organization. His insider's account of how power is brokered and maintained lends a unique perspective to our understanding of the party in Communist society today.

The Communist Party in Power

A Profile of Party Politics in Czechoslovakia

Karel Kaplan

Edited and translated by
Fred Eidlin

Westview Press / Boulder and London

Westview Special Studies on the Soviet Union and Eastern Europe

This Westview softcover edition is printed on acid-free paper and bound in softcovers that carry
the highest rating of the National Association of State Textbook Administrators, in consultation with
the Association of American Publishers and the Book Manufacturers' Institute.

Published in 1987 in the United States of America by Westview Press, Inc.; Frederick A. Praeger,
Publisher; 5500 Central Avenue, Boulder, Colorado 80301

Library of Congress Cataloging-in-Publication Data
Kaplan, Karel.
  The Communist Party in power.
  (Westview special studies on the Soviet Union and Eastern Europe)
  1. Komunistická strana Československa. I. Title.
JN2229.A5K298 1987   324.2437′075   85-11414
ISBN 0-86531-823-9

Composition for this book was created by conversion of the author's word-processor disks.

Printed and bound in the United States of America

∞   The paper used in this publication meets the requirements of the American National
     Standard for Permanence of Paper for Printed Library Materials Z39.48-1984.

6   5   4   3   2   1

Contents

Tables and Figures

Preface

The aim of this book is simple. It seeks to describe the main features of the internal life and functioning of a communist party. It reflects both the results of a historian's research and the long years of experience of a communist official and party apparatchik.

In studying the postwar history of my country I could hardly avoid paying attention to internal party matters, for which the archives of the Central Committee of the Communist party of Czechoslovakia provided extensive information. I also spent eighteen years working at all levels of the communist party organization—district, regional, and central. Over a period of twenty years I held numerous party functions, from basic organizations through the district level up to membership in the Central Control and Revision Commission of the Communist party of Czechoslovakia.

Although this book deals specifically with the communist party in Czechoslovakia, its internal life and the mechanisms by which it operates are similar in many ways to those of all ruling parties, since they are parties enjoying a monopoly of power. Their common social role and similar internal machinery, organization, and methods of operation all derive from this. They also have a certain ideological dimension in common—i.e., the application of Soviet experience, generally called Leninist principles of party construction or principles of parties of the Leninist type. Regardless of the fact that several communist parties have broken with Moscow, they have held on to these principles. Differences in the methods of operation of communist parties of the Soviet bloc are thus inconsequential.

The Communist party of Czechoslovakia was founded in 1921 and, until 1939, operated quite legally within the democratic system of the Czechoslovak Republic. It was one of the strongest political parties in parliament (representing around 10 percent of the voters) and maintained a substantial membership (around 70,000). Its influence grew substantially after the Second World War, and prior to February 1948, when it established its monopoly of power, it had over 1.25 million members and was the strongest political party in the country.

Soon after its seizure of power it adapted its organization and work methods to its new mission—to be the backbone of a power monopoly, to be above all a party of power. This change stemmed directly from the party's changed mission. While it was engaged in a power struggle with other parties, the communist party had to respect certain democratic principles in its internal life. It had to tolerate differences of opinion among members and low-level functionaries, to take into account their interests and demands. Otherwise, the party organization would not have been an effective weapon in the struggle for power. In the power monopoly the party functions primarily and most importantly as an instrument for imposing the designs and will of its leadership and ruling circles. It has thus been transformed into an organization that is tightly organized and unconditionally subordinated to the power-center, that is, into a true Leninist-type party.

A Leninist-type party has existed in Czechoslovakia since February 1948. Not until 1968–1969 had the party's internal structures evolved enough to represent a new model of a communist party. This model grew out of a new conception of the party's role in society and figured among the most important ideals of the Prague Spring of 1968. Once the Prague Spring had been crushed, the party reverted to old models, even using methods of work that had been used just after its seizure of power twenty years before.

After 1948 the party constituted itself as a power colossus, as an entity capable of taking care of itself, of living in society autonomously, self-sufficiently, and also in isolation. Gradually, it created rules for its own life, for its daily routine, and principles of internal structure. It created mechanisms for internal operations and decision making and has refined and consolidated them, especially since the second half of the 1950s. It has transformed them into an operational model of internal party life that generations of party officials pass on, mostly unthinkingly. They are presented and accepted as tried and tested principles of a party of the Leninist type. They have even become the subject of so-called scientific studies of the party, which are taught as a theoretical subject in all party educational institutions. The models, as well as party life itself, are internally contradictory. Party rules and party resolutions proclaim one thing while the activities of party organs and their apparats are conducted quite differently.

From a formal point of view, the communist party, like any organization or association, is an aggregate of members, organizations, and organs. There are basic organizations in factories, communities, cities, and all institutions, district and regional organizations, a territorial organization in Slovakia, and central organs. This is what party rules provide for. In internal organization it can be said that a system of tens prevails. The proportion of party members to the total population stands in a relationship of 1:10. In the regional apparat there is an average of one apparatchik for ten basic organizations, ten districts make up a region, and the state is divided into ten regions. This system of tens did not emerge by coincidence but resulted from many years of experience, suggesting that units of ten are most suitable for effective management, political control, and supervision.

Behind this formal facade is the real structure of the party—quite a different one. This real structure results from its power mission, from its exercise of absolute power over society, from its efforts to resolve all social problems and direct every movement in society by means of its resolutions and instructions. As the backbone of the power monopoly the communist party is an aggregate of members, elected organs, aktivs, and apparats that, depending on their influence, can be broken down into institutions without power and the holders and wielders of power. The wielders of power are the system of power groups, the party apparat, and the aktiv. The party organism functions as the backbone of the power monopoly, mainly because the members of all its institutions are bound by ideological, power, social, or existential ties to the party. The tie operates at all levels and in all areas of the party organization. However, its substance and effectiveness vary. Our examination will deal with the latter, that is, with the real structure of the communist party.

Karel Kaplan

Introduction

Fred Eidlin

When Karel Kaplan casually mentioned this book to me over coffee early in 1982, he was quite modest about its significance. All he had tried to do in the book, he said, was explain how a communist regime really works, and he thought the fruits of his efforts might be of some interest to a handful of specialists. As he talked, I began to realize what a gold mine his book must be—and not just for a handful of specialists or for those with a special interest in Czechoslovakia, but for everyone interested in understanding that peculiar genre of political regime that took shape in the Soviet Union between the World Wars and was transplanted to several other countries in the aftermath of World War II.

Kaplan's qualifications to write such a book are unique and impressive. Although others, including other former insiders, have written about the inner workings of Soviet-type regimes, few if any can match Kaplan's remarkable background of participant observation, access to privileged sources, and training. Kaplan experienced the Czechoslovak communist regime in several different capacities—as worker, party functionary, historian, and political prisoner. As a party functionary for eighteen years, he held positions at all levels of the communist party from basic organization on up to the Central Committee apparat. In addition to what he learned from personal experience, he is also an experienced historian who has conducted extensive research into party history in many different archives. Particularly noteworthy are the three years he spent as head of the commission charged with preparing for the rehabilitation of communists persecuted during the Stalin era—a task that gave him access to the party's secret archives and unprecedented insight into the internal workings of the regime. He also managed to take with him into emigration thousands of microfilmed documents from these secret archives and has written several books based in part on these documents, which deal with the party's seizure and consolidation of power and the trials.

By his own description a former convinced Stalinist, Kaplan's faith, like that of many other communist "true believers," was shaken by the revelations of the Twentieth Congress of the CPSU (1956). Exposure of the crimes of the Stalin era, research in the party's secret archives, and the continuing clash of his ideals with his experience of the reality of the regime all contributed to the collapse of his faith. He had joined the party as "a worker inspired by ideals of social justice and humanism, convinced that the communist party had the will and the capability to realize them." It was those same ideals that led him to oppose the regime this party had instituted and that help explain his commitment to find out and make public the truth about what had happened and how.

The Communist Party in Power is thus the work of a historian writing with professional detachment and impressive analytical skill about a system he knows intimately, based on his remarkable access to information through both personal experience and years of archival research. He explains the workings of a communist party regime in a simple yet penetrating way, in terms of ordinary human motivations and readily understandable organizational structures.

Although the book deals in particular with the communist regime in Czechoslovakia, its author sees all communist regimes as basically similar, and thus considers the insights contained in his book generalizable to all such regimes. Ruling communist parties, in his view, all play a similar role in society and have similar institutional machinery and methods of operation due to their common Leninist principles and monopoly of power. Even communist parties that have broken with Moscow hold to these principles, he contends, making differences in their methods of operation insignificant. Moreover, Kaplan also insists that the essential features of communist regimes have not changed fundamentally over time. He thus sees the institutional-ideological framework of the Czechoslovak regime as essentially unaltered since the establishment of the party's power monopoly in 1948.

This perspective is both a strength and a weakness of *The Communist Party in Power*. On the one hand, Kaplan has his finger on something very real and important, namely, the crucial role in politics and society of the institutional structures and ideological culture shared by all communist regimes. To be sure, advocates of the totalitarian model long ago stressed such an essential similarity. Yet totalitarianism has been substantially discredited as a framework of analysis, and attention tends nowadays to focus on the changes that have been taking place in communist regimes since Stalin rather than on elements of continuity. Moreover, differences among communist regimes have become so obvious over time that it has become increasingly difficult to make a case for their fundamental similarity. Still, it cannot be denied that there are significant constants running through communist regimes. Kaplan's book makes a significant contribution in describing and analyzing these constants in a manner that is more or less consistent with what is now known about Soviet-type regimes and that is free of the obfuscating teleological strains of the totalitarian perspective.

Kaplan advisedly employs the term "power monopoly" to characterize such regimes in which all lines of authority run through the power group and each level of the power group hierarchy effectively dominates its own apparat and the power groups and apparats below it. The power groups control all the instruments of power as well as all the organizations of civil society and can meddle in any aspect of politics and society whenever they choose to do so.

Yet power monopoly though the regime may be, the picture Kaplan presents of it is sharply at variance with the familiar image of totalitarianism. This is not a regime controlled by an omniscient, omnipotent elite single-mindedly united in pursuit of clearly defined goals. Rather it is one in which the ruling elite is ridden with conflicts and personal rivalries, continually faced with apathy and hostility among the rank and file membership of the party. It is a power monopoly in which top decision-making bodies are unable to obtain accurate information from subordinate bodies, unable to digest the flood of materials that form the basis of their decisions, and unable even to keep track of the execution of their own decisions.

Despite the richness of Kaplan's analysis, however, I think he is overly pessimistic and underestimates possibilities for fundamental change within the confines of the institutional-ideological framework described in his book. He believes the internal life and routines of the party are too conservative, too deeply rooted, and too accommodating to the power group for there to be any change. He is even skeptical about the possibility that a new generation of communists will "revolutionize the party." New members have to prove themselves by defending and carrying out party policy, he writes, meaning that even when new blood enters the party, it "flows in old veins, and it flows in them obediently." Although the book is full of information and insight relevant to the factors driving change in communist regimes, Kaplan seems, on balance, to deny that the communist party's power monopoly might gradually erode. Although he explicitly recognizes that the party's structures had, by 1968, evolved enough to represent "a new model of the communist party," readers may wonder how this ever happened. Kaplan simply does not marshal his own evidence to inquire into the dynamics of change in communist regimes. He seems rather to attribute to them an almost supernatural capacity of being able to preserve forever their power-monopolistic essence.

This perspective is no doubt due in part to Kaplan's lack of familiarity with regimes other than the Czechoslovak—either communist or liberal democratic. This is a lacuna to which he freely admits. When I suggested to him, for example, that there seemed to be a great deal of similarity between his descriptions of political practice within the framework of the power monopoly and the politics with which we are familiar in liberal democracies, he allowed that this might be so, but said he couldn't judge because he wasn't well-acquainted with political practice in the West. When I asked whether recent reforms in Hungary might not amount to an abandonment of the party's power monopoly despite persistence of the institutional and ideological forms described in his book, he admitted the possibility, but said he didn't know enough about the current state of affairs in Hungary to make such a judgment.

In generalizing from his experience in Czechoslovakia and in the absence of any comparative analysis, Kaplan fails to give proper weight to the peculiarity of the circumstances accounting for the exaggerated, atypical rigidity of that country's ideological-institutional structures. Stalinism ran a particularly severe course in Czechoslovakia because of a combination of factors, including, among other things, the popularity, mass character, and deeply rooted democratic traditions of the Communist party of Czechoslovakia and the foreignness of Stalinism to the Czechoslovak political culture. The magnitude of what had to be done to Stalinize, the strength of the organizational weapon available to the Stalinizers, and the foreignness of the resulting regime to Czechoslovak political traditions—a foreignness even to the political traditions of the communist party itself—all were factors that help explain why the Czechoslovak regime long remained among the most rigidly orthodox Stalinist regime in the Soviet bloc—one that long resisted de-Stalinization and reform, even under pressure from the Soviet Union.

When pressures had, by the early 1960s, built up to the point where reform could no longer be put off, the rigid orthodoxy of the system described so nicely by Kaplan systematically stymied implementation of urgently needed reforms. Because Stalinism was such an artificial, forced set of practices in the Czechoslovak context, there was no comfortable middle ground between rigid adherence to practices established under Stalin and outright abandonment of that system of practices. This persistent dilemma and the paralysis of policy resulting from it served to compound the anger and frustration widely felt toward the regime throughout the population and the communist party itself. It also helps explain the sudden collapse of Stalinist orthodoxy in 1968. Because the sudden political decompression that came with the Prague Spring turned out to be unacceptable to the Soviet leadership of that time, and because no intermediate fallback arrangement turned out to be workable, the only available option for postintervention Czechoslovakia seems to have been regression to old, familiar, stereotyped patterns reinforced from the outside.

Thus, although Kaplan may be right about the continuity of the ideological and institutional structures of the Czechoslovak regime, I would not stress their continuity as much as he does. I would rather stress their under-the-surface degeneration in the short period of fifteen years between Stalin's death and the Prague Spring and their unnatural reimposition due to external factors after the 1968 intervention.

In offering this criticism I should make clear that many specialists in Soviet-type regimes will disagree with me and find Kaplan's frame of analysis entirely congenial. Yet it seems to me important at least to raise some questions about the widely held assumption underlying Kaplan's work that communist regimes are somehow immune to fundamental change. Why should it be assumed that the institutional and ideological formulae underlying such regimes have some permanent, magical capability to prevent their own evolution and mutation? After all, even most liberal democratic regimes have evolved from various forms of absolutism. Liberalism wasn't very democratic until quite recently. The doctrine of popular sovereignty evolved and gradually took root in England alongside the contradictory doctrine of divine right of kings. In fact, most of the rights and privileges nowadays taken for granted by the citizens of liberal democracies—and especially their broad extension to most of the population—resulted from protracted struggles and have not been established all that long.

Furthermore, why should it not be possible for fundamental change to occur without some dramatic overthrow of the "essential" institutional-ideological structures of communist regimes? After all, the Roman Catholic church of today, although certainly fundamentally different from the church of the Inquisition, has preserved enough "essential" institutional and doctrinal features so that it would be possible to argue that it has not changed essentially at all. Why should it not be possible for regimes of the genre described by Kaplan to succeed in shaking off the bonds of Stalinism while remaining Marxist-Leninist in some meaningful sense simply by stressing other aspects of Marx's and Lenin's teachings than those emphasized by Stalinism? During the Prague Spring, for example, communist ideals and institutions were not overthrown; rather, ideals that had long been present in communist tradition simply began to be taken seriously, and institutions began to function more as they were supposed to function, that is, according to straightforward reading of the communist party's own rules.

It has long been well-known that the secretive, overly centralized, overly bureaucratized, overly corrupt system Kaplan describes is highly inefficient, crisis-prone, and poorly adapted to the needs of modern society. Severe criticism of the fundamental ills of the power monopoly system has long ceased to be an exclusive monopoly of regime outsiders. It has been especially interesting to be working on Kaplan's book while a steady stream of fundamental criticism of the ills he describes has been coming from Moscow itself. Rather than being a new phenomenon, *glasnost, perestroika*, and *uskorenie* should be seen as slogans of another chapter in a continuing process of recovery from the devastating shock to society of Stalin's rule. Although the reform movement currently going on in the Soviet Union is certainly not identical to the Prague Spring or the Solidarity movement in Poland, the diagnoses of the ills of the system and the forces driving change are very similar in all these cases.

The principal lesson usually drawn from the Prague Spring is that its forcible suppression constituted "definitive proof of the unreformability of the system and confirmation of its totalitarian character."[1] But this view is too simplistic. The kinds of reform advocated by the Czechoslovak reformists had long been under discussion and were being experimented with and implemented throughout the countries in the Soviet sphere of influence. This process did not stop with the suppression of the Prague Spring, although that certainly had a temporarily dampening effect. The tragedy of Czechoslovakia was that the time was not quite ripe. The pace of change was too quick for the allies, but, unfortunately, having been so long repressed by Novotnýite orthodoxy, it probably couldn't have been slowed down. It was precisely because the program of the Czechoslovak reformists found such resonance in Poland, East Germany, and the Soviet Union itself that the conservative leaderships in ascendancy in those countries at that time felt so threatened. Yet the military intervention in Czechoslovakia changed few minds about the need for reform; it only led some to abandon hope about the very possibility of reform and others to wait and rethink their strategies.

Those who believe that communist regimes cannot possibly reform themselves usually argue that no matter how much reforms are discussed and attempted, they cannot be carried through because consistent implementation would undermine the very foundations of the regime, and this the ruling elite will never allow. The ruling elite, it is insisted, cushioned anyway from the hardships of everyday life, cares only for preservation of its special privileges and monopoly of power, regards a permanent state of disaster normal, and remains indifferent to it. As Robert Conquest has put it, the Soviet Union (and presumably Soviet-type regimes in general) is "a society continually under martial law, a siege polity, a permanent emergency dictatorship."[2] Sometimes, appeal is even made to the whole of Russian history to support the thesis that the Soviet system is unreformable. Russian history is full of terrible rulers and full of futile attempts at reform.

Although there is, historically, a large measure of truth in such a view, no one has, to my knowledge, offered much argument that would justify such extrapolation from the past into the indefinite future. It is certainly not obvious why Soviet-type regimes should continue in perpetuity systematically to favor party hacks over competent, educated individuals interested in doing public good and to defend policies and institutions that do not work well. Nor is it obvious why some combination of experience, changes in the character of society and ruling elites, and perhaps skillful leadership might not eventually bring the Soviet Union and its associated states out of their protracted times of trouble.

"It is safe to assert," said Abraham Lincoln, "that no government proper ever had a provision in its organic law for its own termination."[3] Regime maintenance and the maintenance of order are fundamental problems for any regime, and, as Milan Šimečka has put it, "There are no greater partisans of order than victorious revolutionaries."[4] Yet, although there may be unanimity among communist ruling elites about the importance of maintaining the party's hold on power, we ought to realize by now that members of these ruling elites can disagree fundamentally as to what constitutes order, what constitutes preservation of the regime, and how such ends can best be realized. Among the major factors driving the current reforms in the Soviet Union is precisely the serious erosion of authority, due, at least in part, to efforts to preserve the kind of orthodoxy Kaplan describes. Clinging to orthodoxy may be a strategy that can, under some circumstances, secure the elite's power position; yet, if maintained at the expense of addressing urgent problems facing society, such a policy may court disaster for the regime and its ruling elites in the slightly longer run.

Thus, although some members of the ruling elite may oppose fundamental reforms as subversive of the fundamental order of the regime, others may see just the opposite threat, namely, that it is opposition to fundamental reform that poses the greatest threat to order and the very survival of the regime.

1

Institutions Without Power

Members

The Communist party of Czechoslovakia (CPCz) has about 1.5 million members, and they can be categorized according to their reasons for joining the party. Participants in the struggle to establish the monopoly of power are still heavily represented. They joined believing in the rightness of party policy. This mass, once a million strong, has become differentiated over time. Some, thanks to the party, attained advantageous positions of power and prestige and became firm supporters. Others later became disenchanted and either quit or were expelled. Still others lost their earlier enthusiasm, remaining members while lapsing into a total passivity accentuated by their old age. The second category consists of members who joined under pressure and out of fear, or for careerist reasons, only after communist rule had been established. In this period only a small proportion joined out of political conviction. The third category consists of those who became communists after the Soviet occupation of Czechoslovakia in August 1968. The communist leadership at that time sought to make up for the loss of the half million expelled members and functionaries by bringing in new workers, mainly young ones. Most of these are motivated by the privileges they see as associated with party membership rather than by political conviction.

A member's situation in the party is determined by the party's role as backbone of a power monopoly. He has to defend and implement policies that he had no part whatsoever in formulating. He is little more than an instrument, implementing the will of the party leadership. He cannot even express his opinions about party policies, since these are presented to him as instructions intended only to be carried out. Binding party resolutions and instructions also contribute to establishing limits to the political thinking and behavior of communists.

Most members either do not fulfill even their basic party obligations or do so lackadaisically and purely as a matter of form. They remain

9

passive or limit their activities to occasional attendance at party meetings and fulfillment of a few other basic obligations, such as subscription to the party press and participation in party training. Sometimes local and district functionaries attempt to get rid of passive members, whom they regard as ballast that drags them down. They want a party of action, a party of true, faithful, and obedient wielders of power, a party of functionaries—small, but ideologically firm. Their demands encounter resistance from higher-level party institutions, which intentionally maintain the mass character of the party. In this way they are able to bind a tenth of the whole population and a quarter of the adult population to the communist leadership by various organizational and ideological ties and to subordinate them to its influence. It makes possible the existence of a network of party organizations extensive enough for the leadership to be able to impress its will into all the pores of society and for there to be a party organization or a sufficient number of communists in every factory, workshop, office, school, and university secretariat. It also serves as a permanent reservoir of functionaries and an entity capable of living a life of its own, as well as being a substantial source of income for the party.

Most members react to their powerlessness by passivity. This is the way they express distaste for carrying out policies in which they do not believe. They also know that they can play no role in policy formation or even influence policy in their own situations. Yet they do not want to break with the party or are afraid to. Most communists thus live at odds with themselves. They behave one way at party meetings and at work, where they mechanically voice agreement with party policy, and quite another way among family, friends, and colleagues, with whom they do not want to talk about politics at all. Only a few give vent to their convictions and express their criticisms of party policy among those close to them.

The reasons for their reluctance to get out of the party are similar those for joining. Most common is the fact that party membership gives a certain protection from the political persecution to which the majority of citizens are exposed. Members of the intelligentsia view membership as a kind of professional obligation and fear the social consequences of leaving the party. For some, membership offers or facilitates the way to a career. Only a small part of this passive membership is bound to the party by ideas and the inertia of long years of membership. Nevertheless, despite the costs involved, tens of thousands of members break with the party, thus giving public expression to their dissatisfaction with party policies and practices.

The proportion of passive members is difficult to determine accurately because it depends on the criteria used. If we use regular participation in meetings as the criterion, 40–50 percent are passive. If the criterion is that someone, although present at meetings, avoids party life and holds no position entrusted to him by the party, the proportion rises to at least two-thirds. But of those who have had to accept functions in the factory or community, a majority does not exercise them. Thus, around 25–30 percent of party members are active communists. Of course, only part of them participate in the exercise of power or in the realization of party policies in public.

There is another aspect of the passivity of a large part of the membership that is unpleasant for the party leadership. It blurs the boundary between the politically conscious communists and those outside the party. It weakens the ideological resistance of the politically conscious and makes it possible for the views of outsiders to seep into the ranks of the party. This problem constantly disturbs the ideological stability and monolithic character of the party for which the leadership strives so much. This state of affairs becomes very dangerous in times of internal party crisis, when (in Czechoslovakia in 1956, 1963, and mainly in 1968) the passive members are set in motion. Their repressed opinions and pent-up dissatisfaction burst out and are vented at the party leadership.

The communist leadership keeps watch over the development of the membership base, especially its social structure. On the basis of resolutions from the center, the district and regional organizations deal with these matters every month, the center at least twice a year. They pay special attention to the proportion of workers and farmers in the party. This is partly attributable to ideological motives, i.e., awareness that a party proclaiming itself to be the vanguard of the working class has to demonstrate this, at least by having a preponderance of workers in its ranks.

There are, however, power motives at work too. The communist leadership strives to maintain its influence among workers and to keep them as an important social support for its power. The top leadership of the party labors under a cultivated self-deception that the highest proportion of supporters of its policies is to be found among the workers. For these reasons workers enjoy a privileged position within the party. Many of the party offenses they commit are regarded more mildly. They can get away with more criticism and can criticize more audaciously than others. Furthermore, their opinions are considered to be the most important in determinations of the reactions of communists to various measures.

As soon as the proportion of workers in the party falls below a certain level—usually one-third—an alarm goes off at central headquarters, and an organized membership campaign is launched. The numbers of workers to be recruited is established for the regions, which then distribute these quotas among the districts, which in turn assign them to the organizations where the actual recruitment plans are prepared. In factories workers are sought out and persuaded to join the party. Promises of advantages as well as threats are held out to them.[1] Despite all efforts it has not been possible to put a stop to the decline in the number of worker-communists, let alone to significantly raise their numbers.[2] Thus the basis for party membership has changed conclusively from political conviction to the party's status as a social institution.

This constant decrease of worker-members was a natural consequence of the party's becoming the backbone of a power monopoly. It became a party of power wielders and overseers of society. This process began immediately after the establishment of communist power and was completed during the years 1968–1970. During this period the absolute numbers of worker-members also declined, from 47 percent in 1947 to 32.9 percent in 1966. On January 1, 1970, they made up only 26.1 percent (431,000). Then, while the absolute number continued to decline, the relative decline in participation slowed due to massive expulsions of nonworker members. The proportion of workers leveled off at 25–26 percent, i.e., about one-fifth the total number of workers in the country. Such numbers of worker-communists suffice to constitute "a class ornament or facade" for the party and a base for the selection of functionaries for the party, state, and economic apparats—a solid foundation for the party's power. This mass of worker-communists also serves to break the unity of opinion among the workers.

The true significance of working-class party members is completely different from what the communist leadership understands it to be. Workers represent the largest group of members and functionaries who are socially independent of party organs. Party organs neither determine what their employment is to be nor approve their appointments to positions. This makes it possible for workers to criticize the policies of the party without much risk. This accentuates the fact that it is workers' demands alone that can compel the respect of the leadership, and their political activity evokes the greatest fears within the power elite.

The changes that have been taking place in party membership since the establishment of communist rule affect both the party's internal profile and its internal relations. More and more of those who join and control the party see membership as a job requirement; as a necessary prerequisite for their careers or improved social status; as a source of privilege or as the only possibility for their social and political fulfillment. In the final analysis most workers who join do so to obtain various advantages. The party leadership accepts this state of affairs, knowing that such social and existential bonds are the most solid and that they are an especially strong source of unconditional allegiance. However, the situation also has its drawbacks. It undermines the determination, even of functionaries, to defend and enforce unpopular party policy—a problem that becomes especially apparent in the party's difficult moments.

Significant changes have taken place in the relationship of members to the party leadership. Although elements of mistrust have been increasing on both sides, it is much more pronounced on the part of the members. They receive every significant decision of the leadership already doubting its rightness or not believing that it can be realized. Thus, at party meetings, remarks expressing the annoyance of members are not infrequently heard: "We've already heard that." "You tell us that all the time," and the like. Perhaps the following example most typically illustrates this change in the relationship of the membership to the leadership. At the beginning of the fifties, communists still used the expression, "our leading comrades, our leadership"; just ten years later, only "those up there at the top." The party leadership and its apparat have to use considerable force—compared to earlier days—to convince the party's own members and lower-level functionaries of the rightness of party policy.

Furthermore, the ideological stability that characterized the party during its struggle for monopoly of power and in the early days following the establishment of this power monopoly no longer exists. The everyday bitter experience of members with the regime has resulted in a shrinkage of the once-numerous group of sincere party fanatics who acted out of enthusiasm and belief in ideals, to no more than a handful of functionaries. Historical experiences have been accumulating in the consciousness of communists—for example, revelation of the crimes of Stalin, partial criticism of the party's own policies, and denunciation of former leading comrades suddenly abandoned for advocating political principles that had only recently been extolled—and act as a warning sign and permanent source of lack of confidence. Such gaps in the party's ideological stability have, over time, taken on a magnitude that ideological education and campaigns can only partly remedy, perhaps temporarily improve, but in no way eliminate.

The Supreme Authorities— Democratic Facade

Party rules proclaim that the annual members' meetings, the biannual district and regional conferences, and the party congress (which takes

place every five years) are the party's highest authorities and that the
party's policies are established within their respective spheres of authority. In reality the members' meetings are purely ceremonial, and
the conferences are merely more ceremonial, more formal, larger, and
lengthier gatherings of district and regional functionaries, most of whom
know each other from a host of similar meetings. Participants do not
make decisions about anything. They merely listen, deliver reports
about activities, and approve resolutions placed before them by the
bureau of the basic organization or the presidium of the district or
regional organization.

Meetings and Conferences

Party institutions view the roles of the annual meetings and biannual
conferences as portrayed by party rules, not as they really are. Some
functionaries even believe that they actually perform the key role they
are supposed to play of maintaining the leading role of the party
(others pretend they do). Great care is devoted to preparing for these
gatherings, a care that many times exceeds their significance. Preparations play out like a ceremony. They are carried out according to
directives and under the supervision of superior party organs. For
each of these events, central headquarters issues directives for the
election of delegates in the form of formulalike resolutions defining
the main tasks upon which the report on activities and the discussion
are to concentrate. The regions and districts receive still further detailed
instructions through internal party channels. These instructions usually
contain a draft of the report on activities delivered by the chairman
at the members' meeting or the leading secretary at the district and
regional conference, and they determine the social composition of the
newly elected committees. In the party organizations, district-level
instructors attend to preparations. Special brigades of political workers
come from the regional and central organizations to prepare the conferences.

The meetings and conferences traditionally break down into three
parts. First, participants listen to two lengthy speeches—a report about
the activities of the committees and a speech given by the leader of
the Central Committee delegation at the conferences or the representative of the district at the annual meetings. The report on the activities
of the basic organizations is prepared by the chairman along with the
instructor and in the districts and regions, by a commission made up
primarily of leading party officials. The report is approved, first by
the presidium, then by the whole district or regional committee. It
contains an enumeration of successes in the main areas of the life of

the locality, the district, or the region; critical remarks directed at lower-level functionaries, and a summary of future tasks. The representative of the central party organization usually reads verbatim the report he has received, in which the successes of party policies to date are brought out and urgent tasks are "introduced."

The second part of the conference is devoted to discussion. Delegates, for the most part, give dull news regarding activities of their organizations that is almost completely ignored by the others. The so-called obligatory discussion, dealing with the assignment of members of the presidia of the regional and district committees, consists of news about the activities of the institutions which they administer. In many of these contributions to the discussion, usually approved by someone, a tone of self-criticism and criticism can be heard. As a rule the criticism deals with lower-level party functionaries or higher-level functionaries in the economic and state apparats. Only rarely is it aimed at higher-level party officials or at the political guidelines of the center and the region. The organizers of the conference take precautions against the possibility that someone might deviate from the rules and criticize the higher authorities or even their own policy line. Requests of "uncertain delegates" to participate in the discussion are postponed so that they are never gotten to, and the discussion ends due to lack of time. An unwritten law of party life requires that no opinion officially considered incorrect or critical of party policy is to go unanswered. So whenever, despite all the careful supervision, such an opinion is expressed, the secretary of the district committee (DC) or regional committee (RC) immediately assigns a functionary to respond to it. Moreover, the leading secretary is supposed to "deal with it firmly" in his concluding speech.

In the third part, the resolutions are approved and the new committees elected. Party institutions strive to make the resolutions concrete and to specify a responsible person and period of realization for each item. Accordingly, drafts are nicely worked out and approved beforehand by the presidium of the DC or RC. Most delegates don't read them at all, and should someone occasionally happen to have comments, they will be completely insignificant. He can let the proposals commission know about them, but no one is interested in the resolutions, which the conference approves formally and unanimously. Only the district or regional apparat analyzes them. (It determines, for example, that the resolutions adopted by the annual meeting dealt 88 percent with internal party matters and only 12 percent with public matters).

Election of the new committees also plays a part in the overall scheme of the conferences and annual meetings. It is governed by the basic principle that appointments to the most important positions (from the point of view of political influence) are approved, even initiated, by the superior organ. The DC presidium does this for the chairmen of the basic organization. In some districts this practice extends to all the members of the bureaus of large and significant organizations. In each case the instructor or the responsible DC secretary expresses an opinion.

Lists of candidates for the district and regional committees are put together according to tried and tested practice. Sections of the party apparat recommend functionaries in their respective areas of responsibility who may be prospects for membership in the committee. DC and RC secretaries prepare lists of those recommended, which they modify with the assistance of the district or regional instructors so that they fit guidelines from the center regarding social composition. The required proportion of workers is achieved with difficulty since most those nominated decline the position. In the end the secretaries are happy to be able to find the prescribed number of workers. The list of nominees goes to the DC or RC presidium, which completes and approves it. The presidium also decides which candidates have to be elected at all costs. Responsibility for this falls to the chairman of the electoral commission—a member of the presidium. The electoral commission of the conference receives the list along with cadre profiles. At the commission's meetings, often attended by a district or regional instructor who follows the process of putting together the lists of candidates, the chairman of the commission makes sure that certain candidates designated by the presidium are elected, and the commission chooses the remaining members from the list placed before it. Only rarely do the conference delegates get someone elected who is not on the list.

The conference votes on each nominee individually and by acclamation. Several attempts to introduce the practice of election by secret ballot have been decisively rejected out of fear that many functionaries, in whose election there is special interest,[3] would not make it.

Evaluation of the conference begins immediately upon adjournment. Each DC and RC presidium reviews its own conference even though, according to party rules, such action does not fall within their competence. This common practice is a reflection of the secondary status of the conference and its subordination to the presidium. Presidium members evaluate the interventions of the delegates, rate their "political correctness," and decide with which delegates to discuss their "mistaken" interventions.

The concluding item is an extensive evaluation by the spokesman of the Central Committee. This is prepared by the responsible department, that is, by the Organizational-Political Department. The evaluation praises the high quality of the conference and represents it as proof of the unity of the party around the Central Committee and as confirmation of the rightness of the party's policies. It makes mention of isolated cases of critical remarks of delegates and declares them to be an expression of insufficient maturity and inadequate understanding of the party's political positions. The party leadership accepts the report with solemnnity and pays close attention to the political evaluation given to it in its subsequent decision making.

The evaluation of a conference also includes statistical data concerning the social composition of the body of delegates. These figures show that worker-delegates—socially independent of the party institutions—make up about a third at the district conferences, and less than 25 percent at the regional conferences, while functionaries constitute 45 percent at the district level, and two thirds at the regional. The proportions of workers did not increase even when "the district committees were given clear instructions, . . . according to which workers were to be given priority in selection." However, workers show no interest in participation in the conferences, which most consider a waste of time.

The Congress

Proclaimed as the party's highest authority, the party congress is actually a big, long, well-prepared, and well-orchestrated pageant, a huge undertaking of self-celebration of the party and its leadership, or the largest and most festive meeting of party functionaries with international participation. Every five years, its production is governed by well-established principles.

First of all, the task of a congress is to demonstrate the unity of the party behind the Central Committee (CC) and absolute confidence in the leadership. Second, no controversial matters are dealt with at a congress. It merely approves matters that have already been decided by the leadership or that would be accomplished even without a congress. Third, nothing is left to chance. Thus, different variants of proposals are not presented and all kinds of incidental matters are subjected to thorough and comprehensive preparation. Fourth, those congresses at which something would be at issue and at which confrontation would occur are not allowed to take place.

Preparations for the congress are directed from beginning to end by the secretaries of the Central Committee. In concrete terms this begins with the meetings where it is decided which questions the congress will deal with. Then various groups and committees of specialists work under the leadership or supervision of the CC secretaries, carrying out analyses, making calculations, and preparing data and draft resolutions. Other groups prepare the report on activities to be delivered at the congress by the general secretary and the speech dealing with economic tasks. Both speeches are approved, first by the secretaries, then by the CC Presidium and the Central Committee itself. Extensive technical and organizational work goes on simultaneously (e.g., CC secretaries even approve the decorations for the hall). In the final phase a scenario is prepared with a schedule for each day of the congress, designating by name those who are going to run it. Even the texts of the introductory remarks are prepared for them.

Each congress is usually preceded by internal party discussion. The CC Presidium transmits to the party membership an enumeration of successes to date and tasks for the future, expressed in numbers and percentages. The nature and scope of these materials are such that few members can say anything at all about them and only a few even bother to read them. Their remarks deal only with local grievances or the activities of institutions immediately superior to them, not at all with party policies. At most they deal with perennial complaints, e.g. about supplies, shortages of spare parts, inadequate living quarters, and the like.

The precongress discussion, which is represented as a manifestation of democracy, takes the form of a massive campaign. Each party organization is required to submit a protocol of the discussion with a compendium of comments. Their total number reaches several thousand, and they are pretty much the same. A whole machine emerges to process them. In the districts the party apparat puts together the first compendium of comments from the basic organizations. Those that concern district institutions are picked out and assigned to be dealt with. Procedures are the same in the regions and in the central organization. No one ever remembers all these submissions after the congress. They live on only as a thick volume with the title, *Results of Precongress Discussion*. The procedure is repeated before the next congress.

Special attention is paid to the preparation of personnel matters relating to the congress. Before the regional conferences, which elect the delegates to the congress, the regional leadership receives instructions for their selection. In them appeals are made to maintain a certain proportion of "comrades from the sphere of production," mainly workers and farmers. Other instructions call for "working with delegates," i.e., calling them together and informing them of the significance of the congress. The delegates as well as the congress divide into regional delegations. Each has its leader, the leading secretary of the

RC, and secretaries. It is only through the head of his delegation that a delegate has the right to make known his views on what is going on at the congress. Only the delegation head is in contact with the working presidium of the congress.

Nominations for membership in the Central Committee, which is elected by the congress, are prepared even more carefully. The selection procedure resembles the corresponding selection procedures preceding the conferences. Every department of the CC Secretariat evaluates the current members of the CC within its own area of responsibility and recommends changes. New nominations are submitted along with substantiating arguments and cadre profiles by the CC Organizational-Political Department, which also receives the prescribed number of proposals from the regions and puts together a preliminary list. This list is modified at a conference of CC heads of department and submitted to the CC secretaries. After modification the list goes to the CC Presidium and from there to the elections commission, whose composition is proposed to the congress by the CC Presidium. More individuals are proposed for membership in the CC than are actually elected. The chairman of the Elections Commission, who is a member of the CC Presidium, is responsible for making sure that those individuals are appointed whose membership in the CC is linked to their positions—for example, members of the next CC Presidium, CC secretaries, the ambassador to the Soviet Union, the representative to COMECON, some ministers (defence and interior). This he is able to accomplish without difficulty.

About 1,200–1,500 regular delegates (one delegate for every 1,000 party members) attend the congress, along with about 800 guests and delegates with advisory status. At the last five congresses 30 percent of the delegates were workers, but 75 percent were workers by original profession. About half of the delegates hold their positions and practice their professions thanks to the party, and 20 percent of them are even paid party functionaries. Half of the delegates are thus totally dependent on party organs for their livelihood and social status. An additional 15 percent of the delegates belong to the intelligentsia and the army—i.e., positions to which appointment requires the approval of party institutions (see Table 1.1).

Still another, no less important division shows up in the congress. Among the delegates there is group of experienced functionaries, "movers," who have long occupied high-level positions. They think of the congress as just another party meeting with somewhat higher attendance and more festivities. The small group that runs the congress comes from their ranks and consists of the members of the CC Presidium, the secretaries, the heads of two CC departments, and the heads of

TABLE 1.1
Social Composition of the Delegates to Party Congresses

Congress	Total	Original profession Worker	Workers	Agric.	Tech.- econ.	In Party and state apparat
XII	1568	67.2%	432	285	224	413
XIII	1477	68.5%	327	184	332	466
XIV	1195	74.5%	382	124	93	352
XV	1213	76.8%	390	163	150	334

the regional delegations. In contrast to their views, most of the delegates consider it an honor to participate in the congress, to be present at this great show, and to be able to exchange greetings with leading comrades. Many even feel that they are taking part in a historic event and behave accordingly in the way they sit, listen to speeches, clap and create and enjoy a festive atmosphere. They agree with everything said and vote for everything put forward. The atmosphere at the congress binds them even more strongly, and most important, it binds them emotionally to the power group.

The greater part of the five-day proceedings is taken up by discussions and speeches by guests. The extent of participation of guests is always considerable, as is shown in Table 1.2. The discussion by the delegates is divided into the mandatory and the assigned. Presentations in the mandatory part are given by members of the CC Presidium, CC secretaries, and secretaries of the regional committees, whose institutions have given them the task of making contributions of a "fundamental character" to the discussion. The assigned discussion consists of those contributions that central headquarters requests from the regions or from high officials of central institutions (e.g., the Academy of Sciences or mass organizations). Before the congress, each region

TABLE 1.2
Overview of Discussions at Congresses

Congress	Number of Discussants	Number of Guests	Members of Power group	CC secre- taries
10th (1954)	95	44	8	9
11th (1958)	105	63	7	9
12th (1962)	126	75	8	7
13th (1966)	137	82	9	8
14th (1971)	127	75	4	11
15th (1976)	61	18	5	11

receives recommendations as to which problems its delegation should address. The regional secretaries choose a delegate and prepare a discussion contribution with him. Any contribution to the discussion by other delegates is approved by the head of the regional delegation. Thus the number of delegates able to take part in the discussion without prior censorship is minimal—for all practical purposes only guests from the ranks of former CC members. Even for these delegates, however, the CC Presidium can exercise ex post facto censorship. On one occasion the Presidium was upset with the presentation of a CC member. In 1966, the managers of the congress intentionally let Ota Šik speak only as the last speaker, and they omitted from the record the passage of his speech containing proposals for democratization of the life of the party.

Only a negligible part of the delegates reads the draft documents prepared for the congress. More of them familiarize themselves with those parts relating to their own responsibilities, and it is these delegates who are the source of most of the remarks made in the discussion. Their remarks do not, however, conflict with the draft texts. The drafting commission accepts only a few of them, informing most authors that their comments will be taken into account in the process of implementing the decision—meaning that no one will remember them. In the end the congress approves the resolution unanimously and demonstratively.

The CC Presidium attributes great importance to the congress documents. Immediately after the congress the party apparat, lower-level party institutions, and the leaderships of central extra-party institutions have to deal with these documents. They have to work through them, formulate work plans based on them, and report on all of this to the competent divisions of the party apparat. Despite all these efforts there is always a danger that the congress will get lost in the problems of everyday life and fall into oblivion. The leadership tries to prevent this by launching extensive propaganda campaigns that constantly repeat the congress resolutions and stress their historical significance. This also happens at party meetings and training courses, in public speeches, and in the mass media. As soon as the leadership again notices that the congress is no longer being talked about, it criticizes its apparat and launches a new campaign in which it stresses the dependence of its own resolutions upon the policy line of the congress and invokes resolutions of the congress at every possible opportunity. Agendas for CC meetings are conceived in a similar spirit. Matters dealt with earlier—e.g., concerning tasks of the party in industry or in agriculture—are brought under a heading of fulfillment of the aims of the congress in the industrial or agricultural sector. Commentaries in the mass media, lectures at meetings, etc., also take on a similar congress slant.

Such revival of the spirit of the congress has several motives. Proclaiming that the congress has established policy for the further development of society, or that the government, parliament, and all institutions consider their main task to be fulfillment of the congress resolution, is supposed to serve as evidence of the leading role of the party. The CC Presidium uses the congress campaign to strengthen its own position, since it presents its own policy line as reflecting congress resolutions. Since the Presidium also determines how those resolutions are interpreted, it can also counter occasional criticisms of its policy under the slogan of maintaining the policy line of the congress. This is how the game is routinely played in the life of the party. Those who know precisely how the congress is put together and are aware of its true role treat congress resolutions as if they were resolutions of the supreme party authority—not only in public, but even among themselves and in private discussions. Of course, this is true only to the extent that the resolutions correspond to the needs and interests of the moment of the party leadership.

Broadly Elected Authorities: Auxiliary Aktiv of the Powerholding Groups

According to party rules the district and regional committees are the supreme authorities between conferences. In the basic organizations this role is performed by the members' meetings. These are supposed to be held once a month as a rule; the district and regional committees are supposed to meet at least once every two months. Regular meetings of the DC and RC committees are maintained without great difficulties; the members' meetings are a different story. Every month a considerable number of organizations are found not to have held members' meetings. The presidium of the district committee has to prepare a monthly report on meeting activities. In addition to statistical data on participation, this report also includes the number of organizations that have not held members' meetings, sometimes even mentioning them by name. The chairmen of these organizations that miss meetings are often summoned to the district secretariat for consultation.

Regularity of meetings is also supposed to be provided for by plans of activities. The idea of having plans of meeting activity emerged immediately after the establishment of communist rule. It then developed into a planning mania, which subsided somewhat at the end of the 1950s and the beginning of the 1960s, but the planning wave reemerged and has persisted. The initiative comes from the center, and plans of meeting activities are worked out by the party organ at each level—the central, the regional, and the district. They contain the dates of meetings, the main points of business to be dealt with, and the names of the functionaries who are going to present reports. The duration of the plans differs—three months, a half or full year, or sometimes even longer.

The central plan serves as a point of departure. The individual departments of the central party apparat put together lists of questions in their respective areas of competence with which the Secretariat, Presidium, or Central Committee should deal. These proposals come together in the Organizational-Political Department, which puts them on the calendar and presents them to the CC secretaries for approval. Once modified the proposals begin to circulate as the draft plan for activities of the central organs, moving step by step toward formal approval by the Secretariat, the Presidium, and finally the Central Committee. Plans are prepared in a similar way in the regions on the basis of the central plan. These plans take over most of the items from the central plan, and the center's Organizational-Political Department looks after the coordination of the regional and central plans. The districts take their cues from the regional plan, copying most of its items, and the region controls the coordination of the district plans with its own.

District functionaries call for plans of activities from the basic organizations, but their efforts meet with little success. Some organizations make no plan at all; most make one that is purely formal in the sense that it in no way guides them; only a few try to take the plan seriously. However, the organizations are required to deal with so many decisions of higher party organs that they couldn't possibly follow their own plans. Nevertheless, the district continually calls for plans.

Members' Meeting

Neither the members nor the bureau of the party organization see the need for members' meetings, since they know that nothing is decided at them. They are held mainly because the district committee, party rules, or the plan of work requires it. Most members regard participation in the meetings as a membership obligation or habit. Functionaries also see it as a job-related responsibility and an integral component of their profession. The agenda for a members' meeting is prepared by the organization's bureau, usually in consultation with the district instructor. The matters dealt with consist of those imposed "from above" and domestic matters. Those imposed from above predominate and are gladly adopted by the members of the bureau, who are thus spared the worries of preparing the meeting since "the official from the district" fills up the program. Domestic matters differ in character. In factories they deal primarily with fulfillment of the plan; in villages with the work of agricultural organizations. Apart from these matters, a great deal of time in the members' meetings of all organizations is taken up by internal party problems (training, admission of members, press subscriptions, etc.).

Only part of the membership participates regularly in members' meetings—a kind of solid core consisting of bureau members and some local functionaries—but some additional members also attend. Relatively few of "these additionals" work in productive organizations; on the contrary, a large number work in bureaucratic or educational institutions. (In 1971, more than 400,000 communists did not take part in even a single meeting.) Since the district keeps track of participation in meetings, the bureaus of the organizations exaggerate the numbers in their reports on participation. Even according to these figures, participation varies between 50–60 percent of the party membership.

Analysis of the time spent at several hundred members' meetings during the sixties shows that 23 percent of the time was taken up by waiting for meetings to begin, 48 percent with speeches and information, only 17 percent with discussion, and 12 percent with the conclusions of representatives from the higher-level party organs. The speeches and information deal mainly with uninteresting news and resolutions, which are mostly repetition. The speeches are mostly so general in character that no one can say anything about them.

Every organization has one or, at the most, two perennial talkers, in party jargon called "maintenance men." They always have something to say about everything, and insofar as the party line is concerned, what they say usually only positive. Most of those present keep quiet for many reasons. Either they are in a hurry to get home and don't want to prolong the meeting, they have nothing to say, or they consider it futile to say anything. For many members the main reason for keeping quiet is fear of saying something wrong and being criticized. There is also a feeling that critical remarks and proposals presented will go unnoticed. Finally, many members are equipped with a self-censorship acquired through long years of experience, and they would rather keep quiet than risk falling out of favor with their superiors by making critical remarks. Contributions to the discussion that go beyond local affairs are rare, and almost no one takes the liberty of criticizing the political line and course of action of higher party organs. This is permissible only for those "trained" communists who consider party policy too liberal. On the other hand, critical remarks directed at economic or state authorities are heard from time to time, for the most part from members who are not socially dependent on the party—i.e., workers, farmers, and retired people.

From the point of view of the party member and his rights, members' meetings are formal gatherings and accordingly without significance. This line is crossed during periods of internal party crisis when meetings reflect the will of the membership and serve to pressure the leadership. The members' meeting serves as an instrument for the implementation of the will and initiative of the party center. It makes possible a rapid flow of information from the center, and conversely, it expresses agreement with the policies of the leadership and simultaneously reminds members of their duty to defend and implement those policies.

The District and Regional Committees

The district and regional committees do not in any way function as party organs that actually exercise control within the realm of their authority but rather as mere auxiliaries of their presidia having insignificant actual power. They are conspicuous for the fact that they make no decisions but obediently approve whatever their presidium or the center puts before them. This is due to the low level of significance of the matters they are given to deal with and because of the composition of the membership.

Matters that are important from the point of view of power politics—like cadre or security affairs—do not get on the meeting agendas of the district and regional committees, which are guided by their plans of work. General economic matters or narrow internal-party affairs predominate, and most items on the agendas have to do with the results of CC plenary meetings or the fulfillment of guidelines of other central institutions.[4]

The membership of the district committees averages around 60 (i.e. 5000 altogether) and the regional committees average around 80 (700–800 altogether). Of these members, only a fifth is socially independent of the DC or RC presidium. The level of worker representation in this total number is 20–21 percent for the district committees and 18–19 percent for the regional committees.[5] The percentage of DC and RC members who were originally workers, but took up paid positions in various apparats is about 70–80 percent.[6] Their social dependence on the DC or RC presidium is absolute, and many of them hold membership in these committees by virtue of positions they have held for a certain period.

The responsible instructor and a representative of the higher-level organ also take part in meetings of the DC and RC. For the most part these are functionaries of the party apparat, including CC secretaries, who are responsible for various portfolios. Their task is to take part in the discussion with a "statement of principle," and to react on the spot should any incorrect opinions be put forward by any of the members present. Both the representative and the instructor submit reports on the course of the meeting, independent of each other, to the political-organizational department of the RC or CC that delegated them.

Speeches for DC and RC meetings are drafted by the party apparat. The DC/RC presidium discusses and transmits them. They are usually limited to detailed information with copious figures on the state of the economy, mixed with well-known political proclamations and tasks. Most of those present are unable to say anything at all about such matters presented in specialists' terms. Those present thus break down into a few perennial and long-winded talkers who deliver their rhetorical exercises, on the one hand, and their passive listeners, on the other hand.

The contents of the discussion, especially the limits of criticism, are predetermined. Each participant in the discussion is guided by the principle, fixed in the minds of functionaries, that party resolutions are not discussed, they are carried out. Discussion is allowed only about the means of their realization. For this reason, they refrain from criticizing, not only resolutions of the Central Committee, but even the course of action of their own presidium. Exceptions to this rule occur only on rare occasions. Criticism most exceeds its usual limits in periods of internal party crisis, during which, however, the most obstinate defenders of previous policies are to be found among members of the DC and RC.

All attempts to increase the role of the district and regional committees in the life of the party and the district or region have been unsuccessful. The presidium sees no need to call meetings of its committee; that is, it treats the members of the committee as mere executors of its instructions, which are in turn derived from the guidelines of the center. The public is largley unaware of who the members of the DC and RC are, and, in the party, no one asks anything of them except that they formally approve the way their presidium carries out the resolutions of the center in the district or region. At the same time, these are mostly well-known resolutions that are, in the final analysis, carried out through other channels (state and economic institutions).

Members of the district and regional committees enjoy certain privileges—although these are not very substantial compared with the privileges enjoyed by members of the other party institutions. They are protected from the persecutions afflicting the majority of citizens, and they and their families achieve success in their careers more easily. The "doors of power in the district and region" open for them. They meet with members of the presidium and employees of the state apparat, whom they recognize as the local representatives of the party since, among other reasons, it is these people who determine their work assignments. For those who hold paid positions in institutions other than the party, membership guarantees their positions and, in addition, makes their position in the workplace a more advantageous one. For these reasons they strive to remain members of the committee, and at meetings they show the essential amount of activity in harmony with the interests of the presidium and party apparat. For "unpaid" functionaries, membership represents the opportunity to have requests of one's community, factory, or school fulfilled.

Although members' meetings and meetings of the district and regional committees attract little attention in the locality, party headquarters pays considerable attention to them, drawing conclusions from them as to how the party's policies and directives are being received and carried out. It is considered sufficient merely to note that the district or regional committees have dealt with this or that resolution and taken a stand on it. News releases dealing with a resolution's implementation are issued as proof that the resolution has come to life. Only in exceptional cases is mention made of incorrect or deviant points of view in the minutes of the district and regional committee meetings. If headquarters determines that there has been some inadmissible deviation from its decisions, it will intervene. Only rarely does it keep track of the fate of the resolution, and even then it does so in a purely formal manner.

Discussions of the district and regional committees, guided by the basic principle that it is inappropriate to criticize resolutions that have been adopted, are represented as agreement by the entire party. The discussion at members' meetings is thus the main source of information about the attitude of all citizens toward party resolutions. The bureaus of basic organizations are required to report remarks made at the members' meetings and to transmit them to the district. The central party organization requires an analysis from a district of remarks made and a report on what has become of them. Every year, however, it is found that the committees have hardly taken down any remarks at all, since they know that no one will do anything with them in any case and that the higher authorities pay no attention to them.

TABLE 1.3
Members and Candidates Elected

Congress	Number of members	Party employees among them	Functionaries from central institutions
X	113	25	40
XI	147	44	47
XII	147	45	43
XIII	166	55	42
XIV	160	39	45
XV	175	35	43

The Central Committee

The Central Committee is responsible for the direction of all party activities between congresses. Its exact size is not fixed, and it varies between 80 and 130. It meets at least three times a year, but didn't meet at all from 1949 to 1952 under Klement Gottwald's leadership. This practice was considered a manifestation of the "cult of personality," and for this reason the CC Presidium has subsequently convened the CC in conformity with regulations.

The CC only minimally fulfills the tasks set out for it in the party rules. It is not a decision-making body, but rather one that ratifies unanimously and ceremoniously. The Presidium and secretaries of the CC stage manage the meeting all the way from the preparatory phase to adoption of a resolution so that the CC can successfully fulfill its role of ratification without deviation. The leadership has an effective instrument for this. Most CC members take belief in the Presidium for granted. They consider such trust to be a party obligation and are convinced in any case that the Presidium is better informed than they are. The structure of the Central Committee, from the point of view of positions held by its members, also helps explain the Presidium's hold over it. Over two-thirds of CC members hold positions in party, governmental, or economic apparats or mass organizations that are filled by the CC Presidium (see Table 1.3). These functionaries make up the hard core of the CC and break down into several strata according to the extent of their power. At the extremes are the all-powerful Presidium members and secretaries of the CC (18 percent of the membership) and those without significant positions of power (25–30 percent). Between these groups is the influential group of RC leading secretaries (around ten) and the group of vice premiers and ministers (around eighteen). Less important is the group of members of the National Assembly.

TABLE 1.4
Issues Dealt with at Central Committee Meetings

	1948-1952	1953-1958	1958-1963	1969-1978
Number of CC meetings	9	24	43	34
ISSUES DEALT WITH				
Economic	5	14	29	22
Internal party affairs	2	6	10	6
International affairs	--	3	6	3
Elected organs of power	1	3	6	6
Cadre affairs	3	2	8	6
Ideological	--	2	6	2
Other	--	2	8	4

The character of the CC's meeting agenda also contributes to its being a mere ratifying body. To be sure, the main thrust of the agenda is determined by a long-range plan of work, but the particulars are proposed by a conference of leading secretaries and approved by the CC Presidium. The CC has to meet at least three times a year, and themes are thus sought and chosen for it. These are never determined on the basis of a thorough analysis of the condition of society or urgency of needs. Among the factors playing a role in theme selection are the interests of the party apparat and the conflicts within it. Proposals come from the individual sections of the CC, and two conflicting tendencies vie with each other. Some departments don't put forward matters having to do with their areas of competence but, on the contrary, even try to prevent them from coming up since this means a great deal of work on preparations. Against this, however, stands the conviction that the influence and authority of a department increases when matters within its competence are dealt with by the CC. For this second reason it is the less significant departments above all that push to have their issues put on the CC agenda. However, they run up against opposition, mainly from the CC secretaries who, themselves, determine some themes for the CC meeting. Thus the work plan and program of the CC meeting result from conflict among various interests within the CC Presidium, the CC secretaries, and the party apparat.

Economic, as well as narrowly technical questions predominate on CC meeting agenda as indicated in Table 1.4. (At some meetings several points were dealt with.)

The narrowly technical character of all questions dealt with results in speeches that teem with figures and technical terms which 5 percent of the members of the CC, at the most, can understand or say anything about. Economic matters include, for example, the five-year and annual plans for economic development and their fulfillment, the development or tasks of machine industries, construction, food industries, chemicals, electrotechnology, agriculture, etc.

All materials are provided to the CC by its presidium, which jealously guards this prerogative. Along with the CC secretaries, its control is already manifest in the preparation of speeches and resolutions. In the first place it elaborates their theses, which are drafted by the responsible CC secretary or a member of the presidium. After approval (sometimes including a schedule for further elaboration), their preparation continues under the direction of the responsible CC secretary. Groups of specialists, as well as some members of the CC and its commissions, participate in this process. They compile the supporting materials as well as the subjects of the resolutions. Then those items are worked on by the responsible section of the CC in technical matters together with functionaries from extra-party institutions responsible for portfolios. (When a long-range or short-range economic plan is involved, the materials are prepared by the Office of Planning in collaboration with the party apparat.) The individual who is to give the speech puts it in its final form. Then, along with the draft resolution, the speech goes through a process of elaboration within the central party organs (the Secretariat and commissions of the CC), but the Presidium has the last word. It either approves the final draft or has parts reworked, elaborated, or modified. These modifications are made by the "speaker," by the responsible secretary, or sometimes by a committee appointed by the CC Presidium. The length of time the preparations for a CC meeting require varies. At most, they take a year (as on the position of the party in society, October 1967); at the least, two months (as on the standard of living, April 1967).

CC members find out about the questions to be dealt with by means of the speeches. Before this they don't even know precisely what will come up. The invitation to a meeting usually comes at the last minute and contains only a list of the points to be dealt with. The members of the CC can thus only anticipate the contents of the speech and have no opportunity to prepare for the meeting by consulting with specialists. Only in rare instances are they given additional, mainly statistical, data at the meeting. Never are they given two or more options for a solution, nor are they made aware of differences of opinion that came up in the preparatory stages. They receive only the standpoint of and solution approved by the CC Presidium. The nature of the discussion conforms to the ratifying role of the CC. Those who take part express agreement with the contents of the speech and the correctness of the proposed resolution. The CC Presidium, which controls the meeting, influences and to a certain extent orchestrates the discussion. This begins with its predetermination of the length of the meeting, which is indicated on the invitation. Its intervention in the discussion continues with the establishment of a list of those who are to participate. It prepares this according to its own criteria—in no way according to the chronological order in which requests to speak are received—and is able in this way to exclude "inconvenient discussants." Quite routinely, the members of the CC Presidium, themselves, criticize participants in the discussion with whose views they disagree, or they recruit other CC members to do so for them.[7]

Their final intervention occurs during the publication process. Contributions to the discussion that the CC Presidium doesn't like are either not published at all, or the press committee elected at the meeting abridges them in such a way that their substance is altered. In addition, during the meeting all contributions to the discussion are immediately transcribed from magnetic tape, and every participant is authorized and able to make modifications for the record.

The result of such practices is that CC members are afraid to participate in the discussion for fear they might say something wrong. Or they read prepared texts of their contributions to the debate. It is mainly, even exclusively, those CC members who are interested because of a connection with their departments who take part in the discussion and deliver long speeches written by their ministries or some other apparat. Participants in the discussion reflect the opinions of such agencies more than their own. A third of the members of the CC take no part in the discussion, or they speak up once at the most. Nonetheless, it is precisely these members who are reelected to the CC. This practice is in line with the principle, widespread among party apparatchiks, that the best CC member is he who shuts up and votes.

Despite all the constraints, critical tones can sometimes be discerned in the remarks of CC members. They do not, however, depart from the spirit of the speech, i.e., such remarks are aimed at lower-level party and central extra-party institutions and do not relate to the political course of action or activities of the Presidium. High officials are criticized by name only after they have been relieved of their positions. Those exceptional cases in which they are criticized are generally regarded as presaging their fall from power.

Beginning in the mid sixties, some CC members began to make critical remarks that even touched upon the activities of the CC Presidium. This became much more pronounced in 1967 and became one of the sources of the Prague Spring. This novel practice in the CC was rooted in the mounting crisis in the party and society, which "rebellious" CC members reflected in their speeches. Out of this state of affairs grew the efforts of part of the membership to make the CC play the role it was supposed to play according to party rules. On the eve of the Prague Spring, this aim was achieved. The immediate cause of this success lay in the weakness of the Presidium, which split into two camps and lost the capability and strength to run everything. This made it possible for the CC to temporarily come into its own in a power-political sense.

The process of approval of resolutions and decisions is an entirely pro forma one. Until 1954, the CC adopted resolutions to the effect that the speeches delivered were guidelines for the activity of the party. Since 1954, the CC Presidium has submitted proposals for resolutions and decisions on matters to be discussed either directly or by means of the proposals commission elected at the congress. Most CC members don't read a proposed resolution, due either to apathy or to a belief that it says nothing about their area of expertise. Their occasional remarks deal only with stylistic modifications.

The CC adopts wide-ranging decisions and resolutions, most of which are forgotten in the course of daily events. Only those sections of the party apparat responsible for the corresponding portfolios work through them and make plans for their fulfillment. However, lower-level party organs also work through these resolutions. The responsible CC section submits a report to the CC Presidium or Secretariat, and sometimes the item, "Report on the fulfillment of the resolutions of the last CC meeting," also appears on the work agenda. To a certain extent, CC resolutions have a different fate in state and economic institutions, which have often played a role in formulating them. These institutions work through the resolutions, deal with them, and are governed by their interpretations of them. Sometimes they have to submit a report for information to the CC section responsible for them, which is received by a secretary or the CC Secretariat. Conversely, the heads of extra-party institutions themselves invoke resolutions as the need arises. They use them as an important argument in getting the requests of their own departments (e.g. financial, more investment, allocation of labor, etc.) through in the government and in their conflicts with central agencies.

The true relationship between the CC and its Presidium is just the opposite of what the party rules stipulate. The CC does not supervise the activities of the Presidium at all. The Presidium fulfills its obligation to report to the CC on its activities, as laid down in party rules, in a purely formal manner. Members of the CC receive a *Bulletin* containing the resolutions of the CC and governmental bodies (also called blue), actually it contains only a small portion of the less significant resolutions of these organs. There is no information in this brief bulletin about why a resolution was passed. Only in exceptional cases does the CC receive additional information about Presidium resolutions, and even then the information is fragmentary. Presidium members have no access whatsoever to information about the situation in the party organizations, the districts and regions, or about the views of party members.

On the other hand, contrary to the rules, the CC Presidium assesses every single meeting of the CC. It has no interest in initiatives or critical remarks, rather it evaluates members' contributions to the discussion. Contributions to the discussion are classified as positive or negative according to whether they are in agreement with the Presidium's point of view. In the negative cases, the hidden aims and intentions of the authors are sought.[8]

On the one hand, membership in the CC entails only an imperceptible amount of participation in the exercise of power. On the other hand, it entails no political responsibility, and attending meetings three times a year carries little obligation. Members of the CC know very well that membership doesn't require them to do anything and that to raise their hands in favor of a resolution will lead to no consequences whatsoever for them. This is consistent with the generally applicable principle in the party that it is not he who voted for a mistaken resolution who is responsible but he who proposed it. This helps to explain the apathy of CC members toward questions discussed and toward voting on resolutions. Let me illustrate this conception, using as an example the case of party General Secretary Rudolf Slánský.

In September 1951, all the members of the CC voted to strip Slánský of his position. Three months later, they applauded his imprisonment and, a year later, his execution. In 1957, they adopted a resolution again proclaiming him a criminal and his execution as justified. Five years later, they approved his judicial rehabilitation, denying him party rehabilitation, and five years after that, they requested his party rehabilitation as well. Throughout all of this procedure, a large part of the membership belonged to all or at least several of the Central Committees that dealt with the case, always unquestioningly raising their hands for something completely different.

Nonetheless, CC membership grants a measure of social status to those who have it. It serves as a criterion of social and political prestige within the party as well as outside it, facilitates access to the center of power, and brings with it many privileges. However, in the discussion of reports and the assignment of tasks to ministers and other functionaries, the CC Presidium takes no account of CC membership, nor does it solicit CC members' views. But the relationship of CC members to the central party apparat is a different story as CC members have much easier access to leading functionaries in the apparat, including leading CC secretaries. According to the accepted rule, a secretary has to receive a CC member if the latter requests it, and he has to do so without the mediation or presence of the CC section head responsible for the portfolio. This rule doesn't apply to others, including ministers. And, the other way around, the majority of CC members head institutions whose activities are followed and assessed by the section of the CC responsible for the portfolio, which has a good deal to say about who remains in their positions and in the CC. CC members adapt their relationship "to their section" in the party apparat to this hard reality.

Among the privileges that come with CC membership, three are among the most significant: first, being better informed; second, having relatively strong protection against losing one's position; and third, advancement along the social ladder and in the party hierarchy. A CC member belongs to the category of higher cadres, and changes in his functions usually take place within this category. For those who hold high positions in central institutions, CC membership ranks them above functionaries in the same position. For lower-level functionaries, membership makes it possible to come into contact at meetings with ministers and other high officials with whom they would otherwise not come into contact. For many communists, membership is the peak of their party careers, fulfillment of a dream or going beyond what they had allowed themselves to dream. They thus feel grateful to the Presidium and indebted to it for having recommended them for CC membership, or at least having allowed them in. Every functionary, once he gets into the CC, tries to stay in as long as possible.

One further remark should be made about the relationship of the party apparat to meetings of the Central Committee. Most employees in the central apparat consider the meetings to be purely a matter of form; some consider them to be useless. And no one is interested in a meeting except for those from the department that prepared it. Only a small number regard the meetings with seriousness and respect. Although a few actually read all the published documents, they are truly the rare exceptions. Party apparatchiks in the regions and districts don't read the speeches and resolutions of the CC at all; instead they become familiar with the contents of these at consultations and meetings. The exceptions are some (not all) employees with responsibilities relating to some portfolio, who read at least those portions of the documents that bear directly upon their work.

Auxiliary Structures
and the System of Control

Since the 1960s, it has again become the fashion to set up commissions at the district, regional, and Central Committee levels similar to those that were abolished in 1949 when the party's monopoly of power was established. At that time, their functions were absorbed through expansion of the party apparat. Fifteen years later, commissions for the widest variety of party and social life appeared once again. Among the permanent ones are economic, agricultural, ideological, and youth commissions and, at the central level, a legal commission. They consist of members of the DC, RC, or CC, and specialists. Heading each is the secretary of the DC, RC, or CC responsible for the portfolio.

A commission has two main tasks and pays special attention to the first, which is to prepare the supporting materials for action by the presidium or its committee and to prepare reports concerning the activities or guidelines of the institutions that fall under their area of competence. Its second task is to keep tabs on the realization of party resolutions.

The commissions are auxiliary institutions of the DC, RC, or CC, which approve their work agendas. In practice, however, they are under the control of the DC, RC, or CC presidium, work according to presidium directives, and deliver their reports to it rather than directly to the committee that elected it. A commission has no executive authority, and the fate of its proposals or recommendations is determined by the presidium. The presidium's interests are achieved in the commission through the commission chairman, i.e., the responsible DC, RC, or CC secretary. If the presidium rejects or modifies the commission's proposals, the commission has to comply. Conflicts of opinion often take place in the commissions between party apparatchiks and specialists.

Despite their limited authority, the commissions can influence the decision making of the presidium and its committee. They express their views on those basic reports that fall into their area of competence to the presidium, and they pose questions they consider important to the presidium on their own initiative—often questions the presidium would not otherwise deal with. Their remarks and proposals are taken into consideration and dealt with, even though they are not always accepted. In addition, the commissions take part in the preparation of speeches and resolutions for meetings of their committees.

The control and revision commissions have a completely different standing in the party. They exist in the districts, regions, and at the central level; they are elected by the conference and the congress; and their chairmen are employees of the party apparat with the right to take part in meetings of the presidium. According to party rules, they are supposed to constitute an independent system of control within the party, to keep track of how the resolutions adopted by party organs are being fulfilled, to check up on the management of the party, and to deal with disciplinary cases. In reality, they deal only with marginal matters. In the regions and districts their activities are limited to supervising management and disciplinary matters. Not even the Central Control and Revision Commission fulfills the role of an independent institution of control. Although elected by the congress, the commission isn't responsible to it but rather to the CC. However, plans for control are approved by the Presidium, and the CC Presidium and Secretariat discuss its results. All of the commissions' reports destined for CC meetings go through the Presidium. In addition, the Presidium, the Secretariat, and even the general secretary assign tasks to it. Due to this dependency, decisions of the central authorities and initiatives of the secretaries of the CC are not subject to control. The Central Control and Revision Commission's authority is limited to checking into how well decisions of central party organs are being carried out by lower-level, especially basic, organizations.

Within the organs of the power group, reports of the Central Control and Revision Commission are considered to be of secondary importance. They are reviewed without much interest, except for disciplinary matters involving important functionaries. Aside from the fact that these reports deal mostly with marginal matters having to do with the internal life of the party, their quality is not as high as that of reports prepared by other departments. This is partly due to the fact that worn out functionaries are transferred to the control and revision commissions.

Notes

1. When I was employed as a worker in a factory from 1971–1976, I experienced a membership recruitment campaign. There were 42 employees in the boiler room where I worked. The enterprise committee chose eight young workers for recruitment and got six of them. The real reasons for their joining were these: One was promised the position of foreman, two were promised an enterprise apartment, one was threatened that the enterprise would not approve a program of study by correspondence at an institution of higher education. One had career ambitions and left shortly afterwards for service in the State Security. One showed no ambition for the time being. One woman, an engineer, attempted to be accepted into the Party, but was rejected due to her "class origins."

2. In 1948, after the conquest of power, there were 1,555,000 workers in the Party; in 1966, only 557,000. In 1949, there were 256,000 farmers; in 1966, only 93,000. After the crushing of the Prague Spring in 1968, the decrease in workers continued. In 1971, it fell to 312,000 (26 percent) and the number of farmers declined to 60,000 (4.9 percent). Only in the mid-1970s did they succeed in stopping it. If we take into consideration that more than 200,000 worker-communists went over to the ranks of the intelligentsia during the period 1948–1954, more than 800,000 workers left the party primarily out of disagreement with its policies. In 1969, an additional 150,000 left for similar reasons, and 100,000 were expelled.

3. In 1968, delegates from 107 out of 119 district conferences decided to vote secretly. Only at twenty-seven conferences were the proposals submitted approved without changes. At seventy-nine of them, no fewer than six failed to get elected, and thirteen of them made more than ten changes in the candidacies proposed. Among the functionaries who were not elected were eight leading secretaries and eighteen secretaries of district committees.

4. For example, in 1975, out of forty-two meetings of regional committees, economic questions were dealt with at twenty-nine of them, internal party matters at four, and national committees and trade union organizations in one case. Out of sixty-six meetings of district committees, economic matters were on the agenda at forty-six of them, party work at eight, and national committees, trade union organizations, culture, and schools at twelve.

5. For a year after the establishment of the power monopoly (1949) workers made up 58 percent of the membership of the district committees. Then their proportions declined with a corresponding increase in the proportions of white-collar workers (to 30–35 percent) and political employees (to 22 percent in the district and 34 percent in the regions).

6. In 1951 they made up 78.6 percent of the membership in the CC, in 1952, 82.5 percent, in 1953, 82.9 percent, in 1958, 77.7 percent, in 1960 also 77.7 percent. The proportions of white-collar workers, according to their current profession, rose during the period 1951-1954 from 41.4 percent to 70 percent. In 1953 76.6 percent of the regional committees consisted of workers by original profession, but only 5.5 percent of them were not advanced to some position.

7. In 1953, the Minister of Education was attacked for having stood up for teachers against the arbitrary and capricious behavior of local functionaries. In 1955, the Minister of Agriculture was attacked for having made use of pricing policy to raise agricultural production, and in 1967, so was a Minister who drew attention to the "dying out of agriculture" due to the old age of farmers. On top of this, the General Secretary routinely takes participants in the discussion to task, either while they are speaking or immediately after.

8. Novotny, for example, in response to remarks made by a CC member said: "I am surprised by his performance and understand his motive, but I am not going to talk about this. . . . "

2

The System of Power Groups

The Backbone of Power

The supporting backbone of the communist power monopoly is its system of power groups. I make use of this term advisedly, since I believe it best captures the essence of the system, namely, that party organs occupy a key role in the machinery of power, and are organized in a self-contained system. The party's power is concentrated in the activities of the party organs, based on a constitutional provision for its leading role in the state.

The key position of the power groups derives from the reality that it is they who formulate party policy and guidelines, determine the methods for their implementation, and assure their fulfillment, as well as the fact that they can make decisions concerning all aspects of social life and even personal life. As representatives of the party, the power groups control all the instruments of power as well as all the organizations of civil society. They attempt to control every detail from the center, to work out specific tasks and assign them to all lower-level power groups right down to the basic power groups, to control and watch over every institution in society that has power and exercises control—every extra-party institution, that is—and to bind not only the lower-level party organs but also the organs of the state as well as the organs of the mass organizations—directly, authoritatively, and administratively.

Three factors characterize the power groups' decision making. First, decisions on all matters—including those involving expertise—are made from a power-political point of view. This influences the selection and resolution of issues. Second, their decisions are subject to the aims of the moment or to whatever political campaign happens to be in progress. To be sure, this makes it possible to concentrate all efforts on the realization of one or two aims, but it can create serious difficulties for the future. For example, if the leadership proclaims a goal of paying more attention to agriculture, machine industries, etc., all decisions, even those relating to quite remote sectors, will be seen in the light of this aim, regardless of long-term consequences. And third, the power groups make decisions with unwarranted self-confidence. Their members are convinced that they have a monopoly of truth as well as a monopoly of power, and they conduct themselves according to "the basic principle of the infallibility of party organs." They make decisions about the broadest range of matters with great self-confidence and stubbornly stick to their positions, only extremely rarely revising their earlier decisions.

The power groups consist of the "core" of the bureaus of the basic and enterprise organizations and the presidia and secretaries of the district, regional, and central committees of the party—roughly 88,000–90,000 communist functionaries. The system of power groups is like a power pyramid, with a hierarchical structure extending from the lowest to the highest fifteen- to twenty–member group. The position of each component, its authority over subordinates, and its obligations toward superiors are clearly defined. The center monopolizes power over the whole of society and enforces its will and decisions uniformly by means of an extensive network of power groups reaching into all areas and corners of social life. The groups implement their guidelines in two ways: by means of extra-party institutions within the domain of their authority and by transmission of the guidelines to subordinate levels of the power system.

The central group delegates part of its power to lower levels, doing so in a manner that reinforces its monopoly position and prevents the lower levels from getting out of its control. The amount of power delegated to the lower levels and the way power is decentralized depend on what the center decides at its own discretion. Control is assured by the facts that the higher-level group approves the composition of lower-level groups and that the latter are responsible for their actions to a higher-level group—the district to the region, the region to the center.

Delegation of power is guided by three basic principles. First, all lower-level components exercise their power exclusively within their own domain of authority. They are not allowed to infringe upon the authority of other groups at the same level, even less upon the authority of higher-level groups. Second, lower-level components exercise their power exclusively within a framework of the will and guidelines of the central group, which are adapted to suit local conditions. The lower levels keep track of the implementation of guidelines by state and economic institutions and mass organizations within their jurisdiction that receive orders from their superior organs and inform the higher-level power group about such matters. Third, the central power group has the authority to compel the obedience of subordinate groups as it can take measures against any such groups that do not enforce its will according to its conceptions. It can limit their authority, transfer it to a higher organ or to itself, or replace the disobedient group. Decentralization ensures that the lower-level power groups will act within the limits of their authority and to the extent assigned to them as bearers and executors of power and simultaneously constitute the basic framework of the power mechanism.

The central power group takes pains to make sure that its will and guidelines are interpreted uniformly and consistently by lower-level power groups. This is primarily accomplished through intra-party channels, among which the Corps of Instructors plays an important role. The instructor looks after the party organization and stimulates and directs its activities to a significant extent. The district committees try to install an instructor for each basic organization, but since they cannot accomplish this aim, they concentrate on so-called weak organizations, i.e., those that would, for practical purposes, not function at all without an instructor. The district corps of instructors consists of about ten unpaid activists, who carry out their functions in addition to their profession, and instructors who work in the party apparat, for whom taking care of several basic organizations constitutes the substance of their work. The regional committee has an instructor for each district in its party apparat, and similarly, there is an instructor in the center for every region.

The responsibility of the district instructor to the basic organization is to transmit and assure the fulfillment of tasks assigned to it by the district party institution. He attends meetings of the executive and members' meetings of his organization and reports on the meetings to the responsible party apparatchik. The regional and central instructors keep track of how resolutions and guidelines of the center are being implemented in a district or region. Instructors are alerted to decisions that are considered especially important at conferences organized for them by the organizational-political department of the RC or CC to which they are attached. The instructor discusses the resolutions and guidelines with the DC or RC leading secretary, discusses their concrete application with him, and draws attention to deficiencies in measures proposed by him even before they go to the DC or RC presidium. The instructor also keeps track of how the party apparat and the extra-party institutions are ensuring the implementation of resolutions, even at the lowest levels. He informs his organizational-political department in detail about all of these steps and measures as well as about all important events.

The instructor is not the only agent of the party apparat who intervenes in the activities of lower-level power groups, influences, predetermines, and controls their decision making. Every apparatchik, working through comrades subordinate to his department at the district and/or regional level, asks for reports to be submitted and recommends resolutions as needed. Heads of department in the CC and CC secretaries ask this of RC secretaries, and they in turn ask the same of the leading secretary in each district.

The system of power groups conforms to Lenin's teaching on the party. It represents that form of party unity which Lenin called "the material unity of the organization." A second form is unity of ideas. Since the bond of ideas linking functionaries and members to the party is not firm and is constantly weakening, organizational unity has to be reinforced, above all the unity of its backbone—the system of power groups. However, not even this system is free of internal tensions. In addition to controversies within groups, there are also controversies among groups. The most frequent occur between the lowest and the district levels, less frequently between district and regional, and only exceptionally between regional and central. Controversies and conflicts only rarely have to do with the policy line or contents of guidelines from the central (and this only at the lowest levels). Most have to do with concrete measures of daily politics (predominantly cadre measures) or with methods for the realization of resolutions and instructions from superior institutions. These superior institutions try to resolve their controversies with the lower levels by means of agreement. If this doesn't work, they enforce their will uncompromisingly, acting according to the principle of democratic centralism. This figures among the most important principles of party organization and serves to justify the necessity of a unified system of power groups. It stems from a symbiosis of two elements—the democratism of elections (merely formal) of organs, from the bottom up, and centralism (real) obedience from the top down, all the way down to the membership.

The Lower-level (Basic) Power Groups

The system of power groups penetrates into the basic units of society by means of its lowest levels. The power groups are made up of a hard core or portion of the membership of the bureaus of the basic party organizations and the bureaus of the enterprise and local organizations. They are found everywhere—in communities, cities, factories, offices, schools. The upper-level party organizations strive to have a communist cell functioning in every place of work or in every community. Wherever there is no cell, they instruct the appropriate director to establish one by transferring cadres.

The number of party organizations hardly ever changes. There are about 45,000 basic organizations, enterprise, and local committees, and 315,000–316,000 members of bureaus. About 70–74 percent of the bureaus (between 32,000 and 33,000) exist in factories and institutions, between 21 and 25 percent in villages, and the remainder in cities. Each year, about 30 percent of the members of bureaus are replaced, and 45 percent of them have been elected to their positions more than four times. Each year, difficulties arise in putting together the bureaus, and in no mean number of cases, a bureau with the full complement cannot be put together at all. The people the party leadership wants to have in the bureaus refuse to accept positions. Thus, more-willing individuals are put forward, though of course they are fully aware that they are being appointed merely to achieve the prescribed number.

The social composition of the bureaus of basic party organizations is as follows: one-third workers, about a quarter white-collar workers, 8–9 percent farmers, about 5 percent teachers and political employees, and the rest pensioners and others. The picture becomes clearer if we look at social composition by types of basic organization. In production and transportation, workers constitute about 40 percent of the bureaus, and white-collar workers make up the majority (around 37 percent are engineer-technicians). In rural organizations, workers are more than a quarter of the membership, farmers and pensioners about 19 percent each. In neighborhood organizations, pensioners (about 60 percent) and housewives (about 10 percent) predominate.

The more than 300,000 strong mass of party bureau members can be broken down according to type and amount of their activity, as well as according to level of participation in the exercise of power. Members can be divided into three groups. In the first are those who participate in almost no activities inside or outside the bureau, and who do not even attend meetings regularly. They accept their positions knowing that they are going to avoid all their obligations. The second group consists of those responsible for the party organization's domestic affairs, such as the agent, the treasurer and the official responsible for culture and education. These positions are intended for nonpolitical individuals (white-collar workers, teachers). Most members who regard their positions as a professional obligation and a guarantee of job security, or even as the basis for a career or to gain various advantages (e.g. university admission for their children), come from these two categories.

The third group consists of a few active members, upon whom all the work of the committee and the basic party organization as a whole actually depends. Decison making and power are also concentrated in their hands. This concentration is not always intended by them but is often a result of lack of interest in working on the part of the other bureau members. The active group consists of two to four bureau members, depending on the size of the organization and local conditions. It includes, first and foremost, the chairman of the organization. In production, it also includes the chairman of the works council, the factory director or his deputy, the political commander of the people's militia, the head of the personnel or special committee (for army and security affairs). In the village, it includes the chairmen of the national committee and the collective farm; in schools, the director; in offices, two or three leading officials. The active group is the power core of the bureaus and the lowest level in the system of power groups.

Bureaus are supposed to meet weekly, or at the least every other week, something the district party apparat scrupulously keeps track of. The active group regularly takes part in meetings, the other members very irregularly. The bureau and chairman can also invite other people, who may be not only local functionaries (from the community, factory, or office) but also functionaries from the district organization. If the bureau deals with some issue affecting a district institution, it can request, by means of the district party secretariat, that a responsible district functionary (chairman of the district national committee, director of a factory or business, school inspector, etc.) be delegated to its meeting.

The meeting agenda is set by the chairman. Almost four-fifths of it consists of carrying out tasks imposed by higher organs. Even the organization's own local matters tend to be recommended "from above." In 1964, one basic organization's bureau received about 120 pages of resolutions from superior organs and 308 letters. From among these resolutions and instructions the chairman selects only a few to submit to his bureau for decision or for information. The party control commission often complains that official letters have been found with the chairman that have not even been opened.

Issues dealt with by the bureau can be divided into internal party matters and public matters. The internal party matters include, first and foremost, preparation of members' meetings and public meetings, admission of new members, party education, subscription to the party press, the status of visual propaganda, etc. The public matters most often include reports on the situation in the factory, workshop, agricultural cooperative, or office, discussion of the results of the school year or elections to works councils, the work of national committees; mass organizations; and preparation for various celebrations. But they also include more concrete matters—the state of supplies in the community, observance of the established hours of work in factories, the status of socialist competition, etc. Personal evaluations of fellow citizens and fellow workers, recommendations for studies and appointments, and opinions regarding the appointments to positions within the organization's own enterprise are routinely discussed. Matters that the district wants discussed are put on the meeting agenda by the instructor.

Most of a bureau's decisions merely implement guidelines of superior party institutions and are uncontroversial. Matters having to do with operations of the factory, workshop, and office, or the work of national committees and mass organizations can become sources of conflict. Party bureaus in production exercise their right to check up on the management. This is usually done by the director or his deputy's giving a monthly report on fulfillment of the economic plan. Management is required to take heed of the comments of the bureau, and usually does. Discussion of the management of agricultural cooperatives and the work of national committees and mass organizations is similar. However, it is common for a bureau to criticize the management of an enterprise, the chairman of a national committee, or a mass organization or ask that they take measures with which they do not agree and are reluctant to carry out. In such cases, the bureau can make use of its power prerogatives and achieve its aims through the district party secretariat.

Generally the position of the lowest-level power groups derives from the statewide power position of the party. The power group represents the party, its power and its leading role, in the place where the group exercises authority. Its position is viewed and understood this way not only by most citizens but also by the communists themselves. The power group bases its position on three factors. First, it has the right to intervene in all matters within the domain of its authority. It can take up any issue of public and economic life and is encouraged by party rules and instructions of the party leadership to adopt and implement resolutions on such matters. Second, the bureau can, and sometimes must, inform superior organs about the situation in its region and can use the authority and support of these organs to make its own demands prevail. The leaderships of extra-party institutions are, for the most part, powerless to do anything about this, and they try to stay on good terms with members of the power group since any unfavorable report sent "upwards" by members of the power group makes a bad impression, and sometimes even has personal consequences.

The third source of power is the bureau's authority in cadre matters. It has the right to have a say in appointments to all positions, and in the promotion and demotion of all employees, regardless of whether such action comes under its authority according to cadre procedures. Cadre procedures spell out only those matters on which the bureaus must take a position but in no way limit what they can do on their own initiative.

The chairman of a bureau, the principal figure of the power group, has an especially privileged status. There are about 45,000 chairmen, about a third workers, more than a quarter white-collar workers, 7 percent farmers, teachers, political employees, and soldiers. More than a third are replaced every year, but over 10 percent stay in their positions longer than four years. The power position of the chairman also usually derives from the party's position in the state. Concretely, the chairman's power is based on his relationship to the center of power in the district. He is in contact with the district party secretariat, which gathers information as well as providing it. He can discuss matters relating to his place of work or domicile with secretaries of the DC, including the leading secretary, all of whom consider his opinion to be very important. The head of an enterprise or office is well aware of this aspect of the chairman's position and tries to win him over and make him dependent. This is done either by recommending a subordinate official or by granting favors—e.g., pay raises or plum jobs for his relatives.

The chairman's power position is further reinforced by the fact that he makes decisions about many things by himself, without getting prior approval from the bureau. And when he needs approval, he usually gets it easily. Among such decisions are, for example, approval of appointments to positions that fall outside cadre procedures—the heads of enterprises and offices ask for at least oral approval from the chairman regarding these positions. He can also give citizens various recommendations. When the district secretariat requests cadre evaluations, the chairman presents their final wording to the bureau for approval, or even formulates them himself.

Higher state and economic institutions, the police, and especially State Security turn to him for information about fellow citizens and fellow workers. Because of this, the practice has evolved that many chairmen have become informers for State Security by virtue of their position. The communist leadership at first considered this practice natural, but by 1956, it no longer had an entirely positive view of it. Its members noted with displeasure that State Security "has recruited the best members and functionaries of our party organizations. The chairmen and others are informers for security. In several organizations there are five to eight informers" (Alexej Čepička at a meeting of the CC politburo on April 17, 1956). This practice was too deeply rooted, however, and changed only to the extent that the numbers of informers declined. The chairman, however, remains first and foremost among them.

District and Regional Groups

The power group in the districts and regions consists of the members of the presidium (formerly the bureau) and the secretaries of the DC and RC of the party. The composition of the next presidium is thrashed out by the leading secretary along with the secretaries of the DC and the RC and his instructor. He presents names to the current presidium for approval, and then the superior institution gives its views—the regional for the district, the central for the regional. The procedure ends with a formal vote conducted by the district or regional committee at its first meeting after the conference. The selection and election of the DC and RC secretaries takes place in much the same way. In the regions, the secretaries make up a body called the RC secretariat; and though no corresponding institution exists in the districts, meetings of DC secretaries usually perform its functions.

Central headquarters recommends the number of members and functionaries to be in the presidium. In addition to the leading secretary, the membership includes one or two secretaries, the chairman of the district/regional national committee, the chairman of the district/regional trade union organization, and two to four other functionaries from a factory, the city, or an agricultural cooperative or the leading functionaries of some mass organizations. The number of secretaries ranges from three to five. The district or regional power group thus consists of ten to twelve people.

As in the bureau of the basic organization, two types of factors contribute to the power position of the presidium. One is derived from the party's power position in the state. In addressing its decisions to the district and regional presidia, the central group intentionally strengthens their authority as the heart of the power mechanism. Ordinary party members and citizens are less aware of the role of the presidium as the representative of the party and of power—they attribute this role mainly to individual leading functionaries. On the other hand, the role of the presidium is fully appreciated by those whose job appointments it approves and by those in charge of institutions it receives reports on.

The second factor is the authority of the DC and RC presidia to make decisions relating to all matters in the life of the district and the region. If they do not actually deal directly with some matters, and leave them to the apparat, it isn't because they cannot take them up but only because they don't consider it necessary. They have great authority in cadre matters. According to cadre procedures, they approve a whole host of appointments to positions and can freely go beyond this limit at their own discretion as long as doing so doesn't encroach upon the authority of some superior organ.

At the beginning of the sixties, party rules called for weekly meetings of a presidium, this requirement later being changed to every two weeks. In addition to regular presidium members, the heads of the departments whose reports are under discussion always take part in meetings, as well as representatives of those institutions affected by the reports. For some matters, someone representing the portfolio from a higher-level party institution, usually from the party apparat, also attends. His presence emphasizes the importance of the questions under consideration. In exceptionally important and urgent matters, secretaries and members of the CC Presidium may take part in meetings of RC presidia.

The meeting agenda is put together, or at least approved by, the leading secretary. The work plan is taken as the point of departure, but supplementary matters predominate over those determined by the plan. These are proposed by the secretaries and heads of departments in the party apparat. Other members of an RC presidium can also give reports.

The DC or RC presidium deals with a wide range of matters—from the utilization of tractors to theater programs, from the fulfillment of the plan to atheistic propaganda, from distribution of supplies to higher education. Party functionaries don't mind at all that the presidium makes decisions on matters its members know nothing at all about. On the contrary, functionaries are convinced that presidium members have the political qualifications and the obligation to express a party position. In contrast, the specialists who prepare the materials for the discussions do not have a very high opinion of the presidium's qualifications for making decisions. Occasionally, efforts of the DC or RC secretaries to restrict a presidium meeting's agenda to important political questions come into conflict with the principles and practice of central headquarters. According to these, party organs are supposed to keep track of all urgent matters and to watch over them, since what they do not discuss "escapes." All higher-level functionaries suffer a deeply rooted self-deception that the presidia, by their decisions, prevent or eliminate shortcomings, and their members suffer the conceit that they uphold the leading role of the party in this way.

The issues that most frequently appear on the agendas of the presidium meetings can be divided into three categories. First, there are those imposed by higher-level party organs. The district leadership gets them from the region, which in turn gets them from the center, where the responsible party apparatchiks keep track of how their decisions are dealt with "below." The number of such decisions is quite formidable, but the leading secretary picks only a few. After consultation with the responsible secretary and the instructor, he decides what to do with these decisions. In some cases, this amounts to no more than oral or written information from the presidium about what has already been done in the way of implementing them. Others are passed on to the party apparat or the secretariat to be dealt with. Only when a resolution explicitly stipulates that the presidium has to deal with it does it get on the meeting agenda.

Apart from such resolutions, important decisions of the government or the central organs of mass organizations adopted on the basis of CC Presidium resolutions also get on the agenda, but lower-level party organs are not required to deal with them. They have only to administer them within their respective regions. They will submit a plan for the realization of these decisions on their own initiative or on that of DC or RC secretaries, the chairman of the district or regional national committee (DNC/RNC), or the secretary of a mass organization. Such plans deal, for example, with investment, with construction in agricultural cooperatives, with the preparation of annual meetings and conferences of mass organizations, with reorganization of veterinary services, with competition among national committees to make theirs be the best community, and the like.

The second category consists of those items that come up regularly on the basis of earlier instructions so that dealing with them has become routine. Cadre and internal party matters are first and foremost among these. Cadre proposals appear on the agenda of every meeting, and internal party matters include such things as the regular monthly assessment of meeting activity and reports on the movement of members, on party education, and on subscriptions to the party press. A frequent item continues to be the political-organizational preparations for various campaigns, which are worked out in detail. These include, e.g., the campaigns accompanying elections, important party decisions, the First of May, celebration of the October Revolution, and the liberation of the Czechoslovak Republic as well as campaigns of lesser significance—Press Day, Army Day, etc. Among the traditional regular ones are those for fulfillment of the plan in industry or in agriculture, purchase of agricultural products, evaluation of the school year, and, bound up with the last, the religiosity of the youth, the scheduled shows of theaters, etc.

The third category consists of matters that are peculiar to each organization, ranked according to its own considerations and needs.

Among these are, for example, reports on the activities of national committees and mass organizations, on the work of some industrial or agricultural enterprises, on some party organizations, on business and trade networks and the supply situation, on the state of health care services, on cultural facilities, and on sports activities. But there are also even more specific items, for example, the restructuring of workers' wages, the election of enterprise councils, apartment construction, or the situation in the universities.

The presidium acts on the basis of written reports. In the districts, it also acts on the basis of oral information, as it also does in the regions in exceptional or urgent cases. Reports are presented by a secretary or the head of a department, in isolated cases by a member of the presidium. This procedure is not followed as strictly in the districts as it is in the regions, but nevertheless, in the districts, too, every report presented by functionaries outside the party apparat must contain the position of the responsible secretary. The quality of the reports varies greatly. Many of them look more or less like appropriately adapted copies of reports of higher organs. Most of them are extensive and marshal statistical data or factual details (including those of a technical character). Members of the presidium often complain about the excessive length of the reports, which makes it impossible to read them thoroughly. They are thus aimed only at those people who are personally interested in them.

Presidium meetings are chaired by the leading secretary. First on the agenda are cadre matters and, if necessary, internal party information from higher organs. Discussion of reports follows. Participating in the discussion are mainly those whose area of responsibility is somehow affected, as well as those who, although they have not read the report, have had a position prepared by their respective apparat. Those who do not have such means and are not at all interested in the subject either remain silent or "join in" the discussion already in progress. Since there is no clear-cut division of responsibility among functionaries at the district and regional levels, most members make some more or less significant comment regarding almost every report. The amount of discussion determines the length of time it takes to deal with each matter. With some reports that period lasts ten minutes; with others, as much as several hours. Sharp controversies often occur during the discussion between members of the presidium and those invited to discuss their reports. The former often criticize the heads of nonparty institutions. Those concerned defend themselves, contesting the reprimands and accusations leveled at them and striving to explain the causes of the phenomena criticized—however, mostly in vain. They usually carry on a battle that is lost from the start, since members of the presidium are not accustomed to backing down and would rather fire or transfer comrades who are not subservient enough. Conflicts between presidium members and representatives of high-level nonparty institutions (in the regions, with a minister or a high official from the central office of a mass organization; in the district, with the head of a national committee and the like). When presidium members are unable to convince these officials, they get their way by means of high-level ties in the party apparat: the head of a department, a CC secretary, or an RC secretary.

Responses to the discussion are made by the person who presented the report and by those asked to assist. The session is closed by the leading secretary. He also formulates the resolution, the draft of which has to contain every written report. The resolution deals only with the organizational implementation of matters discussed. Secretaries ask that they be concrete (i.e., detailed) with time frames and specification of personal responsibility for their fulfillment. This practice results in a large quantity of resolutions, which no one is able to control, and many of them immediately become merely formal. As soon as the report and resolution are approved, anything else that is done with them becomes the responsibility of the party apparat.

Many reports and proposed resolutions get through the DC or RC presidium without difficulty and without changes. The members approve whatever is put before them, either because they agree with it, or because they don't understand the material discussed and rely on those who prepared the report. Some ask that the report be modified according to their remarks, and the proposed resolution is often changed and expanded. It also sometimes happens that they don't agree with some remarks and ask that they be deleted from the program and completely reworked, or they may reject them entirely.

The RC secretariat and DC secretaries are responsible for internal party affairs. However, they also go beyond their authority and make decisions about matters falling within the competence of the RC or DC presidia. Conversely, the presidia delegate to the secretaries part of their authority, entrust them with various questions, and give them the task of completing or reworking its resolutions. Most significant, however, is the fact that at the meetings, the RC secretariat and DC secretaries deal with reports prepared for the RC or DC presidium and make decisions regarding their inclusion in the program. With important reports they discuss their contents, establish a unified position, and thus predetermine the decision making of the RC or DC presidium.

Initiatives for matters to be dealt with by the power group in the region and district come from a superior organ from within—especially from the RC or DC secretaries, from the party apparat, and from extra-party institutions. The method and character of decision making is influenced and predetermined to a considerable extent by the contents of the reports and proposed resolutions, that is, in the first instance by the work of the party apparat. The power group is not, however, entirely dependent on that work. It can always reject or return reports and change resolutions. On the other hand, the influence of the party apparat on the decision making of the power group is considerably reinforced by the fact that its most important members—the DC and RC secretaries—constitute the core of the presidium and possess considerable clout within it.

On paper, all DC and RC presidium members are equal. In reality, there are two kinds of membership—representatives of power apparats and functionaries without apparats. The former possess considerable advantages. They have information from their superior organs as well as from lower-level functionaries, they receive an overview of the widest variety of matters throughout the entire district or region, and politics is their profession. The latter represent either a kind of specialist in pulling strings—in industry, the director of an enterprise; in agriculture, the chairman of an agricultural cooperative—or a "voice of the people." Conflicts occasionally occur among representatives of power apparats based on the power groups to which they belong, which reflect the differing points of view of their respective agencies. This happens mostly between DC or RC secretaries, as representatives of the party apparat, and the chairmen of the DNC or RNC, as representatives of the state apparat. Differing, even opposing, views turn up between these kinds of functionaries as to the solution of various questions, as well as differing evaluations of deficiencies and responsibility for them. DC and RC secretaries and their apparats like to shift the responsibility for mistakes and deficiencies to other institutions and apparats. But the representatives of these in the presidium put up resistance and point, on the contrary, to insufficient activity of party organizations and functionaries, and to mistakes of the party apparat.

In advocating their points of view, the power positions of the DC or RC secretaries and DNC or RNC chairmen are evenly matched in that both the secretaries and the chairmen are members of power groups, dispose of information obtained by their own means, and command apparats that work out and ensure the fulfillment of what are often the same guidelines in their own way. They also hold equivalent rank in the cadre nomenklatura [a list of positions in the state administration and in social organizations for which party bodies are responsible, i.e., to which they may name personnel or for which their assent is needed]. Because of their position in society, the DNC and

RNC chairmen stand higher and form a kind of "tandem" with the DC or RC leading secretary. When conflicts occur, leading secretaries cannot overrule or silence DNC or RNC chairmen or have them removed from their positions since they belong to the party apparat. The leading secretary is not entirely without recourse, however. He can complain to the chairman's superior or to an RC or CC secretary. A chairman's removal has to be approved by the superior party organs, and reasons for it have to be given. Concern about the reaction in a district or region also tends to restrain any radical resolution of conflicts among these members of the power group.

Conflicts even occur between representatives of the unions and the DC or RC secretary responsible for industry. Most of these conflicts arise from the confrontation of demands and conceptions of the latter with social reality, as represented or interpreted by the former. There is no lack of conflict among the DC and RC secretaries themselves either. These controversies do not occur on a regular basis, and aren't always heated, but they reflect differing opinions, as well as personal power interests, of the secretaries. Such conflicts take place within the confines of the power group and are also appropriately resolved within this framework. Occasionally they break out of this closed circle, but even then, only a small proportion of functionaries find out about them. They remain hidden from the public. The power group behaves outwardly as a single, harmonious entity, as established by the unwritten law of party life.

High-level party organs pay a great deal of attention to maintaining unified action on the part of members of a DC or RC presidium, especially to preserving good relations between the secretaries and the DNC or RNC chairman. His collaboration with the DC or RC leading secretary is seen as an essential prerequisite for the functioning of the power mechanism. The regional and central instructor reports any discord and antagonism among the members of the power group assigned to him. As soon as conflicts reoccur, become permanent, and risk becoming public, the higher-level party institution intervenes—especially when there are frequent breakdowns in the collaboration of the DNC or RNC chairman and the leading secretary. The higher-level institution usually makes personnel changes, and it is often DC or RC secretaries, rather than power group members outside the party apparat, who are the victims.

The privileged position of the DC or RC leading secretary stands out against the background of the relatively equal positions of power apparat members. Everyone recognizes this, including members of the power group. This privileged status is tied to the position rather than to the individual, and it holds true regardless of the professional level or political competence of the individual in question. This state of affairs was established by the supreme party authorities, which strive continually to maintain it. For them, the leading secretary is the most solid and secure instrument for the enforcement of their designs and their will. Mainly for this reason, reinforcement of the authority of the leading, and thus most powerful, man in the district or region is exceedingly important to them. The leading secretary is also responsible to the higher power group for everything that happens in his "territory." In figurative terms, he receives this territory to administer knowing that he will unquestioningly carry out the will of the center. The privileged position of the leading secretary is stressed by the superior organs in the course of his selection and installation.

The district leading secretary is chosen by the regional organs; the regional, by the central organs. Before each district conference, the RC political-organizational department submits to its presidium an evaluation of every DC leading secretary, as well as of the other DC secretaries. The first version of the evaluation is prepared by the RC instructor, and it is then revised by the district head of department and the RC secretariat. The report for the RC presidium contains a proposal for confirmation of the incumbent DC leading secretary or for his replacement. If a change is foreseen, his successor is named in the report after recommendation by the political-organizational department or by secretaries of the RC. Selection is limited to three sources: (1) members of the DC presidium or DC secretaries, (2) a leading secretary or DC secretary from another district, (3) regional party apparatchiks. The DC leading secretary is chosen from the same sources when a change takes place between two district conferences. In such cases a functionary from another district or region is usually appointed. The departure of a DC leading secretary is negotiated with him by the RC leading secretary or, in exceptional cases, by one of the RC secretaries, who likewise negotiates with the proposed successor. The change is approved by the DC presidium, which is informed of it by a secretary or RC head of department. The procedure at the central level for selection of an RC leading secretary is similar, with a greater role being played by the Secretariat and CC secretaries.

The leading secretary is the only one at the district or regional level whose appointment is confirmed by the central committee, and the higher-level presidium makes a direct proposal to the appropriate committee. His first meeting after the conference is chaired by a representative of the region or the center, who announces, "The regional (or central) committee proposes Comrade XY to you for the office of leading secretary." This clinches his election. The leading secretary enjoys a host of special privileges. He is the best-informed functionary, as central headquarters shares some especially secret information with him alone. His position is crucial in the resolution of all matters of serious consequence in the district or region, and he often has the "last word." Functionaries at higher levels of the state and economic and party apparats regard it evidence of their importance, even a high honor, if they can discuss their areas of responsibility directly with the leading secretary. The leading secretary's concurrence with their position, presented as "the party's opinion," carries great weight.

The position of the leading secretary in the power group is based not only on support from higher authorities but also on a host of additional factors. He stands at the head of an exceedingly powerful party apparat. He establishes the agenda for meetings of the RC presidium and secretariat and the DC conference of secretaries, chairs those meetings, and formulates their resolutions. His privileged knowledge from central headquarters is supplemented by his own sources. Especially valuable in this respect is his exclusive information from State Security as he has the right to ask State Security for information on the situation in any institution or locality or about any person. Matters having to do with security and the military are among his responsibilities, and he doesn't have to inform his presidium about them.

He alone has regular direct relations with members of higher-level power groups, including their leading secretaries. It is difficult, in some cases even impossible, for the other members of the presidium or the secretaries to have such contacts. And conversely, members of higher-level power groups turn mainly to the leading secretary, some rely on him exclusively. For all functionaries in the region and district, it is he, first and foremost, who symbolizes the party and its policies. They turn to him with matters having to do with their functions, and his opinion or advice is regarded as the binding party policy. Furthermore, an awareness of his considerable authority in cadre matters is strongly in evidence in these relationships. Finally, an RC leading secretary is assured membership in the CC as well as a seat in the National Assembly.

Presidium of the Central Committee

Composition

The basic characteristic of the communist monopoly of power is the most extensive concentration of power in the hands of a narrow group of people history has ever known. It is a total hegemony over society, in which this group stands out as absolute political ruler, owner of all means of production and national wealth, and proprietor of cultural facilities as well as the supreme arbiter of criteria for the value of works of art and for standards regarding information of the citizenry. This holder of absolute power is the central power group—the Presidium, Secretariat, and secretaries of the Central Committee—twenty people in all. Nominations for membership in it originate at conferences of CC secretaries, are approved by the current Presidium, and members are elected or, more accurately, ratified by the Central Committee.

After its seizure of power, the core of the communist leadership consisted of "old veterans," members of the prewar Politburo or CC. They also simultaneously held state offices. During the course of ten to fifteen years they gradually left their positions due to age or other reasons and were completely replaced by a new generation of functionaries.[1]

After this shift in personnel, especially the generational shift, profound changes took place that affected the character and mission of the power group. It metamorphosed from a power-political institution into the supreme unit of a politico-economic directive regime, into an organ of direct decision making over all areas of social life. The whole party devotes itself to fulfillment of this role—one the power group appropriated for itself, thus usurping the right to make decisions about everything according to its own interests. The composition of the group's membership also conforms to this role as it resembles a representative institution consisting of representatives of the power apparats. The general secretary, two or three CC secretaries; the leading party secretary in Slovakia and in the city of Prague; the chairmen of the federal, Czech, and Slovak governments, the minister of planning; and the chairmen of the central office of the trade unions and the parliament are standing members by virtue of their positions. (In the particular circumstances of Czechoslovakia, the Czecho-Slovak relationship is also reflected in the composition of the Presidium, but this is not significant for our consideration of the anatomy of the party.) It is significant that the proportion of party apparatchiks in the Presidium has increased. In 1954, of the eleven members of the Politburo, there were only two representatives of the party apparat; during the seventies, they made up half the membership. Of course, members who had earlier worked in the party apparat but held another position during the period of their membership in the CC Presidium always predominated.[2]

As a result of bad experiences with membership in the Politburo of a minister of defense in the mid fifties and a minister of the interior in the early sixties, and especially because of a recommendation of Nikita Khrushchev, the Central Committee passed a resolution in 1962

(Antonín Novotný proposed it) prohibiting their membership in the Presidium. This resolution reflected an interest common to all its members, not to have in their midst a representative of an especially powerful and controlling apparat. That is to say, membership of the minister of the interior or defense alters the power relations within the Presidium. Their power positions are inferior to that of the general secretary; their power is greater than that of the other Presidium members since they have their own sources of information, otherwise available only to the general secretary (and sometimes not even to him). They also have important links to important power-political forces in Moscow (military and security), either in the course of their work or through "their" Soviet liaison officer.

CC secretaries, vice-premiers in the government, and other high-level functionaries long for membership in the CC Presidium and go to great lengths to get in. Because membership is linked to certain state and party positions, conflicts often take place in connection with the filling of these positions. Appointments to the Presidium are the exclusive prerogative of the general secretary, a significant instrument of power for him. He can use this instrument to build a power group according to his own conceptions. The process begins with criticism of the work of an institution or department headed by some functionary the general secretary wants to get rid of. This is followed by the functionary's removal, which automatically means departure from the Presidium. The general secretary can then easily replace that person with someone he wants in the Presidium. This is very often someone who would never have attained a high position without being the general secretary's "horse." The new appointee feels much obliged to the general secretary, first out of gratitude, later because he also comes to see the linkage between his own position and that of the general secretary. The general secretary tries to build up a hard core of his own men, consisting of this kind of member, to maintain it for several electoral periods, and to modify the remaining membership.[3]

Some fundamental principles guide the general secretary and CC secretaries in their choice of Presidium members: Only individuals whose views are in full agreement with theirs and whose devotion to their policies is beyond doubt are admitted into the power group. It is only within these limits that struggles occasionally take place among secretaries as well as among other members of the Presidium to get "their people" into the power group.

Consistent maintenance of these criteria functions as one of the main elements ensuring continuity of the leadership. These criteria can be labeled "ideological-political." An additional element providing continuity is the fact that the power group is only gradually supplemented by new members or members from the younger generation, and this happens in such a manner that the core remains intact. These new members, whether or not they are consciously aware of it, accept responsibility for the policies of the past and feel bound to them. They can't detach themselves since they see in the defense of party policy, including that of the past, the prerequisite for maintenance of the party's position in society and, most important, of their leadership within the party. Established methods of work are the most significant element of continuity, and these have deep roots, growing out of the social role of the party and the power group. These work methods emerge and live on as a product of the regime and the mechanism of power. Every new member enters the power group with an awareness of unconditional subordination to its routines, intensified by the feeling of being a novice among party veterans. And no one resists these routines. They either regard them as quite normal or lack the courage to oppose them due to fear of losing their membership in the group of the most powerful, and they justify their actions by the necessity of maintaining the unity of the leadership.

The above-mentioned elements of continuity are among the sources of the conservatism that is so pronounced in communist leaderships after their accession to power. The power group knows no family inheritance of position, but it has mastered the process of "inheritance" of the power system, policy, ideology, and historical experience of the party, which matter much more to it. This "inheritance" is transmitted, guarded, and cultivated.

Substance of the Proceedings

The Presidium deals with a broad range of problems, and two problems of general character arise in connection with the broad scope of its decision making. First, the Presidium makes decisions on matters for which constitutional organs are responsible yet bears no responsibility for its decisions. Responsibility rests with the constitutional organs and heads of state institutions. Since 1948, there has been a running conflict about authority between the government and parliament on the one hand and the CC Presidium on the other hand. This is a concealed conflict that usually works to the benefit of the CC Presidium. The Presidium substitutes its own authority for that of state organs, not only in general orientation, i.e., in determining the course of state policy, but whenever it wants to. It reserves the right to make decisions, broad as well as specific, having to do with any portfolio or specialized matter at all coming under the authority of the government and its ministries. No division of authority has ever been clearly defined, and all efforts to do this have met with disinterest, especially on the part of the CC secretaries. They know that they would lose the possibility of arbitrarily selecting matters to be removed from the authority of the government.

Second, the Presidium adopts binding resolutions concerning matters about which its members have no specialized knowledge at all. They justify their behavior by insisting that, as members of a political organ, they have the right to make political decisions. However, most of the issues with which they deal are specialized, economic, or even technological in character and can only be evaluated by specialists. Their so-called political decision making works to the detriment of expertise. It is a clear paradox, but a reality, that they particularly like to make decisions about things they know nothing about, above all about agriculture and culture.

Resolutions of the CC Presidium often conflict with analyses and proposals that are the result of many months of work by specialists. Despite this, only rarely does the Presidium receive alternative proposals to choose among. If any alternative exists at all, it is the position of the responsible department or a CC secretary, and is usually drafted so as to agree with the views of the members of the CC Presidium, or at least the general secretary. For especially important questions, expert opinion from scholarly institutions or individual specialists is included, along with the views of CC commissions. However, most of these merely confirm the proposal that has been presented. Alternative proposals of resolutions are quite unusual.

Suggested changes to measures proposed by specialists evoke incomprehension, surprise, and astonishment among the specialists. They cannot understand the motives, nor do they know the reasons for the decisions of the CC Presidium. Let me take two especially blatant examples from the fifties. Czechoslovak economists had worked out a proposal for the First Five Year Plan (1949–1953) on the basis of the established fact that Czechoslovakia is a country poor in raw materials. In 1951, Stalin proclaimed that there was a significant wealth of minerals on Czechoslovak territory. The Prague leadership suddenly changed its mind and adapted its economic policy to conform to his view. In 1954, Prime Minister Viliam Široký was to go to Moscow for consultations regarding the Czechoslovak economic plan. On the basis of their calculations, the planning office foresaw an increase in production of 3–4 percent. Široký argued that he couldn't go to Moscow with such a low rate of growth, and the Politburo raised it a further 4 percent on the spot.

The CC Presidium justifies its political decision making on the grounds that it protects the Marxist-Leninist orientation of party policy and the true interpretation of Marxism. It thus sets itself up as the supreme arbiter in the interpretation and implementation of Marxism-Leninism. However, no one, with the partial exception of the CC secretary for ideology, has ever studied the works of Marx or Lenin. Their libraries contain attractively bound "classical works," which have never been touched. None of the Presidium members knows any of Marx's works. Lenin they have encountered at party schools and training courses, and this mostly according to the interpretation of the times—i.e., Stalinist. They even acknowledge this weakness themselves.[4] They read no more than "applied Marxism"—mainly what is contained in resolutions of the Soviet party. There, however, Marxism is "applied," as in Prague, very simply. Every leadership proclaims its policies to be the only true Marxism-Leninism and themselves to be crystal pure Marxist-Leninists, something given to them by nature as a kind of christening present.

It would be doing the members of the power group an injustice to overlook the fact that they sometimes actually do look at Lenin's works. For this "theoretical act" functionaries make use of the established expression: "I took Lenin's advice, I consulted Lenin." Lower-level functionaries say, "I studied the Lily Marlene method" (I leafed through the Marxist-Leninist literature). In actual practice, this means that the high-level functionary looked up, or had looked up for him, quotes from Lenin in order to "give theoretical support" to party policy.

The power group does not use Marxism-Leninism as a theoretical perspective to help shape their policy but, rather, as the theoretical facade in which they wrap their policies. It is very important to them to make use of the Marxist-Leninist attribute. The party apparat is aware of this predilection and thus caters to it in reports and documents. There are, however, real reasons for this predilection. First and foremost, it is well received in Moscow, where the Soviets pass themselves off as the arbiters of the world through Marxism-Leninism. Moscow is very sensitive to the use of ideology. One typical example: In 1955, during Khrushchev's first visit to Yugoslavia, the Soviet Premier, Nikolai Bulganin praised Tito as a great Leninist. However, the visit didn't turn out according to Moscow's expectations, and Tito didn't appear to be such a great Leninist after all. For this reason, the Soviet leadership later wrote to Prague that Bulganin had made a mistake.

However, the Prague leaders also have their own reasons for stressing the correctness of their interpretation of Marxism-Leninism, apart from concern regarding Moscow. If they proclaim their policy—and thus themselves—to be the only Marxist-Leninist one, they can, if need be, declare all deviating views to be un-Marxist and anti-Marxist. Since it is the duty of the party leadership to protect the purity of Marxism-Leninism, there naturally exists a right to level criticism or disagreement, or, if need be, to launch a campaign against deviationists. Furthermore, the expression of reverence, belief, and fidelity to Marxism-Leninism is taken by all functionaries as a matter of course, whether or not they know it or believe in it. It is simply the law that everyone recognizes. Only the rare individual inquires into whether Marxism actually is everything it is made out to be, and whether party policy is Marxist; most functionaries don't worry about such things. They accept as Marxism whatever is transmitted to them, and they believe in it.

A brief analysis of the questions the CC Presidium deals with shows that Marxism is not used at all in a practical way as a method of understanding. The Presidium agenda contains no analyses of the condition of society, of its political consciousness, of the economic interests of groups in society, of the situation in the party itself, or similar matters. Instead, proclamations and phrases about the socialist unity of the people, the nation, and nationalities and superficial, empty statistical surveys of the class and social composition of the population substitute for a search for answers to such questions. It wouldn't be hard for the Presidium to get hold of the kinds of analyses mentioned, since several scholarly institutions deal with these kinds of questions. The Presidium believes that its own information is adequate to form a picture of society, and that thorough research and analysis is no better. Fear of the truth also contributes to the members' disinterest. Experience with the occasional study of conditions in the economy evokes fears that similar glimpses at other areas of social life would place a mirror in front of their own policies. There is also concern that those who carry out such studies can exploit them in order to make negative phenomena public.[5] Cadre proposals appear on the agenda of every Presidium meeting—sometimes there are more than ten. These are dealt with first, and they can be broken down into three groups. First, there are those for which the Central Committee is given responsibility under cadre procedures. The CC Presidium makes these nominations and therefore has to discuss them. A larger category consists of cadres belonging to the Presidium's nomenklatura list. These include high-level cadres, such as vice-ministers, radio and television high officials, the general procuracy, the supreme court, the churches, the noncommunist parties, the minister of defense, the parliament, the chairmen and secretaries of the most significant mass organizations, generals, heads of security, permanent representatives to COMECON, Warsaw Pact institutions, and individuals to be sent to study at the party university in Moscow or the Soviet military academy.

The third group consists of persons being elevated or honored. These are nominations that, according to the constitution, are made by the president of the Republic (university professors, ambassadors, national artists, etc.) as well as nominations of distinguished artists, ministers of sport, and the holders of orders and distinctions. Establishment of the personal pensions of high party and state officials can also be considered as cadre decisions. Cadre proposals are submitted by the CC secretary responsible for the portfolio.

Matters having to do with internal party life appear relatively seldom on the Presidium meeting agenda, as they tend to be the responsibility of the CC Secretariat. They are prepared by the Organizational-Political (the First) and the Ideological (the Second) Departments of the Central Secretariat and, in exceptional cases, by the army's Main Political Administration. These departments deal mainly with evaluation of conferences and annual meetings and preparation of political campaigns, but they are also concerned with proposals having to do with changes in systematization of the party apparat and in party life and overviews of party administration. They also deal with publication of resolutions having to do with the most important internal party campaigns, such as annual members' meetings and conferences, the social composition of the membership base and cadre and personnel work (adopted in December 1964 and November 1970). The initiatives for reports dealing with internal party life come not only from the experience of the above-mentioned departments but frequently at the request of the regions and districts.

Only in exceptional cases does the Presidium deal with the activities of interest organizations and mass organizations. When it does so it is just before their national congresses and relates to only the most important of them. Otherwise, this concern is left to the CC Secretariat. Two exceptions are the trade unions and youth organization, which appear frequently on the agenda of Presidium meetings. In the case of the youth organization the Presidium is fulfilling an obligation arising from one of its own resolutions dealing with party administration of the youth organization. Reports on the activities of mass organizations are prepared by the leaderships of the organizations and the CC department responsible for this portfolio.

The CC Presidium has an ongoing interest in the activities of parliament, even though this doesn't come up frequently at its meetings. The Presidium's involvement begins with preparations for parliamentary elections. It makes a key stipulating the political and social distribution of deputies, which the regions use as a guide. It assigns central candidates to the regions—such as ministers, members of the power group, and chairmen of mass organizations. It approves nominations for membership in parliament and appointments to high positions in parliament. It approves the entire agenda for the most important sessions of parliament, such as the opening session or the presentation of the government's program, including the text of the government's declaration, as well as the members who are to participate in the discussion. In the early fifties, it also dealt with what participants in the discussion would say. Until 1965, it approved the final wording of all draft laws even before the parliamentary committees had dealt with them. Members of parliament could not then make any changes.

In 1965, the chairman of the parliament succeeded in changing that procedure, so that the Presidium would first deal only with the basic principles of a law, giving it final approval only after parliament had expressed itself, i.e., after the parliamentary committees had dealt with it. The basic principles and comments are returned to the government, with the actual wording of the law being left to the government and parliament. Only for especially important laws does the Presidium continue its earlier practice. In preparation of the law dealing with the five-year plan, parliamentary committees take part in shaping the draft plan after its basic principles have been approved by the Central Committee, whose resolution is already binding for the members of parliament. For some laws, as well as the activities of justice, the CC legal commission informs the CC Presidium of its views and suggestions.

The Presidium often deals with matters related to the military, which has not always been the case. Up to 1953, most military questions were decided upon by Minister Čepička along with President Gottwald and Soviet advisers. For the most part, these were matters that had already been settled within the Soviet General Staff. The CC Presidium and Secretariat controlled only the fulfillment of plans for military production and provided for the army's economic requirements. After 1954, Čepička also submitted some matters having to do with military organization to the Politburo. After his departure, this was done with greater frequency through the general secretary. Since 1957, with insignificant exceptions, it has not been the responsible secretary, i.e., the general secretary, who has given reports having to do with the army but rather the minister of defense himself or the head of a CC department. Since the general secretary does not even make decisions about those matters that come under his authority as president, many reports of the minister or the CC Defense Commission come to the Presidium. Among these are the texts of festive orders, salary adjustments for officers, results of conscription of recruits, and celebrations of Army Day. There are also organizational matters, such as equipping and training the army; dates for the equipment and training of units assigned to the Warsaw Pact; preparation and conduct of military exercises; and party work in the army. During the years 1955–1968, the Presidium discussed an average of eighty reports dealing with military policy or the army annually while the government discussed only twenty-seven to thirty such reports a year, and more than a third of those had to be dealt with first by the CC Presidium.

Security matters do not often come up at Presidium meetings, and even when they do, they mainly involve reports about the organization and material security of the police and the overall state of criminality. Only rarely do reports concerning the situation in State Security, statistical overviews of persons under investigation for or convicted of political and criminal infractions, or reports on the course of the investigation of individual political cases get on the agenda. The general secretary decides whether to include them, upon proposal by the minister of the interior. Until the mid 1950s, the CC Secretariat made decisions on the arrest of officials and approved the dates of court proceedings, the wording of the indictment, and the severity of the sentence, but this practice has been abandoned. Members of the CC Presidium do receive information on the preparation and then the outcome of the most significant political trials, but concrete details are elaborated within a narrow circle of officials.

During the 1950s, matters having to do with justice were frequently on the agenda. The minister of justice first submitted for decision matters relating to the most important political trials, later matters having to do with the rehabilitation of their victims. The quantity of such reports has gradually declined, but the most common ones include reports on the activities of procuracies and courts (mostly statistical), including evaluations of crime policy (especially economic crime) and the maintenance of legality. The minister also submits for decision death penalty cases and proposals for amnesty to be granted by the president. Such proposals for amnesty set forth precisely the crimes to which the amnesty applies and the number of those to be given amnesty. They also include a list of names of political prisoners being considered for amnesty, with which the Presidium deals especially carefully.

Although members of the CC Presidium set themselves up with pleasure and enthusiasm as critics of artistic works and work in the social sciences, cultural affairs come up at their meetings as routine items, usually in a a general form. The Presidium deals with reports on television broadcasting, i.e., on the political orientation of its dramaturgy, as well as those on the film industry. The Presidium members also go through reports about dramaturgy in the theater (including breakdowns into the number of Soviet, contemporary, and classical plays), the activities of the Academy of Sciences, education in general or higher education in particular, church policy, and similar matters. The reports also contain statistical data on cinema attendance (according to the criteria under review—Soviet, Czech, Western films), the theater, religiosity of citizens, social composition of the student population in higher education, the television broadcast day as it breaks down into entertainment, political commentary, etc. The discussion usually "slides" into criticism of some particular television programs, films, theater performances, or books. Participants in the discussion also express their opinions of authors and show interest in the financial aspects of cultural activities. The CC Presidium deals with conceptual matters relating to the activities of cultural institutions and often publishes the results of its deliberations as basic resolutions of the Central Committee. For example, on August 30, 1966, it published the document *On Current Questions of Party Guidance of the Press and Other Mass Media Having Influence on Ideas.* In 1975, there were resolutions on the unified program of social sciences and on the role and management of institutions of higher education.

The special attention elicited by writers' congresses has become a tradition. The Presidium deals with preparations for them and even more with what happens at them if criticisms of party policy are made. In cases like the writers' congresses in 1956 and 1967, it intervenes harshly against the critics and attempts to destroy them socially by banning publication of their works. During the 1970s, the Presidium dealt several times with the situation in the cultural domain. Hundreds of artists and scholars were placed in a situation of existential distress on account of its decisions, because they refused to identify themselves with the official policy of liquidation of the Prague Spring and collaboration with Moscow.

Reports in the cultural domain are prepared by the responsible CC department in collaboration with the leaderships of cultural institutions, which provide the supporting material. The Ideological Commission participates in many of them, itself providing suggestions for reports to be prepared.

Most numerous, as already noted, are reports on economic questions. These are extremely varied, from the quality and price of bread to ideas for economic development over the next ten to twenty years, from authorization of weapons exports to cattle raising. Most reports come from the ministries responsible for the areas with which the reports deal. Materials from the planning office predominate both in content and importance. Its minister or responsible vice-premier is a member or candidate member of the CC Presidium, with the right to present reports. A relatively smaller number of reports of a fundamental nature are produced by the Economic Department of the CC Secretariat, the CC Economic Commission, and special and occasional commissions of specialists and ministers.

The CC Presidium discusses and approves all short- and long-term economic plans and submits most of them to the Central Committee. The former also deals with the fulfillment of these plans on a monthly, quarterly, and yearly basis, as well as the state budget and the financial condition of the country, including saving and spending by citizens. Questions having to do with the standard of living and social situation of citizens, all significant price adjustments, wage policy, the state of health care and social security, private consumption, disturbances in supplies to the commercial network, the problem of living quarters— e.g., it approves the level of investments, the construction of large settlements in Prague and Bratislava—all such reports contain concrete resolutions. In the area of foreign trade it regularly discusses the quarterly balance of trade, balance of payments, and all significant interstate treaties dealing with economic matters.

In addition to such questions of a more general character, there are also more specific matters that get on the agenda. One category of these can be called portfolio related. Among them are reports on the condition of various branches of production—such as in the chemical, electrotechnical, mining, smelting, and machine industries; animal production; state farms; agricultural mechanization; meeting the needs of the population; cooperatives and communal enterprises; supplies of several kinds of goods; technical development; trade with Warsaw Pact and Third World countries; fulfillment of deliveries to the Soviet Union; and arms production and arms sales abroad.

An additional group consists of concrete economic questions, e.g., routine reports on the construction of major investment projects already approved by the Presidium and proclaimed as governmental projects of the highest priority, such as the Prague subway, the Bratislava bridge, the superhighway, large power plants, dams, mines, several agricultural investments, and particularly important deliveries to foreign countries. Reports of this kind—which are verificatory in character, called for by earlier resolutions, or stem from some initiative of a minister responsible for the matters dealt with—contain particularly detailed resolutions that require other ministries and enterprises to obtain materials, technology, and manpower. Also on the agenda are specialized questions such as technological renovation of large factories; changes in their production programs, measures aimed at conservation of energy and materials, including organization of contests among enterprises; the system of premiums; fulfillment of specific production goals; restructuring of workers' wages; plans for reconstruction of the old city of Prague; the state of supplies above and beyond the norm (in factories) and unsold goods (in stores); improvements in the quality of production and of innovation; construction of recreational facilities; and the political and financial aspects of agreements with foreign firms concerning construction of major investment projects.

Only infrequently do comprehensive analyses of the condition of the economy appear on the agenda, usually when disturbances in the economic sphere reach a critical point. From time to time the CC Presidium asks the Office of Planning to work out a long-range conception for economic development or for some branch of production (machine, chemical, or mining industry), which it then approves as guidelines. Most of these economic prognoses quickly reveal themselves to be unrealistic for various reasons and are modified or completely abandoned. The Presidium devotes considerable attention to all changes in the system of economic management, dealing not only with basic principles but even with details. It makes sure that decentralization of decision making does not weaken its authority in the economic domain. Under various pressures, however, it accedes to changes in the system of economic management or even takes the initiative itself as it did in 1951, 1965, and 1980.

The CC Presidium has never concerned itself with analysis of the international situation, the country's status in the international arena, or the government's foreign policy (except for preparation of speeches dealing with international issues for the CC meeting in 1957). It limits itself to specific measures, to reports that are informational in character, and to discussion of the political orientation of the Czechoslovak delegation at significant international meetings and conferences of communist parties. Rather than make its own analyses, it utilizes the evaluations of Soviet institutions and politicians. There is "no disagreement" about decisions in the realm of international politics, "either within the Presidium or within the central committee" (Vladimír Koucký, December 1967). This state of affairs only reflects the overall lack of interest in international politics that is typical among functionaries, including those at the top.

International political issues discussed by the CC Presidium can be divided into two categories: (1) party affairs and (2) matters having to do with the activities of the Ministry of Foreign Affairs and with membership in international organizations. Issues in the first category include approval of the makeup of delegations to meetings of communist parties and their congresses and polemical letters addressed to other communist parties (e.g., the Chinese). The Presidium makes decisions regarding the reception of delegations of brotherly parties and visits of party and state delegations to Soviet bloc countries and receives reports on the results of their discussions. It deals with the situation in other communist parties, mainly when they are experiencing difficulties (e.g., in 1948, it dealt with the Yugoslav situation; in 1956, with the Hungarian and Polish; in 1980, with the Polish) and it determines the extent to which the mass media will deal with them and the substance of what is to be said.

The general secretary submits for approval all official letters from the Central Committee to the highest organs of Soviet bloc communist parties and governments and often letters from the government as well. At his own discretion, he informs the Presidium of the contents of letters he has received from the leaderships or general secretaries of other communist parties. These have to do with national economic relations, political decisions, or proposals of an international nature that some party has made, or intends to make. Letters from Moscow take precedence among these items of information. Similarly, the general secretary puts on the agenda reports on his meetings (if necessary, those of other members of the Presidium too) with high officials of the Soviet or other East European parties.

Questions of state foreign policy, treaties of alliance, speeches and proposals for meetings of the Warsaw Pact and COMECON, and reports on their results take precedence, as do basic principles for the conduct of delegations to the United Nations and other politically significant conferences. This sometimes also includes scholarly conferences and, in exceptional cases, international independence struggle, youth, trade union, and other organizations. The Presidium approves the political orientation as well as concrete matters discussed during state visits abroad of the president, the prime minister, and the ministers of foreign affairs and defense, or of foreign dignitaries in Prague and significant bilateral negotiations (e.g., with the Vatican), as well as important documents (such as proclamations and decisions of the Ministry of Foreign Affairs and the government). In some individual cases, the general secretary includes as information extracts from the coded dispatches of some ambassador or, more often, minutes of his discussions with an ambassador from a Soviet bloc country, especially the Soviet ambassador.

Extensive reports, as well as specific information on international issues, come from the Ministries of Foreign Affairs and Foreign Trade, the CC International Department, and occasionally from the Office of the General Secretary. Following a practice instituted in 1954, and confirmed by its own resolution, the CC Presidium discusses all public speeches given by its own members. In several cases, the CC Secretariat or a special commission is entrusted with this. This practice later gave way to approval, not of the entire texts of speeches, but of their basic

principles. Only for speeches of considerable importance has the original
practice continued. Presidium members know how to follow instructions, and discussion of speeches is limited to comments and a few
modifications or additions. Only in rare cases do the members recommend changes that affect the contents of the speech.[6] Verificatory
reports concerned with how well CC Presidium resolutions are being
carried out don't often appear on the agenda. These are usually presented at meetings of the CC Secretariat, which means that the Presidium does not have an overview of the fate of its own decisions.

About a fifth of the items on the agenda are informational in
character. The members read only a few of them, since they don't
usually consider them very important, but such items do play a role
in shaping their notions of social reality. For these reasons, they can
be, and in fact are, selected with certain purposes in mind. Information
items may be either written or oral, and decisions to include oral
items are made at the beginning of the meeting. Informational items
are extremely varied in character and may contain, for example, no
more than information on the progress of intra-party campaigns or
economic matters. They can, however, also contain information the
general secretary has culled from the reports of intelligence and coun-
terintelligence agencies with certain purposes in mind.

How the Meetings Are Run

The CC Presidium meets on a regular, weekly basis on a fixed
day—Tuesday. It also holds special sessions and occasionally doesn't
meet for various reasons, including having nothing on the agenda. The
regularity of meetings has been maintained since 1954 but such was
not always the case under Gottwald.[7]

The meeting agenda—or more precisely, part of it—is guided by
the Presidium's plan of work. The planned items get lost in the totality
of matters discussed and are drowned out by a great many other things.
The planned items can usually be distinguished from the others in
that they are more general in character and belong to the category of
reports I have called "basic" or "conceptual."

The meeting agenda is put together by the Office of the General
Secretary and approved by the general secretary. The head of the
general secretary's office makes requests that those functionaries assigned responsibilities by the plan of work submit reports. These
requests stipulate not only what the report is to be about but also
who is to deliver it. Very often, however, the reports are not ready in
time. If pressure is not exerted by the head of the general secretary's
office, who usually makes a written request for the reasons for the

delay, the general secretary himself reminds the official of his obligation to submit the report, orally or sometimes in writing. In addition, secretaries, heads of CC departments, and representatives of central agencies give notice of further items they want added to the agenda, and only in isolated cases does the general secretary's office reject reports from central extra-party institutions as being inappropriate for a meeting of the CC Presidium. Although the general secretary has the last word, he rarely removes an item from the proposed agenda.

The CC Presidium operates on the basis of written reports. These include cadre proposals and conceptual, operational, verificatory, and informational reports. They have to be ready in the prescribed format and quantity by Friday noon. They are then delivered by courier to the members of the Presidium. In rare cases the deadline is deferred to Monday, in which case it is rarely possible to distribute the report before the meeting. Items for which no written report has been submitted are stricken from the agenda, and oral reports are placed at the bottom of the agenda. Most of these contain various kinds of information, and most are delivered by the general secretary.

Members of the CC Presidium and CC secretaries have the right to give reports. Ministers and representatives of central agencies can do so only through the appropriate CC department and secretary. The secretary has to attach to the report a statement of his viewpoint or that of his department. The quantity of ministers' reports has increased to such an extent that they completely dominate the agenda. This practice influences the work and decision making of the Presidium considerably. The Presidium deals with an overwhelmingly large number of issues, with operational and concrete matters predominating over those that are conceptual in character. In most cases, not only is the government responsible for these matters, but final decisions on them should have been made by the prime minister, a deputy premier, or even the responsible minister instead of their coming to the CC Presidium.

During the year following the seizure of power in 1948, there were, according to the minutes, 256 items in all on the Presidium agenda, i.e., an average of 4.4 per meeting. This figure isn't quite exact since, at that time, much use was made of oral reports, which are not entered into the minutes. Of the 256 items dealt with, 60 had to do with domestic and 22 with international politics, 34 with internal party affairs, 24 with cadre matters, 92 with economics, and 11 with culture and education. During the period 1954–1958 there was an average of 29 items per meeting on the Politburo's agenda, with the exception of a few meetings (not more than ten), that dealt with only 1 item. Roughly 5 or 6 items were informational. During the first half of 1965,

433 reports were submitted to the CC Presidium; for the same part of the following year, 385; and at mid-year of 1967, 429. On average, there were 19 items per meeting in 1965, 18 in 1966, and 21 in 1967. During the same period, members also received the following number of reports "for information" (i.e., not requiring a decision on their part): 158 in 1965, 151 in 1966, and 147 in 1967. On average this was 7–8 reports per meeting. In the three-month period (February to April) of the years 1965–1967, the CC Presidium made decisions on 471 matters, of which 25 were fundamental in character.

All efforts to reduce the number of reports, especially those submitted by ministers, have come to naught. Appeals to CC department heads and secretaries not to yield to pressure from ministers and to turn back reports dealing with things they are supposed to decide on their own fall flat. A proposal that reports from ministers be presented to the CC Presidium by the prime minister was received unfavorably.

There are several reasons for this inability to reduce the number of reports presented. The main reason is the CC Presidium's position as the center of directive decision making in politico-economic affairs. Another is the fact that CC secretaries consider it necessary to check up on or supervise the broadest possible range of activities of central institutions, and thus themselves request reports in many cases. They are convinced that the CC Presidium's decisions establish the right way to solve problems and that it has things under control. Furthermore, they think the Presidium's playing this role is part of maintaining the "leading role of the party." The idea that ministers' reports might be submitted by the prime minister is unacceptable to CC secretaries. If implemented, it would mean not only loss of control but also of a source of information about a significant proportion of the government's activities. It would reinforce the government's power position in relation to the CC Presidium as well as the status of the prime minister within the power group.

Neither are the ministers interested in limiting the number of matters dealt with by the Presidium and thus shifting the locus of decision making to the government and ministries. The CC secretaries know that, in the final analysis, it would be they who would have to decide which reports to turn back, and they would rather shift this task to the Presidium. The minister is similarly motivated, and on top of this, he makes use of reports as a means of getting his proposals to the Presidium without the awareness of the prime minister. Since the Presidium's resolutions are binding for all members of the government, he thus forestalls opposition from other portfolios.

In addition to the large number of reports presented, there is also the problem of their scope and character. Despite all criticism of their size, they are very bulky, ranging from ten to fifty pages. Those from the planning office are even larger. Reports from the party apparat are swelled in size by useless "ideological prefaces," in which the authors try to demonstrate the Marxist-Leninist character of the changes and measures proposed. They know that the members of the power group like ideological jargon (ministers' reports to the Presidium, in contrast, resemble the kind of specialized expertise that comes to the government or to meetings of the minister's advisory committee). Such reports from the party apparat lack a broader political assessment of matters, and heads of department and CC secretaries pass them on to the Presidium in this form along with their own views, which are similar in character. As a result, none of the Presidium members reads all the materials submitted. This would exceed their physical capabilities. (It is typical for the materials for a single meeting to amount to around 500 pages. The record, I have noted, is 1,320 pages for a CC Presidium meeting in April 1954.)

Several members have often complained about this problem. Bohuslav Laštovička (member of the CC Presidium from 1964 to 1968) spoke of the large quantity of materials as well as the additional materials always recommended. "For example, the minister of planning has submitted material containing six or seven appendixes as well. Anyone interested in them can borrow them from the planning office and study them." Martin Vaculík (a candidate member of the CC Presidium from 1964 to 1968 remarked, in a similar vein, "that sometimes the amount of material makes it physically impossible for us to prepare" and that he never felt well enough prepared and preferred not to say anything since he could not read all the material. Vladimír Koucký (a CC secretary from 1958 to 1968) complained that "principles laid down by earlier resolutions are not being followed, such as the amount of material for the CC Presidium. It simply leads to a crushing overload, not to mention a situation that is physically difficult to stay on top of when it is not possible to study matters properly or to make a decision, return to it, look for other variants, etc."

Members thus concentrate on reading those reports that interest them from the point of view of their portfolios. Some have their apparats prepare comments on the reports to read at the meeting. The meeting agenda and quantity and character of the reports predetermine the results of the discussions and the quality of the Presidium's decision making.

The discussion follows procedures adopted in 1955. During the era of Gottwald's chairmanship (until March 1953), the procedures of the prewar Politburo were maintained. Gottwald often did not take part in meetings, leaving it to Slánský to run them; then, after his demise, to Antonín Zápatocký. After Gottwald's death, members of the CC Secretariat adopted the principle of collective leadership prevailing at that time, and chairmanship of the meetings was regularly rotated. Slogans about collective leadership are fashionable in periods when equilibrium prevails, with no member enjoying a dominant power position. In 1955 Novotný tried to gain the upper hand, and the introduction of a new way of running Presidium meetings helped him achieve this goal.

In 1955, Lazar Kaganovich, a member of the Soviet leadership paid a visit to Czechoslovakia, and Novotný wanted to find out from him how meetings of the CC Presidium in Moscow were run. On May 23 1955, Novotný presented the Presidium with a report on his conversation with Kaganovich and a proposal that the Soviet procedures be adopted, both of which were approved. The report stated that

There is no precise demarcation between what is to be decided by the government and what is to be decided in the Presidium. Basic political matters are resolved by the Central Committee. Agricultural matters especially have always been under direct CC supervision, primarily to maintain close ties with the farmers. At meetings of the government, twenty-two to thirty-five items are discussed. The proceedings last about three hours. Questions pertaining to the army are discussed by the government as well as by the Central Committee which, of course, approves all army cadre decisions. As a rule, decisions on cadre matters are not made by the CC Presidium in the first instance. A commission is set up, which then presents the proposal.

As for the agenda of our Politburo, Comrade Kaganovich remarked that it seems to him that many reports on our agenda are unnecessary. He recommended that commissions be appointed to evaluate the reports and inform the politburo whether they correspond to reality and whether the proposed solutions are right. The general secretary plays a large role in preparations for Politburo meetings. He directs the Politburo's work and runs its meetings. He puts together the agenda and has to have a good knowledge of matters to be dealt with. He appoints commissions for the further examination of proposals, etc. The final decision has to be "polished up."

The Politburo's resolution read:

Based on experience, it is proposed that (1) The practice of rotating the chairmanship of Politburo meetings be abolished and it be established that meetings of the Politburo always be chaired by the First Secretary of the CPCz CC, something that is properly his responsibility. (2) The principle be laid down that, immediately after the meeting has been called to order, its agenda be approved and a decision made whether any of the proposals submitted should be deleted from the agenda and not discussed. (3) The procedure be adopted that (a) members of the Politburo will have studied proposals so that it not be necessary to substantiate them unless something new be involved; (b) the first Secretary of the CPCz CC ask if members of the Politburo and candidates have questions about the proposal; (c) they all be answered at the same time by the comrade presenting the proposal; (d) the discussion be concluded by the presenter of the proposal; (e) comments for the resolution be presented; (f) the resolution be formulated by the first secretary. In principle, oral proposals not on the agenda should not be discussed, except for urgent, politically serious matters that cannot be postponed.

These rules have been maintained ever since.

In addition to members and candidates, CC secretaries also take part in CC Presidium meetings. Ministers and other high officials are asked to be present for those reports that they prepared in whole or in part. Those summoned complain that they often have to wait in the antechamber of the meeting room, even for several hours, in order to participate in a five-to-ten-minute discussion of a report. They also voice dissatisfaction that they are not invited for reports presented by someone else that affect their portfolios. And ministers express dislike for the Presidium's practice of evaluating the activity of the government or reorganizing it (i.e., by abolishing existing ministries or creating new ones) without prior discussion within the government.

The general secretary runs Presidium meetings. Following approval of the agenda, the members go through item after item, report after report. For each, there are first questions calling for some kind of explanation. These are immediately answered by the presenter of the report or the invited guest. Discussion then follows. It consists mainly of comments and is not really a discussion in the true sense of the word, i.e., an exchange and confrontation of views, an evaluation of the materials discussed. It takes the form of several members, making a couple of comments, usually specific in character, which they prepared or had prepared. The practice of "commenting" is not restricted to operational reports but also takes place with reports that are fundamental and political in character. The practice of commenting in CC Presidium discussions has became so much a habit that in 1967 several members considered it a manifestation of democratic practice that after having already read their comments, they spoke up again on the item under discussion.

One typical example: On December 14, 1966, the CC Presidium discussed a proposal by Novotný to the Central Committee that dealt with the work of central state organs, above all the government. Although this was a matter that affected all sixteen of those present, only ten spoke up. One agreed fully with the evaluation submitted, two others also agreed fully but added two or three specific comments. Five of the interventions lacked a positive evaluation of the activity of the government, but only three or four insignificant remarks were made. Only one member expressed a critical viewpoint on the activity of the government.

The predominantly commentative character of the discussion is rooted in the belief of Presidium members that reports have either been submitted by CC secretaries or the secretaries at least stand behind them and that the general secretary agrees with them. They thus regard the contents of reports and proposed resolutions as basically correct, as the positions of representatives of the party apparat, with whom they want to avoid conflicts. And so, in the discussion, "they agree basically" with the contents of the report and allow themselves "to make only some specific comments." The upshot of this kind of discussion is that whoever puts together the reports (in the party appart or some other apparat) and especially whoever presents them (a CC secretary) predetermine the decisions of the power group to a significant extent. This important reality is accentuated all the more by the additional fact that CC secretaries and above all the general secretary determine which reports get on the CC Presidium's agenda.

Clashes of opinion are thus isolated occurrences among CC Presidium members. They relate to how the matters discussed are evaluated, as well as to what is proposed for their solution. Given the commentative character of the discussion, however, conflicts cannot be allowed to look too much like two clearly opposed positions. On top of this, the members themselves strive to cover up the contradictions by formulating their positions so as not to give the impression that they are contradictory. That is to say, no one can be sure that a sharpening of differences of opinion in the conflict will not turn against him.[8]

The discussion only rarely goes beyond the usual norm of mere commentary. This can happen when matters of general political character involving criticism of previous policies and its future prospects and their future prospects are discussed, or occasionally during discussion of a speech for a meeting of the Central Committee or of matters having to do with Czech-Slovak relations. On such occasions, the discussion lasts a long time, sometimes into the night, and may even continue at the next meeting. Critical and self-critical tones can also be heard.[9]

Criticism within the CC Presidium has almost no effect on its own policy line and activity. Its effects are limited to party, state, and economic apparats; mass organizations; and cultural institutions. Only once in a great while, when a wave of criticism of the leadership is going through the party, does the feeling of self-satisfaction and self-confidence of its members break down. Only then do Presidium members begin to admit repentantly to deficiencies in their own work—but only among themselves. (This happened in 1953–1957 and 1967–1968.) Such fits of self-criticism have their limits, and criticism stops short of individuals drawing consequences for themselves. Every penitent promises improvement, not resignation. To the extent that resignations do occur, they are the result of pressure from others.

Presidium members usually try to cover up their power struggles, or they characterize them as ideological. They are, however, resolved like any other power conflict. If a conflict occurs between members, it is resolved within the Presidium itself, and its decision is submitted to the Central Committee for approval. This was what happened with Alexej Čepička (stripped of his positions in the Politburo and government in 1956), Rudolf Barák (arrested in 1962), and Viliam Široký (stripped of all functions in 1963). When the conflict causes, or threatens to cause, a split of the CC Presidium into two groups, a final resolution is reached outside the framework of the CC Presidium. Moscow's position is awaited.[10]

There is no real discussion, even between members of the Presidium and officials called in to discuss reports from their portfolios. Those invited usually hear only specific comments, which they accept. Sometimes there is criticism of their institutions and, in isolated cases, of them personally. Every experienced functionary knows how to behave in such situations. In his response at the end of the discussion, it isn't advisable to oppose and disagree too much. On the contrary, it is useful to explain away the problem by citing difficulties and extraordinary circumstances. And the functionary is well advised to admit to having learned from the criticism. Only the inexperienced official disagrees and has the courage to defend himself.

On the whole, the necessary preconditions for open and critical discussion do not exist within the CC Presidium. That is, criticism has its limits, respected by all members, whether they are aware of it or not. These are determined by the views of the general secretary. Many members referred to this fact quite openly in 1967–1968, and blamed Novotný for it. Novotný's supporters, since their thinking was in total harmony with his views, could, without contradicting themselves, affirm the contrary, namely, that in the Presidium "everyone could say what he wanted." Such a state of affairs was quite common during the Novotný era. In addition to those who think the same way as the general secretary, there are also those who do not agree with his views but don't dare take a position that differs from his. They would rather keep quiet than get into a conflict. If the members do not know the general secretary's position, or are not entirely sure that they agree, they wait and enter the discussion only after he has spoken. Should it happen that they have already expressed a view that is not in complete agreement with what the general secretary has said, they will not defend this view against him.

The general secretary has the last word on the report under discussion. He expresses his views on its contents, the discussion, and the proposed resolution. Depending on what has transpired during the discussion, he will either alter the resolution or declare it approved. The Presidium does not vote on resolutions unless manifest differences among its members have emerged. During 1964–1968, only once did a member of the Presidium allow a position to be recorded different than the one adopted by the others.

The CC Presidium approves most reports and proposed resolutions as submitted, or it supplements them. There are also innumerable other cases in which the report is returned for reworking due to inadequacy or is rejected as poor in quality or in which resolutions are modified. Only in exceptional cases does the general secretary propose that a report not be discussed, that it be deleted from the agenda, because he considers it ideologically deficient or inappropriate.[11] The discussion of an item usually concludes with a decision to modify and supplement the report and resolution according to the discussion. Modifications are made by a CC secretary or head of department, or sometimes the minister responsible for the portfolio. Stenographic transcripts of CC Presidium meetings are made only in rare cases, so it is not possible either to make precise modifications or to verify their correctness.

The CC Presidium adopts such a large number of resolutions every year that it is impossible to keep track of them. They often repeat themselves; furthermore, one resolution gives rise to others, since many call for additional reports or give the general secretary the responsibility of "putting the finishing touches on the resolution." On average, about 90 tasks a month, i.e., about 1,000 per year, are assigned. Each task consists of several—ten on the average—concrete points derived from a resolution.[12] Several are intended for various officials. Most tasks are assigned to ministers, around 30 percent to members of the CC Presidium, not quite a quarter to CC secretaries, and a fifth to mass and social organizations.

With few exceptions, CC Presidium resolutions are considered top secret for years. Only a few are contained in the blue bulletin of resolutions of CC and government organs intended for CC members. Except for these, they remain unpublished and, for ten years, are accessible only to a narrow circle of trusted officials. Not even brief reports of CC Presidium meetings are published. The more or less insignificant resolutions that even in advance are intended for the public constitute the exception.

After the Presidium meeting all members have to leave their numbered copies of reports on the table. The reports go to the archives along with the minutes of the meeting, which are very brief. They are put together by the general secretary and contain only the headings of items discussed, resolutions pertaining to them, and the names of those taking part in the discussion. Brief notes on the discussion, taken by the head of the Secretariat, are appended to the minutes.

One copy of each of the reports goes to the so-called active archive, where it is kept three years for the use of the party apparat. Two copies of each resolution remain in the general secretary's office. One is cut up or transcribed, and the resolutions are sent to those officials to whom they have been assigned. The second is used by the official responsible for checking up on implementation of the resolutions. He puts it in a file and, from time to time—at his discretion or on instructions from the head of the Secretariat—asks the appropriate officials for a report on the fate of the resolution. Mainly, he sees to it that verificatory reports are submitted on time to the CC Presidium, if this is explicitly called for in the resolution.

The CC Presidium—the most powerful organ in the state—makes decisions on the basis of written reports and by means of resolutions that are binding for all institutions and officials in the state. Final work on reports and proposed resolutions as well as verification of their fulfillment is first and foremost the responsibility of the party apparat, to whose activities a separate chapter is devoted. Initiatives for reports and resolutions come from four basic sources.

The first consists of the elected party organs, which themselves request that their resolutions be worked through. This is done by the Presidium, the CC Secretariat, sometimes by members of the Central Committee, and often by CC commissions. The second is the party apparat. CC departments and secretaries bring up matters, some of which emerge from requests of regions and districts, others from their own experience.

Third are the state and economic apparats, cultural institutions, and mass organizations. They are the source of suggestions for both conceptual, fundamental decisions and most operational reports. Some of these are routine proposals (emerging from evaluation of their work, preparation of their congress and conferences). Others are requested by the party apparat or, most commonly, submitted by these institutions on their own initiative. Fourth, there is Moscow, which is both a direct and an indirect source of initiatives for decision making. It is direct in the sense that Moscow's resolutions provide leading comrades in

Prague with ideas. Furthermore, comments and recommendations come from Moscow, or Prague approaches Moscow on its own initiative asking for Moscow's views on measures in preparation. Moscow is an indirect source of initiatives since the Soviet Union also realizes its interests through its special status in the international communist movement and Soviet bloc, particularly in COMECON and the Warsaw Pact. These international institutions generate resolutions that are assimilated into the program of the CC Presidium and significantly predetermine its decision making.

Let us look at some concrete examples: The CC Presidium, in discussing reports dealing with the manufacture and export of machinery, orders the machine industry to prepare a long-term scheme for development and specialization of its production. In discussing the results of the economic plan, the Presidium orders that specific proposals be prepared to eliminate certain negative phenomena in the economy. Economic difficulties, pressures from enterprises and ministries, and suggestions from research institutes, specialists, and the CC Economic Commission force the Presidium to allow the groundwork to be laid for changes in the economic management system.

Alerts received from the districts and regions regarding problems in the supply of agricultural fertilizers or spare parts for machinery lead the CC Agricultural Department to instruct ministries to work out so-called fundamental solutions to these problems for the CC Presidium. Criticism of inadequate supervision of publishing activities by party and state institutions is transformed by apparatchiks in the CC Ideological Department into a suggestion that a special institution to deal with supervision be set up. Members of the apparats of extra-party institutions may alert the CC department responsible for their portfolios to negative phenomena and difficulties in the areas for which they are responsible (e.g., wage, social, or housing policy) and recommend solutions. Or, conversely, CC departments may request analyses and reports from extra-party institutions on the basis of their own information.

A CC secretary asks his department to develop a plan for the "strengthening of cadres" in the leading organs and the apparats of a mass organization, the Academy of Sciences, or a ministry. An apparatchik, a department, or the head of a CC section may push for a report that has been prepared on the basis of his own knowledge or reports from the districts, e.g., concerning improvement of party administration, changes in the party's educational system, or promotion and sales of the party press. Tasks for Czechoslovakia emerge from reports on meetings of COMECON or Warsaw Pact organs. These are broken down into detailed proposals for resolutions and submitted to the Presidium through the usual channels.

At first glance, it appears that the CC Presidium is totally dependent upon the apparats of the party and the state in selection of the matters with which it deals, as well as the methods by which it deals with them. Some Presidium members blame this situation on the excessive number of operational reports discussed. They are also critical of the fact that many reports come, not from the political, i.e., the party, apparat, but from ministerial and other offices. However, this is not the truth of the matter. Although the CC Presidium, like any other organ, has to make its decisions on the basis of written materials and proposals,

1. It has the greatest discretion with regard to what it will and will not discuss, and on which matters it will adopt resolutions. If it passes a binding resolution on some issue it is not competent to deal with and about which it knows nothing, it does this by its own choice. It thus voluntarily becomes dependent upon proposals from the apparat. The less the Presidium is able to choose among different alternatives, the more this dependency increases. Nothing and no one determine either the scope or the substance of issues discussed by the CC Presidium, except for the position it wants to have in the power and management system of society—i.e., the position of the most powerful body of power apparat representatives making decisions about and controlling everything by directive.

2. There is also another aspect to the fact that the Presidium, far from being powerless in relation to the apparat, is all-powerful. Conceptual proposals and, most significantly, reports are included in its plan of work and derived from party congress or Central Committee resolutions. The CC Presidium prepares and approves these documents. For the most part, they give expression to the Presidium's own will, opinions, and political conception. Its principles, contained in these documents, are embodied in concrete resolutions prepared by the apparat. Leading apparatchiks are familiar with the views of CC Presidium members and their power-political intentions. They know what kinds of reports the members like, prepare them accordingly, and also cast proposed resolutions into this framework. They want to avoid conflict with the Presidium, which would threaten their social status and career. The mood of the CC Presidium thus remains a live influence among leading functionaries. It is a touchstone for them, setting limits to their determination to tell it the truth and to the boldness of their proposed solutions.

3. Despite the all-powerfulness of the CC Presidium, it is, to some extent, dependent upon apparats. This dependence manifests itself in

two ways. First, the Presidium receives from them inaccurate information about social reality. The party apparat and other sources that provide information to the Presidium doctor it to conform to the views and desires of the power group. This distortion is compounded by the fact that such information is received with great interest by the Presidium. Second, there is the low quality of the reports and proposed solutions. Criticisms of the low quality and lack of objectivity of reports and of inconsistent, politically deficient problem solutions are very often addressed to leading functionaries in all central apparats. These functionaries are, for the most part, appointed by the CC Presidium itself, which thereby creates its own apparat. A prerequisite for improvement of its level of competence would have to be removal of the party-political barriers that make an influx of qualified specialists into leading positions impossible. However, it is precisely upon this socially dependent apparat that the power position of the CC Presidium depends. Hence, the barriers persist, and there exists a mutual dependency of the CC Presidium and the power apparats, in which the Presidium is respected as the only leading organ of the power mechanism.

The State of Affairs
Within the Central Committee Presidium

Members of the Presidium, and CC secretaries, are an extraordinarily privileged group in society. The most significant privilege is membership itself in this supreme power organ. Most Presidium members would never be able to get into it or stay in on the basis of their own political abilities or specialized knowledge. This kind of situation can occur only in the kind of system the power group represents and defends. Other privileges include the considerable authority that derives directly from the scope of the CC Presidium's power. Every one of its members has the right to have a say in decisions about any state official, as well as the most important matters in the life of the state and society.

The CC Presidium strives to emphasize its position of supreme importance in society. In June 1948, Slánský implemented Gottwald's orders that the authority of the CC Presidium should be increased at the expense of state organs. Over time, there gradually emerged a kind of diplomatic protocol to be observed at receptions, festivities, and similar occasions. This protocol requires that a Presidium member's membership in the Presidium be mentioned first, and that his state positions be mention only afterward (e.g. member of the CC Presidium and then President of the Republic). The mass media have to refer to CC Presidium members and CC secretaries by name, something that is not required for other officials (for example, CC Presidium members Novotný, Jozef Lenárt, and Široký and members of the Central Committee and the government took part in the festivities). The press office and mass media are required to take note even of less significant appearances of every CC Presidium member in a manner appropriate to the occasion. Their photographs are published in the press in larger size and in the most prominent positions. Thus, the CC Presidium filters into people's consciousness as the most powerful of organs, and all its members become well known.

Presidium membership is an automatic indicator of high social status, and there is yet another reason why party functionaries find this position at the top attractive. Once someone gets into the Presidium, once his cadre file moves to the highest level, he is shielded against any sudden fall from power. In most cases, a return to the lower ranks is slow, and unless something unusual happens, there is time to make provisions for advantageous living conditions and social status. At the same time, membership in the CC Presidium provides special information about the operations of the state, internal party life, and international affairs. It also facilitates access to the general secretary and the possibility of discussing with him even matters of lesser significance.

There are also material advantages associated with membership in the top power group. In 1948, Stalin recommended to Gottwald that he make the members of the Presidium dependent on him by making them financially dependent. Gottwald had no need to do this, since he enjoyed undisputed authority within the leadership. Novotný, however, did make use of the suggestion. He gave gifts to CC Presidium members in so-called white envelopes depending on their degree of support for his policies. They received these every month for two years. Zdeněk Fierlinger, for example, received 1.1 million crowns during this period on top of his salary, and the others around 700,000 crowns each. Novotný's gifts ended with his fall from power in 1967, but other advantages have continued: e.g., better supplies of goods, high salaries, the right to a personal pension proposed by the general secretary, and various services that are usually difficult to obtain otherwise.

In theory, CC Presidium members have equal rights. In reality, significant differences exist among them. The self-effacement of a novice toward the old veterans of the CC Presidium continues for a long time. All new members are aware of the honor they have received in being chosen by the power group to join its ranks, and, for a certain period, they have a sense of gratitude and obligation toward the general secretary. The principal differentiation among Presidium members follows along the lines of their power bases.

A Presidium member's status depends on the clout of the power apparat at his disposal, as well as his ties to Soviet institutions. Viewed from this perspective, CC secretaries, and above all the general secretary, hold first place. At their disposal is the nervous system of the power monopoly—the party, the party apparat, and through it, all other apparats. They have access to some kinds of information not accessible to other members. To be sure, all Presidium members receive a certain amount of information, e.g., confidential monitoring reports issued by the press office, but only some members have access to certain reports from State Security, some international political information (e.g., coded dispatches from diplomatic posts), and some reports from central agencies. The extraordinarily strong position of the CC secretaries is based on their authority in cadre matters. They can make proposals to fill all high positions (in the government, parliament, mass organizations, and the economy). Furthermore, these officials are also subordinate to them through the party. In the final analysis, even members of the CC Presidium know that the CC secretaries make decisions about them at their meetings, where the general secretary has the main say.

The chairman of the federal government stands at about the same level in the hierarchy as CC secretaries, in fact a bit higher. His representative function, giving him a place in party diplomatic protocol ahead of CC secretaries, works especially in his favor. The other members of the government are much lower in status. They have very limited possibilities to use their own apparats to check the accuracy of reports and proposed resolutions or to obtain their own information. The minister of planning is an exception to this in economic matters. The position of the other members of the government is nicely illustrated by events in 1967, when the crisis in the leadership began to take shape. They were utterly unaware of the conflicts in the CC Presidium, mainly among the secretaries. In fact, they were caught by surprise when the crisis erupted.

Position in the CC Presidium hierarchy is also influenced by ties to the second most important apparat from the power-political point of view—State Security. Officially, only the general secretary has the right to receive its reports and intervene in its affairs, but the prime minister also gets some of its reports. Other members have to rely on relationships with functionaries they know in the Ministry of the Interior or State Security, but not all have such contacts.

This relationship also has another side to it. Presidium members and CC secretaries are objects of interest to State Security. Every one of them has "his file" in the secret archives, to which not even the minister in charge of the portfolio is allowed access, where all information gathered on him is collected. At the beginning of the fifties, State Security received such information quite routinely. The fact that it was being gathered was no surprise to anyone, and those affected were aware of it.

In 1952, the CC Secretariat approved a set of guiding principles, given to the minister of security, dealing with State Security work pertaining to members of the CC and its organs. According to these principles, State Security is not supposed to keep such information but is supposed to transmit it unprocessed to the general secretary. Later, surveillance of all members of the power group was officially prohibited. The minister of the interior is supposed to transmit to the general secretary any "information of an irregular nature" sent by someone to the police. Such information does not exist. In reality, however, the surveillance never stopped. State Security goes on gathering information on everyone, and the "files" continue to grow. Information is supplied by the bodyguards of all members of the power group, who belong to State Security, and other employees of their offices who have ties to security. In some cases, eavesdropping devices are also used, most having been installed in offices in the past. Whether or not the tried and tested practice of tapping telephone conversations is used can be neither confirmed nor denied. Members of the power group can phone each other, as well as all high-level functionaries, through a special telephone system (called Černín). It is usually said that this telephone cannot be tapped. Although this seems implausible, I have not been able to verify whether or not it is true.

Everyone knows that, in the final analysis, it is Moscow that decides whether or not they remain in the CC Presidium. This is among the main reasons why every member takes great pains to avoid conflict with Moscow or to get a bad reputation there. Moreover, status in the Presidium depends significantly on a member's ties to Soviet institutions and power groups. Such ties are partly predetermined by position—the prime minister in Prague to his counterpart in Moscow, and so on. In addition to this, every member strives to extend his relationships to additional Soviet functionaries. This is why they also receive Soviets who hold lower-level positions, give them gifts, and invite them for official as well as unofficial visits. There are also members of the CC Presidium who maintain close relationships with important power-political forces in the Soviet regime—to leading figures in espionage and security units. (Karol Bacílek, Václav Kopecký, Pavol David, Bruno Köhler, Široký, and Barák are among the better-known examples.)

The power group behaves according to the recognized principle that conflicts within the leadership mean the beginning of the collapse of the party. It presents itself to the public as a unified body with comradely relations, friendship, collaboration, and exemplary human relationships prevailing among its members. The true state of affairs is quite the opposite. Two different tendencies come together in the relationships of Presidium members. On the one hand, they are unified by privileges and an interest in maintaining unity within their ranks as a precondition for maintaining their own power authority, as well as that of party and state organs. On the other hand, participation in the exercise of power deforms their characters and stimulates their efforts to achieve their personal power interests and ambitions.

Membership in the power group significantly affects every member as a human being, his status in society as well as in life. Conversely, these factors combine to play a role in shaping the member's political thinking and decision making and are also among the sources of the so-called ideological unity of the leadership.

Members of the party leadership are relieved of all the ordinary daily concerns that bother all other citizens, such as difficulties with transportation and services. They are thus surrounded by an opaque wall of privileges and don't have to worry about looking at everyday life as it really is, with its worries, difficulties, and woes. They also receive the widest range of gifts and can reasonably hope to become wealthy quickly.

Power, social prestige, and privileges—these have been the ever-present motives that motivate high-level party functionaries to try as hard as they can to join the ranks of the twenty most powerful and stay there. Having unchecked power naturally spoils people. It breaks down the character, the will, the decisiveness to struggle for any ideals or goals, since the highest goal in life is to stay among the elect. Social prestige undermines a self-critical attitude and fosters belief in one's own extraordinary abilities and superiority to others. Along with power, it gives rise to feelings of power and omnipotence. Joining the power group means entering a different world—the world of powerholders, with their own narrow set of interests, desires, and subjects of conversation. They create their own life-style, different not only from that of ordinary people but also from the life-style of lower-level functionaries. They have their own morals, their own manner of discussion and manner of speech. Their lives are free of the burdens of ordinary, everyday life. Their thinking intentionally tends to be as close as possible to the thoughts and desires of the first man in the state.

Members of the power group get together, not only at meetings of the party leadership, but also on other occasions. Their families, despite the uniformity of their thinking and life-style, do not get too close, though they cannot entirely avoid each other. They have their own world, within whose limits they move, think, and act. They cannot exceed these limits or rebel against this exclusive world, since doing so would threaten their position and membership in the power group. And this is the main factor that governs their actions, thinking, and even feelings.

The factors that most seriously trouble relationships among members of the power group are power-political in character. Conflicts having to do with power position are most pronounced; differences of opinion are less significant. Duels played out at the statewide level in the CC Presidium are mirrored in lower-level power groups, between party and extra-party institutions or, more precisely, between party and extra-party apparats and their representatives. There are frequent conflicts between CC secretaries and the prime minister and minister of planning and, occasionally, with the chairman of the trade unions. Only in rare cases do conflicts among CC secretaries spill over into the CC Presidium. Most run their course at the secretaries' meetings and within the framework of the party apparat. Frequently, the prime ministers of the Czech and Slovak national governments bring their conflicts with the federal government to the power group, and the chairman of the trade unions brings his conflicts with governmental institutions. When these functionaries or their institutions are unable to come to agreement on important, controversial matters, they submit the matter either directly to the CC Presidium or ask the general secretary for his position, and he recommends that "the matter be decided politically," i.e., in the CC Presidium.

Conflicts among institutions not represented in the CC Presidium also penetrate into the power group. These relate, first and foremost, to the army and security. In Czechoslovakia, the army does not have the kind of power position it has in the USSR. Still, its power is considerable. For example, the economic ministries are not always ready to take on production commitments for the army. This conflict is then resolved at the highest levels—i.e., by the power group. For the most part, however, the army is a political factor whose interests are represented by the general secretary. The army command has close ties to military circles in Moscow, its thinking and assessment of social problems is influenced by them, and it even acts directly to realize their interests. The position of the security forces is similar, though they, of course, intervene much more strongly and directly in the internal life of the party.

Members of the leading circles of the army and security have parochial views, favor a hard political regime, and oppose conspicuous

social reform. They always find like-minded comrades who also fear
any kind of social movement and disturbance of ideological stereotypes,
which they perceive as threats to the regime and to their own power.
Opposed to these "hard-line ideologues," who are unaware of social
reality and hold strongly to existing ideological stereotypes, are people
with practical experience, mainly economists, who insist that necessary
economic reforms be carried out. In periods of economic crisis, the
tensions between these two groups erupt into open conflicts. The impact
of tensions within the ruling circles in the Soviet Union is also important. Every rival group in Moscow has its supporters in the Prague
leadership, and the fate of those supporters depends on the outcomes
of confrontations in Moscow.

The most important source of conflicts over power position consists
of efforts to remain in the power group and to rise to higher rungs
of its hierarchy—for example, the struggle for second place in the state,
i.e., to be recognized as second to the general secretary, or to win his
special favor and the advantages that go along with it. This produces
discord, lack of confidence, and suspicion within the leadership, and
there is no lack of denunciation and slander of colleagues to the general
secretary either. All this gives rise to an atmosphere that is unfavorable
for the activity of the power group. Individuals and groups oppose
and intrigue against each other. Rather than assessing the views, criticisms, and proposals of their "rivals" coolly and objectively, they look
for "bad intentions" every time these people speak up. Factors of this
kind gradually add up and result in leadership crises, which erupt in
full force only in times of internal party crisis.[13] Some members even
gather "irregular information" on others, so that they can bring it out
at the right moment.[14] Thus, instead of comradely relationships, an
atmosphere of suspicion, hostility, and intrigue is created as the fruits
of ambition and appetite for power.[15]

The Central Committee Secretariat and Its Secretaries

The second component of the central power group—the CC Secretariat—is an independently functioning organ of the Central Committee. According to party rules, it is supposed to attend to the routine
work of the party, mainly verification of how well resolutions have
been fulfilled, and cadre selection. In actual practice, its position in
the system of central party organs is rather complicated and has never
been fully clarified. The CC Secretariat doesn't act as a fully sovereign
entity apart from the CC Presidium but more as an appendage to it
and executor of its will. For example, the Secretariat reports on its
activities to the Presidium rather than to the Central Committee as

party rules stipulate. On the other hand, it makes decisions on many things that go beyond its prescribed authority, even on matters for which the Presidium is responsible. For example, it discusses many reports before they get to the Presidium, and, since several CC secretaries are members of the Presidium, it thus predetermines the decisions the Presidium will make on them.

The incompletely clarified status of the Secretariat is a continuing source of discussion among its members, as well as among high-level officials of the party apparat. Some see the Secretariat as complementing the CC Presidium, and thus advocate limitation of its activities to internal party affairs. On the other hand, others argue that it should develop into an independent entity in the power mechanism.

The size of the Secretariat varies according to the number of CC secretaries. They constitute its power core. The number of secretaries has fluctuated between five and twelve—for the most part, between seven and eight. In addition to the CC secretaries, one or two high officials of mass organizations, the editor in chief of *Rudé právo* (the central press organ of the CPCz), and sometimes the head of the CC Political-Organizational Department are also Secretariat members. During the sixties, all CC department heads took part in CC Secretariat meetings. In 1968, this practice, introduced by Novotný, was criticized by CC secretaries, and in the seventies, it was abandoned. The Secretariat is thus the official power organ of the CC secretaries, headed by the general secretary.

Since its manner of acting and making decisions greatly resembles the practice of the CC Presidium, I will confine this discussion to significant differences. Meetings are held weekly, the day after the CC Presidium meeting, and the agenda follows a semiannual plan of work. In it, proposals from CC departments are put together only into time intervals, without any particular selection of issues according to their expediency and urgency. However, these subjects make up only a fraction of the items on the agenda. Unplanned business, emerging out of everyday practice, predominates by far.

The agenda is compiled by the general secretary's office and includes almost all items proposed by the heads of the CC departments that have submitted reports. The general secretary approves the agenda or, more precisely, takes it under advisement. The agenda is characterized by the large number of items to be dealt with, only rarely falling below thirty. The Secretariat's oversight function means that oversight reports make up the bulk of the agenda—either those directly assigned by Presidium resolutions or those indirectly deriving from them. Many reports intended for the Presidium are also discussed, since fundamental reports go through several organs in the context of efforts to achieve

a so-called objectivity. First, they go to the commissions of the Secretariat, are modified again, and sometimes the Presidium gives the
Secretariat the task of "finishing" reports.

The Secretariat's responsibility in cadre selection results in cadre
affairs being especially heavily in evidence. According to cadre procedures, the Secretariat approves the appointments of all high-level
apparatchiks in central (i.e. federal and Czech and Slovak national),
state, and economic apparats; cultural institutions; and mass organizations. Party apparatchiks at the central level, including party institutions, *Rudé právo*, the Political University, publishing houses, the
Institute of Marxism-Leninism—it approves them all. As for mass
organizations and institutions of the National Front, it decides on
appointments to positions in their central secretariats, leading functionaries, the members of their presidia, and the editors in chief of
their press organs.

In the state apparat, it is responsible for making decisions about
several high officials of ministries and central offices, and it expresses
views regarding high officials in the regions. Those ministries "with
strict cadre supervision"—interior (security), defense, and foreign affairs—have a higher than average number of functionaries approved
by the CC Secretariat. In the economic apparat, the Secretariat approves
the top officials of central headquarters; the directors of especially
important industrial, trade, agricultural, and transport enterprises; and
a broad group of positions in foreign trade. In parliament, the chairmen
of parliamentary committees and high officials come under its authority.

In the cultural domain, it approves, among others, the top officials
of institutions of higher education, central theaters, the film industry,
television, radio, and all cultural and educational institutions. It also
approves the editors of publishing houses, editors in chief, and some
editors of newspapers and press agencies; foreign correspondents of all
mass media; and high officials and apparatchiks in physical education,
cultural organizations, and the unions of writers and composers.

Cadre affairs are bound up with the approval of trips abroad. The
CC Secretariat deals with the trips abroad of mass organizations and
central agencies on a semiannual or annual basis, i.e., their entire plans
for foreign travel. In a period of disastrous shortages of foreign currency,
and in the context of efforts to save such currency, it discusses each
trip separately. Thus, every week reams of proposals justifying trips
and expenditures of funds come to Secretariat meetings. Although it
only rejects a few of these, this has the effect that high-level institutions
and CC departments responsible for portfolios themselves effect cut-
backs in trips and eliminate those whose importance they doubt.

Except for a moderate number of cases discussed by the CC Presidium, almost all matters, whether important or routine, come under the authority of the Secretariat. But even those decided upon by the Presidium go through the Secretariat. Internal party affairs break down into three groups. The first includes those discussed regularly, such as reports on the meeting activity of party organizations, the course of party education, and plans for the activity of party institutions (the curriculum and nominations of students for the Political University, the work of publishing houses, the plan of work for the Institute of Marxism-Leninism, the plan for politically significant articles for the press organ of the Central Committee) as well as reports on fluctuations in membership and the payment of membership dues.

The second group has to do with evaluations and guidelines for the activity of party organizations (e.g., in agriculture, in central agencies, in the machine industry, in schools), guidelines for the work of communists in national committees and trade unions, and guidelines for cadre work, for the information system, or for party administration. Occasionally, it discusses methods of work in the district or regional committees, usually on the basis of analyses of a few of them. The third group includes oversight reports, in which information as to how lower-level party organizations are implementing party resolutions predominates. These reports are mostly about the results of investigations (screening campaigns) of selected party as well as extra-party institutions. The Central Control and Revision Commission is a frequent source of oversight reports. In addition to this, it also is the source of disciplinary cases.

Matters relating to interest organizations come almost exclusively under the authority of the CC Secretariat. For the most part, they come up at meetings in connection with preparations for the congresses and conferences of these organizations. In such a report, their work to date is evaluated and their upcoming tasks approved. The Secretariat also discusses all significant campaigns undertaken by this or that organization and almost all measures that are international in character (e.g. the trade unions present some new form of socialist competition for approval, the National Front presents a campaign for international solidarity, etc.).

From among the many aspects of cultural life, some are also discussed by the CC Presidium. However, the CC Secretariat deals with them in more detailed and concrete form. Among them are annual analyses of all publishing houses, which also contain critical analyses of their plans for the coming year. There are analyses of the press, which trace their circulation and evaluate the way they have dealt with matters of party policy (how much space they have devoted to international affairs, economic issues, current political campaigns). Various cultural institutions and their plans for the future are also evaluated (including, for example, enterprises for people's entertainment). The CC Secretariat also deals with plans for all of the most significant cultural campaigns and even the political and organizational arrangements for especially important ones (film festivals, large statewide exhibitions, all the most important exhibitions in foreign countries). A great deal of care and attention is devoted to the preparation and political orientation of congresses of the creative unions (writers, creative artists, composers) and their important international meetings.

Among the activities of the Academy of Sciences, the Secretariat is most interested in the social sciences. It makes decisions regarding the establishment and abolition of research institutions and the aims of their research, as well as the framework plans for the social sciences. It also rules on participation in important international conferences and, when necessary, the orientation of the delegation sent. It discusses proposals for the publication of large encyclopedic works and all collected or selected works of the classics of Marxism-Leninism, of its own leading representatives, and of those of other communist parties. Only in exceptional cases are decisions made about concrete matters. However, the CC Secretariat keeps a close watch on interpretation of party history, and in this connection, it discusses several controversial issues in the *Summary of the History of the Communist Party of Czechoslovakia.*

Economic ministries and central agencies pass on many of their problems to meetings of the CC Secretariat. Most are matters for which the minister or even his deputy have full authority to dispose of on their own. The head of the CC department responsible for the portfolio transmits these matters to the CC Secretariat, even though this violates party guidelines. In this way officials attempt to shift responsibility for a decision from themselves to the party organ, or to win the support of a CC Secretariat resolution to help them achieve what their portfolio is asking for. The Secretariat thus orders ministries or economic institutions to make sure that some particular investments are made, to accept production targets, or to fulfill this or that production commitment. That is to say, reports of the CC economic departments usually deal with important unfulfilled production targets or difficulties, e.g., in the purchase of agricultural products, supply of machinery, provision of investments for building projects that the government is monitoring, and the supply of various kinds of consumer goods.

Only rarely does the CC Secretariat deal with international affairs. In addition to approving the international relations of mass organizations and cultural institutions, and a few kinds of activities of secondary importance of the Ministry of Foreign Affairs already mentioned, international relations with communist parties (more precisely, among their apparats) are dealt with at its meetings. It ratifies proposals for agreements for collaboration of the party apparat with the apparats of the communist parties of other Soviet bloc countries and the dispatch of study delegations that result from such agreements. It also deals with the reception of study delegations sent by other communist parties, including details of the schedules for their visits. And it receives written information on the results of visits abroad of study delegations.

The vast scope and quantity of issues discussed result in the decision making of the CC Secretariat being even more pro forma and superficial than that of the CC Presidium. The members of the Secretariat simply do not understand the issues that come before them, since these are predominantly operational, specialized, and technical-economic in character. Furthermore, it would far exceed their physical forces and capabilities to read the reports submitted. They are dependent on their apparat. Naturally, these materials also present great difficulties for their assistants, who do not understand them either. Their reading is thus extremely limited, focusing mainly on those parts of the reports submitted that have to do with their own portfolios.

The CC Secretariat discusses most items in a pro forma way, without any interest on the part of those present and often without discussion. To the extent that there is any, it consists only of comments. This is how an average of twenty items are taken care of in two hours. The nature of this decision making process gives the general secretary even greater influence in the CC Secretariat than he has in the CC Presidium. The social dependency upon him of all those present is absolute, and they thus adapt their positions to his views. Experienced participants in these meetings advise novices courageous enough to try to oppose the general secretary of the futility and consequences of such behavior. In 1962, for example, two department heads decided to oppose Novotný several times and suddenly "left to reinforce the government."

Nevertheless, conflicts existing in the central party apparat do surface at meetings of the CC Secretariat. CC secretaries like very much to use their comments on reports of CC departments to criticize the work of those departments, and thus indirectly to criticize the CC secretary responsible for the portfolio. This is part of their power struggle. The superiority of the CC Organizational-Political Department is especially conspicuous. Its head either is a regular member of the CC Secretariat or behaves like one, and he is lavish in his criticism of other departments. Their heads defend themselves and reciprocate the criticism.

The CC Secretariat functions as a wholesale producer of resolutions dealing with the broadest range of issues. Most of its decisions, however, consist of ex post facto ratification of decisions made by CC secretaries during the preceding week within their own areas of competence and decisions on urgent matters that are operational in character.

There are several reasons for this mass production of resolutions. They emerge, for the most part, from discussion of a large number of reports that are operational and verificatory in character. The verificatory role of the Secretariat is interpreted very broadly. It is not restricted to verification of things assigned by the Presidium in its resolutions but also includes peripheral matters coming from extra-party institutions through the CC departments responsible for them. The operational character of reports results in every decision's being broken down into a large set of items and elaborated. These are often resolutions presented by the minister responsible for the portfolio to his council of advisers. Since there is no overview of resolutions already adopted, new resolutions are produced that repeat the substance of old ones. Nor is it unusual for the Secretariat to pass resolutions within the context of verificatory reports that do not agree with the original CC Presidium resolution calling for the verification.

The large quantity of resolutions reinforces the character of the CC Secretariat as an organ of operational administration and directive decision making in all domains of social life. A great many detailed resolutions derive from the central party organization's distribution of tasks to lower-level party and extra-party institutions. Since there is no overview of resolutions adopted and no ongoing verification of their implementation, and since these are unqualified decisions, their authority is undermined. Officials affected by them don't consider them important. Many don't carry out the resolutions at all, or they carry them out half-heartedly and in a pro forma way, just to be able to furnish proof that they have done something after all. Exceptions to this are resolutions having to do with cadre affairs and those dealing with matters that cannot be ignored, e.g., congresses of mass organizations, international relations, and plans of work for party institutions.

The CC secretaries have their own separate meetings in addition to those of the CC Secretariat. These meetings have no basis in party rules. They are not meetings of a recognized party organ, they adopt no written resolutions, and no minutes are kept. They are called by the general secretary on an irregular basis, at his own discretion, and it is he who sets the agenda. The subjects of discussion come either from him or from the CC secretaries. In both cases the initiatives usually come from party apparatchiks. In individual cases, they may also come from state and economic apparats, as well as from circles of communist intelligentsia—scholarly institutions and institutions of higher education.[16]

Although these meetings of CC secretaries lack the status of meetings of a party organ, indeed precisely because of this, they represent a very important institution, in a certain sense the most important one of all. One can speak of forces existing and acting behind the official organs of the power group, of forces disposing of the considerable power potential provided by the position of the CC secretaries and the general secretary in the CC Presidium and Secretariat and in the power mechanism of the party apparat, which they control.

At their meetings, CC secretaries deal with general matters having to do with party policy, on the one hand, as well as with concrete, operational matters, e.g., the subject matter of CC meetings and the political conception of party congresses; reforms of the administration of the state, the economy or the culture; conceptions of social and wage policy; evaluations of the activities, reorganization and cadre affairs of the government, mass organizations, and the CC Presidium; preparation of some reports and resolutions of CC organs, providing for and verifying their implementation; internal party affairs, and the work of the party apparat. Concrete suggestions for changes in party policy arise at these meetings, the position of the leadership in response to calls for changes from party members crystallizes, and the limits and forms of such changes are established.

Meetings of CC secretaries differ in many ways from meetings of the CC Presidium and the Secretariat. The discussions are not based on reports that have been thoroughly prepared in advance. Issues are discussed, different opinions are expressed, and a final position takes shape. There is thus real discussion rather than the mere reading of comments. Many internal defense mechanisms of the participants fall, and the boundaries of self-censorship change, even though they do not entirely disappear with regard to the general secretary.[17] To be sure, the participants do not adopt resolutions or vote on anything. However, they do not adjourn without reaching binding conclusions or without distributing tasks. As soon as they agree on the necessity of resolving this or that problem, and how to accomplish it, the CC secretary responsible for the portfolio is charged with preparing a report. There is a long way to go from the first meeting of secretaries to the adoption of a final decision by the CC Presidium, but what is important is that the first step has been taken. Since CC secretaries have the upper hand within the organs of the power group, they get the decisions through that have been reached at the secretaries' meetings. On the other hand, of course, if a CC secretary, including the general secretary, cannot get his proposal or demand through at a secretaries' meeting, he will not try to get it through elsewhere.[18]

There are differences in the power positions of secretaries. Membership in the CC Presidium is the first distinction as it places CC secretaries above other colleagues in the power hierarchy. Some thus try as hard as they can to get into the CC Presidium, and the others try to stay in it. Many factors play a role in determining the success of these efforts—especially the general secretary and good relations with him. Moscow also has an important say. The second distinction, related to the first, is the level of importance of a CC secretary's portfolio. Secretaries who are members of the Presidium hold the most important ones, like the Political-Organizational Department, State Security, the army, the economic departments, and the Ideological Department. The third distinction is a secretary's relationship or, more precisely, his access to the general secretary. In theory, all secretaries have the same right to consult with him, but some get to see him easily, e.g., CC Presidium members, while others have difficulties.[19]

There has been a hierarchy of CC secretaries ever since the Gottwald era when Slánský monopolized all relationships of the party apparat with him, a situation that has been maintained ever since. It was further solidified during the sixties when the number of secretaries was increased (there are nine of them). The group of privileged members of the CC Presidium, or makers of policy, can be distinguished from the second-ranking ones, who are aware of their inferior positions and subordinate themselves to "their privileged" CC secretary. For example, Vasil Bil'ak is a member of the Presidium and, as a CC secretary, is responsible for the entire domain of ideology. Aside from him, there are the secretaries holding the portfolios for culture and for education and scholarly research, both of whom feel a certain subordination to Bil'ak. The situation is similar with the secretary and Presidium member responsible for the national economy and the secretaries responsible for the economic portfolios.

There are also two or three privileged members who are closest to the first secretary who, along with him, make up the subgroup with the strongest position within the power group. CC secretaries struggle for membership in this top group. This shows up in their relationships with each other, motivates their efforts to ingratiate themselves with the general secretary (e.g., the pursuit of Novotný's favor took place at the recreational center where CC secretaries spent their weekends together), and is not without influence on the activity of the party apparat.

From a power-political point of view, the CC secretary stands at the peak of the power hierarchy, and his social position derives from this. He decides which reports go to the Presidium from his portfolio, their content, and which proposals for resolutions. Some of his decisions have the character of resolutions of the CC Secretariat, and, according to cadre procedures, he himself approves appointments to several hundred important positions. Therefore, the transfer of a CC secretary, who isn't a member of the CC Presidium, to a position lower than deputy premier in the government is considered a political demotion. In fact, it is a demotion even if he falls to this level, since a deputy premier is de facto subordinate to a CC secretary. For a secretary who is a CC Presidium member, any position except premier is a demotion.[20]

The General Secretary

The privileged position of the general secretary stands out clearly in the preceding description of the central power group (during the years 1953–1972, the term first secretary was used). Symbolically, it can be characterized as a position of first among the most powerful. It is more than just a position at the head of the power group, more than just ascendancy over the others, more than higher social standing with a consciously cultivated difference and a sharp line dividing the holder from the others. It is a supremacy of power.

The general secretary's position is based on factors of permanent character, but it is also influenced by variable factors. Among the most important of the variable factors are the means by which he got to the top and keeps himself there. His relationship to the other members of the power group and decision-making practices depend on whether his authority derives from recognition of his political skills or merely from respect for the office, and he is thus forced to take various measures to build and maintain authority.[21] The political environment also plays a role, as do his personal character traits, the negative aspects of which are considerably aggravated by the power position of the general secretary.[22]

Finally, every general secretary knows that Moscow makes the final decision on him, regardless of the domestic bases of his power. As soon as the members of the power group notice that the first among them has lost the confidence of the Kremlin, they abandon him, make bold to criticize him, and demand his removal. This was the case with Slánský, executed with the consent of the power group; with Novotný in 1968; and with Alexander Dubček in April 1969. Conversely, when the general secretary himself runs into resistance from members of the leadership, he tries to find out whether Moscow isn't behind it and to exploit Moscow's support or agreement in order to reinforce his position. Novotný tried this successfully in April 1954, and unsuccessfully in December 1967; Dubček did so in November 1968, when he abruptly flew off to consult Brezhnev. And Husák has, several times during his tenure in office, suddenly flown to Moscow to find out where he stood there.

The factors that permanently characterize a general secretary's position are always present in party life. All that changes is the relative strength of their influence. First, he heads all organs of the power group—the Presidium, the Secretariat, and the conference of CC secretaries. He determines their agendas, chairs their meetings, and formulates their decisions. Second, he is in command of the most significant power apparats. He has the party apparat at his beck and call. He regards the Central Secretariat as his "brain trust" and has it prepare expert opinions on proposals of the government and other institutions. Armed units are under his control. He directly commands the CC department for security and the army and is the high commander of the people's militia.

Third, power flows from the general secretary's being represented as the first man of the party. He conducts himself and is recognized as such. This means even more, however, as the general secretary has the whole party at his disposal. This is true both in a general sense, due to his position as its head and as chief of the central party apparat, and in a more concrete sense. He is responsible for the CC Political-Organizational (First) Department, which directs lower-level party units and thus party life. If he hands over this department to another secretary, he weakens his position.[23]

Fourth, cadre policy remains an especially effective instrument for the reinforcement of his privileged position. The general secretary makes, or at least has the authority to make, decisions regarding appointments to all high-level positions in the state, including those held by members of the power group. He possesses substantial means to eliminate opponents and disobedient and troublesome people, and install and favor those who are faithful and obedient to him.

Fifth, relationships within the power group work to his benefit. Khrushchev recommended to Novotný that he constitute the CC Presidium and Secretariat in such a way that its members would inform him about the others. In this way, not only information in general, but also information about conflicts among the others would be concentrated in his hands. He didn't need to act on this advice, since such conditions arise quite naturally within the power group due to the power rivalry that has existed ever since the first days of the communist regime. Not only do members of the Presidium give the general secretary information about others, but their mutual rivalry often also leads to a situation in which, in the course of criticism, "some comrades felt offended, reacted in an irritated manner, and from this ticklish situations arose during discussions" (Novotný). Under such conditions, the general secretary takes on the role of arbiter, above all such conflicts.

Sixth, a strong buttress for the general secretary's position within the power group is his monopolization of relations with the highest authorities in Moscow. He alone maintains written and telephone relations with the Soviet general secretary and those of other Soviet bloc parties. CC secretaries can contact their counterparts in Moscow or elsewhere only after consulting with him. He also receives all information about discussions of the minister of foreign affairs or other high officials with the Soviet ambassador.

The seventh factor, the effects of which are not as strong as those already mentioned, is his accumulation of positions. The general secretary is the chairman of the National Front and, from 1957–1968 and again since the mid seventies, president of the Republic—the highest representative of the state. Eighth, the privileged position of the general secretary is based on his privileged knowledge. He receives an enormous amount of information from various sources. Most of this information is available to other functionaries, but his advantage consists of having everything while the other members have only part of it. Most important from the point of view of power is that he alone receives exceptionally important and top secret information. In addition to official information, the information he obtains from conversations with high-ranking officials of the Soviet Union and other states also belongs to this category.

Information plays a many-sided role in the political activity of the general secretary. In particular, he makes use of top secret information as a means of getting his views and designs to prevail. With this aim in mind, he carefully chooses which secret information to reveal to the members of the power group. In providing such information, he treats its source as a great secret "which cannot be revealed."[24] Information is also important because it plays an important role in creating the general secretary's basic assumptions about social reality, and thus it influences his decision making and actions. Information is selected for him by his office staff, which draws his attention to whatever they consider important or would like him to know.

The scope and amount of information the general secretaries have received change very little. All general secretaries have shown interest in the most important information, intended only for them or the narrowest circle of officials. To some extent, different general secretaries have shown differing levels of interest in less important kinds of information, accessible to more people. Taking the last year of Novotný's rule (1967) as an example, I will indicate the amount of information a general secretary has available to him and how Novotný concretely made use of one particular piece of information.

As a matter of principle, Novotný asked for as much information as possible and devoted considerable attention to it. He made no use at all of the press as a source of information. He didn't read it but showed interest in individual articles if they had been drawn to his attention as politically flawed. Similarly, he followed the daily summaries of the foreign press (monitoring) prepared by the press office. He relied mainly on official information.

As president of the Republic and supreme commander of the armed forces, he received much information that was of special political importance and to which he alone had access. As chairman of the National Front, he received information, most of which other members of the power group also received. This included important information about the noncommunist parties.

As general secretary, he received thousands of reports annually. These can be divided into two categories: reports containing conceptual information and those of an operational character. The first category mostly contained documents prepared for meetings of the Presidium, the Secretariat, and CC commissions and documentary materials of extra-party institutions—such as those prepared for meetings of the Slovak National Council, the advisory committee of the minister of the interior, and the State Planning Commission; analyses of the Ministry of State Control; and research reports of various institutes. From this agglomeration, Novotný paid constant attention to reports for the CC Presidium. Only occasionally did he read anything else, and this only when his attention was drawn to them by his personal office.

He did, however, pay a great deal of attention to information of the second category—that of operational character. This information came from both extra-party institutions and intra-party sources. The general secretary's office logged in 569 reports from extra-party sources in 1966 and 490 in 1967. "Political portfolios" transmitted 440 of these in 1966, 378 the next year; economic portfolios and scientific institutions 120 and 99; social organizations 9 and 13. Many more reports arrived by courier from the Ministries of Foreign Affairs and the Interior, and these are not logged in by his office. The Ministry of Foreign Affairs sent copies of coded reports from diplomatic posts twice daily. Their numbers never fell below 20 a day, i.e., 120 weekly and around 6,000 yearly. Novotný read all of them, even though many were not important, and selected some of them to be reproduced for members of the power group. Aside from him and the minister of foreign affairs, these reports were also received by the responsible CC secretary and some by the premier.

A courier from the Ministry of the Interior brought the daily collection of reports from Public Security [the police] (called DZ), which dealt with all criminal affairs—murders, theft, accidents, etc., in the country. These reports were received by a broader group of functionaries, but Novotný read them regularly. Every day, top secret reports arrived, dealing especially with information from abroad obtained by organs of the Ministry of the Interior. Aside from the responsible minister, only the general secretary had access to these. At least three times a week the courier brought special reports containing domestic political information from counterespionage. On the average, there were about 150 reports annually, each containing about ten pages of dense print. For the most part, they contained information about so-called negative manifestations of a political character, including details about individuals involved and places of occurrence. Only the general secretary received this information, and he alone selected some of it—not more than 10 percent—for information of the power group.

From the intra-party information system (which was by no means limited to description of internal party life) there arrived, in 1967, 380 separate reports and 60 information bulletins issued by the CC department, containing about 360 individual reports. Of the 380 separate reports, 283 came from CC secretaries and departments, 40 from district and regional organs, and 57 from basic organizations. More than half the reports from CC departments were proposals for initiatives, and nearly a third were intended for the general secretary alone.

The overall balance sheet of operational-type information in 1967 looked like this: The intra-party system provided 730 reports, the extra-party system 7,690, thus a proportion of 1:10. Only a small portion of the intra-party information was intended for Novotný alone, most of it being received by CC secretaries as well. Of the extra-party information, that contained in letters from the heads of central institutions and a part of the information from the Ministry of Foreign Affairs were intended exclusively for the general secretary. Only one kind of information—special domestic political information from the Ministry of the Interior, i.e., counterespionage—was not and still is not received by anyone but the general secretary.

Novotný's interest was limited to information of a political character, especially that having to do with power, e.g., most of the reports from security and the Ministry of Foreign Affairs. In reading those reports, his interest was further narrowed. He considered important any information referring to "negative phenomena" in the introduction of innovations, which he could use as an argument for maintaining existing political practices.[25]

At his own discretion, the general secretary gives members of the power group an insignificant fraction of the special reports of the Ministry of the Interior (counterespionage). The selection he makes is good indicator of which phenomena and events he considers to be of primary importance. They reflect his political intentions, since they provide information with specific content. In 1967, he gave the Presidium nine such pieces of information, all of which were intended to confirm the rightness of his position in resolving pressing problems of that time.[26]

The limits of the general secretary's interest in information significantly influences his conceptions of social reality. Reports from security and those regarding internal party affairs play the most important role in shaping these conceptions. Both types of reports are distorted, either unintentionally or intentionally. This information also functions as an important part of the basis for the decisions he makes both within the party and in extra-party organs, especially in discussions with high officials.

Decision making takes place in several kinds of situations. Only in unusual cases does the general secretary ask to meet with a minister to discuss matters relating to his portfolio. The ministers of defense and the interior are exceptions to this rule. More often, however, he will himself invite high officials of extra-party institutions to visit him or talk to them on the telephone. This is provided for by CC Presidium and Secretariat resolutions, which give him the responsibility of discussing various matters with officials, including information he has obtained by reading reports or from written as well as oral notification. In such discussions, the general secretary criticizes various aspects of the work of the portfolio headed by the invited functionary, asks for explanations and proposed solutions, and assigns tasks.

CC secretaries are frequent visitors, some of them coming every day. They discuss many routine matters having to do with their portfolios and everything of political significance. They almost always turn to the general secretary when they are unsure of their decision and want to be covered by the chief's concurrence. Telephone contact among them is limited to taking care of organizational matters of secondary importance. Lower-echelon party apparatchiks hardly ever get to see the general secretary, except for heads of the departments for which he is responsible. Other heads of department deal with him only when summoned and are only rarely received at their own request.

The general secretary's office informs heads of departments and CC secretaries almost daily of instructions and tasks the chief has thought of while reading informational material or on the basis of news he has obtained in other ways. These are extremely diverse, usually requiring that something be checked up on, that a report on some activity be prepared, or that some other matter be taken care of, either directly or by means of some extra-party institution. Sometimes these orders also contain criticism of the work of the department.

CC departments also receive many workers' letters from the general secretary's office. Over the five-year period 1976–1981, the Central Committee received 47,515 of them. These are mostly complaints or requests of ordinary citizens addressed to the Secretariat. They go through a special tracking procedure, carried out systematically by an apparatchik in the general secretary's office. They are put on cards, filed, and sent to the responsible CC department. The responsible apparatchik and the Central Control and Revision Commission check on their status semiannually. The CC department has to respond to the petitioner within a certain time limit, or enter into discussions with him. Also, a semi-annual report is prepared for the CC Secretariat on the status of the resolution of workers' letters. The balance sheet is not usually satisfactory, since CC departments consider workers' letters to be a useless waste of time and they take care of them only because they are checked up on.

Notes

1. The number of members and name of the Presidium have changed several times since 1948. Immediately after the seizure of power, it grew to twenty-eight members, consisting of ministers and CC secretaries. Thus, already in June 1948, as a result of Gottwald's proposal, a smaller, eight-member Presidium emerged which, in 1951 was transformed into the CC Political Secretariat. The Presidium existed in addition to the Political Secretariat until both organs were replaced by an eleven-member Politburo in 1954. During the sixties, it was again renamed the Presidium, having thirteen members and candidates. The name of the CC Secretariat, which used to be called the Organizational Secretariat, has not changed since 1954.

2. A more detailed picture of the composition of the CC Presidium during the period 1946–1966 is provided by some statistical data regarding its forty-nine members. Twenty-four were of working-class origins by original occupation; the others came from the intelligentsia. Four remained in the Presidium more than sixteen years, six from twelve to sixteen years, and also six from eight to twelve years. Fourteen were appointed between the ages of 30 and 40, twenty-two between 40 and 50, and eleven between 50 and 60. Three left their positions when they were older than 60, thirteen between 60 and 70, and twenty between 40-50. The average age of members of the power group was thus not high, as shown in Table 2.1.

Nine died while they were members, six fell victim to purges and political trials, eighteen were eliminated for political reasons, and thirteen left naturally,

TABLE 2.1
Average Age of CC Presidium Members at Time of Election

	Congress					
	X	XI	XII	XIII	XIV	XV
Average age	52.2	55.3	53.3	49.7	50.4	53.6

without political reasons. Only eight of them never worked in the party apparat, twelve served in the Comintern, and eight graduated from a Soviet political school. Of fourteen members of the power group in the seventies (after the Soviet occupation), three are of working-class origin by original occupation, and the others are from the ranks of the intelligentsia. Four hold positions in the government, eight in the party apparat, two in the trade unions and in parliament. Only three had never worked in the party apparat at all. Two were members of the power group before the Soviet occupation (August 1968), twelve after it. Finally, three attained their positions in the power group between the ages of 30 and 40, eight from 40 to 50, and three after the age of 60.

3. The following belonged to the Novotný core group during the second half of the sixties: Bohuslav Laštovička, Miroslav Pastyřík, Michal Chudík, Michal Sabolčík, Otakar Šimůnek, Antonín Kapek. Gustav Husák has also been building up his core group since 1969, including Peter Colotka, Josef Kempný, Miloslav Hruškovič, Josef Korčak, Lubomír Štrougal, Václav Hůla.

4. In 1956, at a meeting of the Central Committee, Zápotocký noted that he had never been a theoretician, that theory had never attracted him (nevertheless, despite this, even because of it, he loved to theorize). Novotný, in the course of a party screening operation, considered insufficient knowledge of Marxism-Leninism to be his weakness, since he knew only what he had learned at party short courses. Jaromír Dolanský, in a friendly conversation, complained that he had not read a book since 1945 since he had to read only reports and supporting materials for meetings of the government and CC Presidium. Široký told me happily in 1968 that he could now at last read the books he had not had any time to read when he held his positions. The last time Husák studied Lenin was during his student years. Drahomír Kolder complained that the last time he had been able to turn to the classics had been at party school. The situation was and still is similar for all the other members of the CC Presidium.

5. In 1953, during the political "new course" in the Soviet bloc countries, the political secretariat let the CC prepare theses on the political and, above all, the economic conditions of society. Although it was not a profound analysis, the overall picture was very bad. So bad that a rebuke came from Moscow, pointing to an unjustified emphasis on negative aspects, and failure to mention successes. The Prague leadership modified the analysis to cover up. In 1962, a group of economists completed an analysis of the condition of the economy, the results of which took the leadership aback. They could not, however, fail

to take account of many of the points it made. Among the most important was a recommendation that more attention be paid to the development of agriculture.

In 1965, after long opposition, the CC Presidium authorized an investigation of inner party life from the point of view of the position of the party in society. The results of a year's work were presented as a report at a meeting of the Central Committee in October 1967. The original report, prepared by a group of specialists and backed by 1,600 pages of analysis, gave a critical view of serious deficiencies in the party's work and drew attention to the clash between its activity and social reality. The CC Presidium modified the report so as to take off its critical edges. It could not, however, disregard all critical views and proposals for change, among which was a recommendation to put an end to the accumulation of positions. The demand for separation of the positions of CC general secretary and president of the Republic in Novotný's case, which eventually happened in January 1968, was based on this recommendation. Furthermore, several regions carried out their own investigations and sent the results not only to the power group in the region but also to the center. It, however, showed no interest at all in these results. The Northern Moravian Region sent its analysis of the political situation to the center in September 1966, where it was decided that the CC Secretariat would deal with it. This did not happen until December 21, and then did not involve participation of representatives of the region. And not until February 7, 1967, was a resolution approved to the effect that the analysis took too critical a view of reality and neglected positive results.

6. In the final period of his rule, Novotný often violated this practice. In 1966–1967, he gave forty-seven of the most significant speeches, of which the CC Presidium discussed fourteen. He gave the others either "on his own authority" or he consulted only a narrow circle of officials closest to him about them. An example of substantial changes being made in a speech was in 1953 when the Politburo discussed Zápotocký's speech for a CC meeting concerning changes in previously existing policy.

7. The Presidium held 61 meetings between February 1948 and May 1949; 22 from May to the end of 1949. In 1950, it still held 45; in the following year, 39; in 1952, only 29; and in 1953, also 29. As of 1954, Novotný, who already held the position of first (general) secretary, insisted on maintaining the weekly intervals between CC Presidium meetings. The regularity of meetings figured among the principles of collective leadership in the party propagated at that time. From July 1954 to January 1, 1957, the Presidium had 162 meetings. And the regularity continued. Only in the mid sixties was it somewhat disturbed, so that at mid-year in 1965, the Presidium had had 22 meetings, in the same period of the following year 21, and in 1967 only 18 meetings.

8. Discussions of this kind took place in 1953 during the change in party policy, in 1956 in connection with the application of the conclusions of the Twentieth Congress of the CPSU, in 1957 and 1963 during discussions of the rehabilitation of victims of the political trials of the fifties, and in 1967 when General Secretary Novotný was under fire.

9. For example, this happened to Fierlinger in 1957, when he was given a party reprimand for having criticized the work of State Security within the CC Presidium, of which he was a member.

10. This happened, for example, in the conflict between Zápotocký and Novotný in 1953–1954, which was resolved in Moscow. It also happened in 1966, when the CC Presidium divided into Czech and Slovak factions during discussions about the authority of Slovak national organs, and in the conflict between backers and opponents of Novotný in 1967 and 1968.

11. I myself experienced such a case. In 1964, I prepared a report on the conceptual background for celebrations of the twentieth anniversary of the Slovak National Uprising (1944) and the liberation of Czechoslovakia (1945). Historians took part in its preparation, and it was approved by the Ideological Commission as well as the party leadership in Slovakia. Novotný took it off the agenda of the CC Presidium meeting due to ideological deficiencies and an un-Marxist approach, which he saw in the report's suggestion that the participation of French partisans be mentioned, as well as the participation of U.S. soldiers in the liberation of the Republic.

12. During the three months (February–April) of the years 1965–1967, the CC Presidium assigned 795 tasks, some to several persons or institutions at the same time. 261 of these were assigned to members of the Presidium, 195 to CC secretaries, 22 to lower-level party organizations, 136 to extra-party institutions and mass organizations, and 768 to ministers.

13. The much-feared Kopecký was a member of the postwar Prague leadership. Even Gottwald was afraid of him, and no one wanted to get into a conflict with him. There was also a conflict in this leadership between Zápotocký and Slánský for the position of second man in the party and state (after Gottwald). In 1953–54, following Gottwald's death, a conflict emerged between Zápotocký and Novotný for the highest power position, and later there was a power struggle between Široký and Novotný. Beginning in 1948, there were various conflicts with Čepička, whose rapid rise in power, due to his position as minister of defense and family relationship to Gottwald (he was his son-in-law), was followed with displeasure by the others. First, Zápotocký crossed swords with him, then later, Novotný and Barák. Three years after Gottwald's death, Čepička was stripped of all high positions. In 1962, all the members of the leadership got together to eliminate Barák, who was aiming at the highest position in the party. A year later, Novotný took care of Široký. In 1967, Novotný's position weakened, and his fall from power ensued, with some of those closest to him—Jiří Hendrych, Kolder, and Štrougal— helping to bring it about. Since the establishment of the Husák leadership in the early seventies, there have been conflicts between the Czech and Slovak members, between Alois Indra and Karel Hoffmann (Czechs) and Husák and Bil'ak (Slovaks).

14. Gottwald received information about members of the CC Presidium from State Security. Barák obtained information about Široký, Čepička, Novotný, and Fierlinger and kept his own notes of discussion at meetings of the CC Presidium. Novotný set up files on those who spoke up against him in the CC Presidium in 1967–1968.

15. The atmosphere prevailing within the power group can best be described by one who was present at their discussions, or had the opportunity to observe the behind-the-scenes intrigues. Two accounts of participants help us to get a feel for it. The first comes from the period immediately after the seizure of power (the period 1948–1950) and deals with the party leadership in Slovakia. The author of the account is one of its foremost members, Gustav Husák. In 1963, in an lengthy complaint to the Central Committee, he described, among other things, how Široký (chairman of the communist party in Slovakia and member of the central leadership) organized his supporters and his methods of dominating the Slovak leadership: "The most frequent and bitterest conflicts in the presidium of the CC of the communist party of Slovakia were between Široký (and his group) and Comrade František Zupka (chairman of the trade unions in Slovakia). For all practical purposes, there was constant fighting, constant tension, constant quarrels between Zupka and the leadership of the unions, on the one hand, and Široký and his group, on the other hand. . . . For this, Široký and his group sidetracked Zupka, wherever possible.

"There were similar conflicts in the Presidium between Karol Šmidke and Široký. These two hadn't liked each other even before. When Šmidke made a presentation to the Presidium or the Central Committee, Široký sent in his closest lieutenants to fight him. They ridiculed and humiliated Šmidke, and made him look like a plain idiot behind the scenes. . . . With certain variations, Široký took a similar approach toward Laco Novomeský and other functionaries. Immediately after 1948, Široký got control of the entire security apparat in Slovakia, mainly State Security. He even prohibited commanders of security from giving any reports at all on security matters to Husák, who was chairman of the corps responsible for security matters. The leading commanders of security in Slovakia went regularly to Široký's apartment, on a weekly basis, to report on security matters, and they received instructions from him personally.

"Pull, the man responsible for food supplies was sharply criticized several times in the leadership. . . . When, after February 1948, Pull saw that he had fallen into disfavor with Široký, he personally made a sharp turnaround, turning away from the Slovak National Uprising group (Husák, Šmidke) and, by means of various denunciations to Široký and Braník, won their full confidence. From this moment, he began to rise rapidly, becoming first a member of the Secretariat, and then of the CC Presidium."

The second case comes from the turn of the year 1967–1968, the period when Novotný came under sharp criticism within the Presidium. Excerpts from the discussion at the Central Committee meeting in December that have to do with personal relationships and the atmosphere within the power group are given.

Kolder (Member of the CC Presidium and CC secretary): "I told Comrade Novotný that I don't know where the clear note of suspicion toward me comes from, or why he sometimes worries about views that don't agree with his own. I have also known since December of last year [1966] that I was to be removed from my position. I waited to be called. I expect it as the consequence of my open views."

Piller (CC member): "I am convinced that most members of the Presidium lacked personal courage. They should have fought for their own understanding of party truth. Comrades, and what about those who crawled to Comrade Novotný and chirped comrade here and comrade there, Tonda [Novotný's nickname = "Tony"] here, Tonda there, you're right, what you said was marvelous."

Koucký (CC secretary): "Of course, on the one hand, it is true that the scope for resolving some things was not established consistently enough for there to be a really open and sincere discussion, the necessary calm and stability in work."

Kapek (candidate cember of the CC Presidium): "I didn't understand, and still can't understand, why Comrade Hendrych, as Novotný's closest associate, didn't see his inadequacies, didn't help to eliminate them but, on the contrary, reinforced them by his uncritical stance, his adherence to Comrade Novotný. It surprised me, and I said it at the Presidium meeting, that the collective of a basic party organization is more sincere and more comradely than the CC Presidium. I can't understand why for ten or thirteen years [Hendrych] couldn't see Novotný's weaknesses and help eliminate them, but only then, afterward, put it all together."

Oldřich Cerník (member of the CC Presidium): "The party leadership or party Presidium was represented [by Novotný] as a body from which things quickly leaked and got to foreign agencies."

Dolanský (member of the CC Presidium): "And I can say this about it: that such fear, such pressure always came over me that I tell you quite frankly that when I went to the Presidium, I felt myself tightening up. . . . I don't know why fear should be necessary. But in a way it is a kind of, not forwardness, but such an awful weight in the whole environment behind which such a thing is probably concealed, so now I have something to dig into, this is being hinted at, this is being turned down, etc. Things have been going on this way for about three years. . . . At these last meetings, I spoke very openly, very strongly. You see, and I then said to myself that it is a kind of different atmosphere. It wasn't only me who could shout and criticize. Everyone could."

Dubček (member of the CC Presidium): "At a meeting of the CC Presidium, Comrade Novotný, when he chided some comrades for not having told him some things earlier, openly said, yes, Dubček told me about it."

In January 1968, Novotný responded to the criticism. Among other things, he said: "I always expressed my views openly to everyone, sometimes very critically, even though I know this sometimes causes bad blood. While these discussions were going on in the Presidium, and all the criticism was falling on my head, I was literally baffled with surprise by the content as well as the form, quite frankly, sometimes even libelous. I resisted, and said I considered it beneath my dignity to go the same way as some others and make public what one or the other had said about someone else. I had to swallow it all, and repress it in the interest of unity and collaboration. But naturally, I had my own opinions."

16. In January 1968, Novotný admitted "as my mistake, that I didn't call meetings of all the secretaries often enough." He did not see the need for this

since, during this period, it was clear to him that CC secretaries would agree with his proposals, and he discussed many matters with them individually.

17. Novotný said about these meetings that he often thought aloud at them, since he wanted the CC secretaries to know his views and he theirs. But he subsequently became convinced that while they knew his views, he did not know theirs at all, since they didn't reveal them.

18. In 1966, for example, Novotný proposed that Dubček be replaced as party chief in Slovakia. He ran up against disagreement among the secretaries and backed down.

19. Concerning this situation, Novotný said in 1968 that "My door was always open to secretaries. They consulted me on various questions. Sometimes they didn't. It was up to them what conclusions they drew from the conversation. When the need arose, I would also summon comrades." Under pressure, however, he said, "Some, like Comrade Hendrych, even came several times a day, sometimes even directly, without notice, even when I had someone with me." On the other hand, "It is true that among the comrade secretaries, I had a reserved attitude toward Comrade Kolder because of some of his character traits and ways of behaving." Koucký expressed satisfaction that Novotný always consulted him on international affairs. Štefan Sádovský as well as Václav Slavík complained, on the contrary, that when they had to see Novotný, they often couldn't get to him at all.

20. The transfer of CC Presidium and Secretariat member Alois Indra to the position of chairman of the Federal Assembly (in 1971) can, for example, be interpreted this way.

21. Gottwald commanded a natural authority in the party. All party functionaries, even the highest, took his position as binding. Also, even in his presence, they made their own opinions known, which did not always accord with his. Slánský as general secretary (Gottwald was the chairman of the party) lacked natural authority with the members of the power group. Some stood against him. He built up his position as second after Gottwald by being Gottwald's closest collaborator, the first interpreter of his views, and intermediary with the party apparat, which he controlled. He succeeded in extending his omnipotence to such an extent that he intervened in the activities of and controlled institutions administered by members of the power group, and thereby ranked above them.

In September 1951, Slánský was replaced by Novotný, a complete unknown in the party. Until Gottwald's death (March 1953), he was a completely insignificant and not much respected figure in the power group. It was only then that his rise to power began. He never rested on recognized authority to which others in the leadership would subordinate themselves in recognition of his political wisdom or experience, but rather on the fact that he held the leading position. Novotný's authority did not carry him to the peak of power, authority gave him the position. With it he acquired the necessary means to subordinate the power group to himself. It took him several years to achieve this, and his efforts to maintain his authority as well as his position were carried through by the removal or demotion of all other aspirants—Zápotocký, Čepička, Široký, Július Ďuriš, Barák.

Dubček based his authority on the greatest support of the citizenry ever attained by a leading communist functionary in Czechoslovakia. Husák assumed the position of general secretary eight months after the Soviet occupation of Czechoslovakia in August 1968, and the power group trusted him to quickly put an end to the unrest and insecurity that reigned in the country after the occupation. They saw in him a man with a strong arm, crowned with the glory of the Prague Spring. This source of his authority began to degenerate quickly, and his authority came to be based only on the highest position, guaranteed by the Soviet occupation, and use of the instruments of power.

22. After 1948, Gottwald voluntarily became an isolated and broken recluse, but hard and ruthless. In Slánský's case, his traits as a cold, feelingless bureaucrat and manipulator of power stood out. Power was an obstacle for Dubček. He was afraid to use it and also easily lost it. For Husák, the possession of power became the meaning of his life. It multiplied his intolerance, hardness, and ruthlessness in pursuing his own interests. He subordinated all his decisions, his personal and friendship relationships, and opinions to the acquisition and maintenance of power. In doing this, he had no moral restraints. On the contrary, his character traits made it easier for him. Novotný entered the central power group as an underestimated party clerk, apparatchik, and left as its all-powerful master. Only a few years after his election as president of the Republic (1957), he changed from a functionary ready to permit and respect even opinions differing from his own into an arrogant representative of the party, superior to everyone, intoxicated by a conviction of the correctness of his views, and with strong dictatorial tendencies. This metamorphosis not only led to a concentration of power in his hands but also changed the behavior of those around him.

Members of the power group did not oppose Novotný's views when they considered them to be wrong. On the contrary, they praised them. Many kowtowed to him, everyone wanted to oblige him more than anyone else. They outdid themselves in boosting his merits and his authority. And thus, his conviction of the correctness of his views was reinforced, and grew progressively into a belief in his infallibility, and it thus became impossible to oppose him. The combination of Novotný's power and the practice of the singers of his praise progressively created a state of affairs in which no one dared oppose him, so as not to risk losing their positions. They agreed with everything he proposed, they voted for things with which they didn't even personally agree, and they sought ways to get nearer to his thinking. It is this kind of behavior that produced the so-called ideological unity of the power group that has been called for and praised, and has perpetuated itself since 1948.

One example: On the eve of Novotný's fall (in December 1967), Bil'ak (at the time the Slovak party first secretary) attacked Novotný's speech of 1963, in which he had criticized some phenomena in Slovakia. However, in September 1963, at a Central Committee meeting, Bil'ak had said of this speech that "the criticism leveled by comrade Novotný is correct. The great majority of party members also took it in this way." And in April 1966, at a meeting of the CC Presidium, he had again assured Novotný that "we really defended what you said in Košice." Novotný's speech to graduates of the military school,

September 1, 1967, which several members of the CC Presidium criticized only after Novotný's fall from power provides a similar example. On September 5, however, everyone agreed with it, and no one protested when it was distributed to the regions as political guidelines.

23. A short time before his demise, Novotný entrusted responsibility for the First Department to another CC secretary. Soon after, he condemned this practice because, in his opinion, under such conditions, the general secretary cannot "work effectively and manage activities, since he isn't fully informed."

24. At a meeting of the Central Committee in September 1967, Novotný proclaimed that the recent Writers' Congress, at which there had been criticism of party policy, had been planned in Paris, i.e., by imperialist enemies. When, at the next meeting, he was asked on what basis he had come to such a conclusion, he answered, "This cannot be spoken about."

25. Two examples can be given. First, in January 1967, a meeting of the heads of CC departments took place that dealt with methods of work in the party apparat. Employees in Novotný's office noted the items they considered important in the minutes of the meetings, and Novotný also checked off those that interested him. The results are shown in Table 2.2. Novotný checked off two suggestions in the minutes as important. The first was a recommendation that greater attention be paid to the work of party organizations in order to correct the existing state of affairs, in which no one was responsible for anything. The second suggestion aimed at properly delimiting relationships between party and state institutions, in which there was not to be any division of powers since the leading role of the party is indispensable. The party cannot divide it with anyone.

The second example has to do with Novotný's interest in reports in the *Information Bulletin* of the CC Organizational-Political Department (in 1967). Out of fifteen reports on members' meetings, he was interested in three; out of forty-four reports on meetings of district and regional organs, in ten; out of five reports on relations among the republic's ethnic groups, in one. In the cultural and ideological domain, information about students and institutions of higher education drew his attention. Reports about living conditions passed without his notice.

26. Their significance becomes obvious if we remember that reform of the economic system began to be implemented during the year preceding the Prague Spring and that Novotný was not among its unconditional supporters. It was also the year of the Fourth Congress of Czechoslovak Writers, at which there was sharp criticism of party policy, and a year in which Czech-Slovak relations worsened, thanks to Novotný.

All nine reports contained mostly negative information from the economic sphere, mentioned in connection with the introduction of reform of the system. The names of factories and individuals from which this information came were given. Individual reports also contained, among other things:

Report No. 1: Reactions to changes in the government, views of former functionaries of the Social Democratic party (with their names given) on the domestic political situation, including views on Novotný's imminent demise from his positions in the party.

TABLE 2.2
General Secretary Novotný's Interest in Issues
Dealt with at a Meeting of CC Heads of Department

Notes by Novotný's office	Novotný's interest
Proposal that the Prime Minister present reports for the CC presidium	none
Proposal for changing the proceedings of the CC secretariat	yes
View regarding the necessity of raising qualifications of CC apparatchiks	none
Proposal that more functionaries from the regions than from central extra-party institutions be taken into the central party apparat	yes
Proposals that CC organs not take all decisionmaking on themselves	none
Criticism that meetings of high-level organs are not held for want of written supporting materials about certain things, although these things are very important	none
Criticism of an improper (behind-the-scenes approach to cadre policy	none
Criticism of inadequacies in the system of information	none
Proposal of social security for old apparatchiks	none

Report No. 2: Views among cultural apparatchiks (with their names given) on the political situation and on discrimination against artists, views on the constitutional arrangements among Czechs and Slovaks.

Report No. 3: Rumors among the cultural intelligentsia concerning the removal of the head of the CC Ideological Department, the preparation of party proceedings against the writer, Ladislav Mňačko, both of which were bound up with the introduction of a harder line in culture policy.

Report No. 4: Reactions to the publication of Mňačko's books abroad, collected under the title, "On increasing manifestations of nationalism in Slovakia" (with names given), views of some professors of the Philosophical Faculty of Prague University (names given), the opinion of engineer X on the disadvantageousness of economic cooperation with the USSR.

Report No. 5: Rumors about the substantial emigration of Czechoslovak citizens after the World Hockey Championships, meetings of former "lud'aky" [members of the People's party, which ruled the Slovak state that emerged after the destruction of Czechoslovakia in 1939 and cooperated with Nazi Germany] in Slovakia, reactions to the Mňačko case, characterization of the new head of the CC Ideological Department from the mouths of personalities in the world of culture (names given).

Report No. 6: Information about the intention of some groups of workers to oppose price rises by means of strikes, also about celebration of a mass in city X in which a large number of communists took part.

Report No. 7: Information that the foreign trade enterprise had received letters from its foreign partners criticizing the position of the Prague government toward Israel, and that these letters are part of a campaign organized by Jewish firms.

Report No. 8: Strong response to the Writers' Congress among the intelligentsia, including copying of speeches of participants; views of writer X on the trial of the Czechoslovak emigré in Paris, editor of the journal, *Svědectví*, Pavel Tigrid. The writer mentioned that he knows of relations of the Czechoslovak attaché with Tigrid and, on the other hand, that he is the object of a criminal trial in Prague (all names given). In the region, X strongly condemns the actions of the writers at their congress and expects that the party Central Committee will take appropriate measures.

Report No. 9: Information about general agreement with the decision to strip Mňačko of his citizenship and the varying opinions on this matter of a whole host of people (names given), especially from Bratislava . . .

3

The Party Apparat

The Role of the Party Apparat

The party apparat—the aggregate of party apparatchiks or system of party secretariats and machinery—is the most important power instrument of the party leadership. This importance stems from several factors. First and foremost, it consists of the most powerful organs and it administers itself according to its own needs. Interrelationships among these organs were established in 1957 as follows: "There must be an unflinching unity of will and action in the party apparat, between party organs and apparatchiks." Linkage between the leadership and its apparat is assured by means of personnel. DC, RC, and CC secretaries are the core of the power group, and they thus stand at the top of the apparat. The power group protects its apparat and defends it against the criticism leveled at it—mainly in times of party crisis. This happened in Czechoslovakia in 1951 after the arrest of General Secretary Slánský, in 1956 after the Twentieth Congress of the CPSU, and in 1967–1968 during the fall of Novotný. In such instances, criticism of the apparat is called a manifestation of Trotskyism, an attack on the backbone of the party.

Moreover, the party apparat alone has the party, its organization, and its aktiv [see chapter 4] at its disposal and uses them to control extra-party institutions as well. It dominates the party and its operations. All party organizations and institutions come under its authority, and it is with its apparatchiks that members and functionaries most frequently come into contact. For most, the Secretariat is the party's principal agency. They meet on its turf, receive instructions and guidelines from its apparatchiks, consult with them, complain to them, ask them for advice, and then treat this advice as instructions and as the party's position. Party apparatchiks are the most important and politically most solid component of the aktiv of functionaries. Without a doubt, all functionaries regard them as "their kind of people." At the same time their special position is recognized. They are regarded as people who know what the party needs and wants and who can take care of a great many things.

Second, the apparat lays the groundwork for decisions of the power group and interprets and makes sure of their implementation. No attempt to limit its activity to merely implementing resolutions has ever been successful. What especially stands out is its role in controlling and supervising all institutions of social life.

Third, the apparat is solid from a political and class point of view. The ultimate criteria for selection of it personnel are unconditional loyalty to the party, agreement with its policies, and obedience to instructions and guidelines of the power group. From the point of view of social structure it has, from the outset, been a working-class apparat. The predominance of workers by profession or members from working class families has been maintained.[1] Since the second half of the sixties, it must be admitted, its social structure has changed in favor of the intelligentsia. Nonetheless, in 1980 about 60 percent of party apparatchiks were workers by original profession and 89 percent came from working-class families.

Fourth, it is a universal apparat. The power group implements its decisions by means of different branches of the state and economic apparats and mass organizations. But only the party apparat is responsible for the overall implementation of resolutions and, simultaneously, of coordinating the activity of all extra-party institutions. Its supremacy over all other apparats derives from the fact that it is the apparat of the power groups. It acts toward all institutions not only as the mouthpiece of the power group but as the mouthpiece of the entire party, assuring its leading role. Since 1948, its structure has been adapted to the organization of the state and society, so that there is a party apparatchik responsible for every domain of social activity or organization. He presses for the implementation of party resolutions in the sector assigned to him, assigns tasks, and keeps track of the activities of "his" extra-party institution. He is politically responsible for it, i.e., to his power group and the party and to no one else, while the leading officials of extra-party institutions are responsible both to the party and to their own superior organs and leadership. Above all they are responsible before the law. The party apparat thus functions as a shadow apparat, replacing or doubling for other apparats. Attempts to limit or abolish this role of shadow apparat have been only partially successful, since each component of the party apparat has extensive authority over all extra-party institutions and apparats based on the support of its own power group and the higher levels of the party apparat.

Fifth, although the party apparat functions as an instrument of the power group, it is also capable of acting as an independent force against the power group. This aspect of its position is quite significant. It is capable of exercising this "independent" role in all phases of its activity—in laying the groundwork for decisions of the power group, in interpreting the will and guidelines of the power group, and in choosing means to implement them.

The numbers of party apparatchiks have changed often. The apparat began to grow immediately after the establishment of communist power and stopped with the systematization of 1967 at 8,499, two-thirds (5,240) of whom were political. Around 4,886 work in the districts, 1,344 in the regions, 278 in the Slovak central headquarters, and 757 in the federal central headquarters.[2] On average, there is one political apparatchik for every 280 communists. If party apparatchiks paid out of factory budgets are included, the ratio falls to one for every 250 communists.

The guidelines governing the party apparat's work give it the responsibility of preparing the foundations for the decision making of party organs, of assuring and checking up on the implementation of their resolutions and guidelines, looking after the activity of all party and extra-party institutions, administering the party aktiv, and selecting and assigning cadres. The party apparat deals with all kinds of tasks, but mainly it implements decisions and guidelines in two ways. It delegates tasks to lower-level party organs and extra-party institutions in the domain of its authority and checks up on their fulfillment. It also supervises extra-party institutions, both directly and through lower-level party organizations which carry out their supervisory roles by means of extensive networks of instructors.

"Delegated tasks," checking up on their implementation, and supervising the activities of organizations and institutions are the kinds of organizational and cadre work for which the apparat is best adapted, as a supreme transpolitical agency with officials working according to routines. On the other hand, laying the groundwork for decision making by the power group requires a level of qualifications and knowledge that most apparatchiks lack. Thus their direct participation in such "creative work" is minimal. They affect the decision-making process more as organizers and coordinators of the activities of others—mainly functionaries of extra-party institutions. They collaborate only to a limited extent in the formulation of reports and proposed resolutions, and only rarely formulate them by themselves.

The nature of the party apparat's work calls for an organizer, a politically experienced and obedient official for whom implementation of guidelines has become simply a routine. These requirements determine the selection criteria for apparatchiks. The ideal type of the party apparatchik is someone who has come up through the apparat in the district and region and then gone to political school. District apparatchiks are sought out mainly among functionaries of basic organizations and extra-party institutions. The DC secretary selects new apparatchiks for his portfolio from the group of well-known functionaries, directly "from production," or from among those who have graduated from party school.

For the most part, it is district apparatchiks who are recruited into the regional apparat. Here, the selection process is more demanding, the standards more stringent. Each head takes care of recruitment for his department with the concurrence of an RC secretary. On the basis of reports from his colleagues, consultations with apparatchiks in his portfolio from the district, and with the concurrence of the regional instructor, he "picks out" one or two possible candidates to work in his department. As soon as the need arises he either discusses with a district secretary the possibility of the individual in question's being made available to the region, or he has him classified "into the ranks of prospective cadres." The individual in question then goes off to party school and joins the department after graduation. Heads of departments and their deputies at central headquarters proceed along similar lines.

In isolated cases, the procedure can work in reverse, with the central sending its apparatchiks to a region and regions in turn sending theirs to the districts. Only in exceptional cases do functionaries of extra-party institutions in the regions and at the central level go directly into the party apparat. This usually happens when positions require a certain level of qualifications (knowledge of music, literature, etc.). Such functionaries are usually of a different breed than routinized party apparatchiks and soon go "back." On the other hand, transfers in the opposite direction—from the party apparat to the apparats of extra-party institutions—are quite frequent. Among those who leave the apparat this way are those who didn't work out, those who are sent "to strengthen the party" in another institution, or those who, for various reasons, go after a transfer themselves.

Promotion of party apparatchiks to higher positions takes place in a manner that resembles the selection process. Heads of RC and CC sections are usually selected from among apparatchiks in that department, and heads of RC departments either from among apparatchiks of RC departments or DC secretaries. Deputy heads of CC departments are chosen from among the heads of sections, graduates of the Moscow party school, or the heads of RC departments.

These principles of selection have gradually led to the formation of a hard core within the apparat that consists of apparatchiks with long years of experience, of routinized professionals—men of the apparat. They are convinced that work in the apparat is the only profession they are able to perform, and that it is the only possible source of existential security for them. This lies at the root of their efforts to remain in the apparat, efforts that result in an obedience to their superiors that is unconditional to the point of servility. They are also the ones who shape the consciousness and atmosphere of the party apparat and determine its work methods and rhythm of operation.

The power groups and the leaderships of their apparats have a vested interest in the stabilization of cadres. Secretaries and heads of departments in the districts, regions, and the central transfer apparatchiks from one portfolio to another and bargain with each other with the sole aim of keeping tried and tested comrades with long years of experience in the apparat. They pay no attention to the expertise and the experience they have acquired. They often don't even pay attention to the quality of their work, since their expertise lies in their current profession: party apparatchik. This is how many who have worked in several departments and sections and "managed" several completely different portfolios vegetate in the apparat. On February 1, 1966, more than 50 percent of political apparatchiks had been in the apparat longer than five years. By the end of the seventies, this percentage had exceeded three-quarters.

The educational level of the apparat has gone up since the fifties. At the end of the fifties university graduates were the exception, but beginning in the sixties their numbers rose rapidly. In 1968 more than 70 percent of political personnel in the central apparat were university graduates. Although there were substantially fewer at lower levels, by 1980 more than 40 percent of apparatchiks had a university education. These were predominantly graduates of the Prague or Moscow political universities. Despite this progress, the level of specialized and political qualifications within the apparat remains low. The specialized knowledge of apparatchiks in portfolios with administrative functions is superficial, and political consciousness is limited and one-sided. Especially typical is a lack of knowledge of international affairs. Apparatchiks make no effort to increase their awareness, and no one particularly expects this of them. It is enough that they have graduated from political school. Knowledge that exceeds the norm by too much is even disturbing to the others. It might threaten deep-rooted ideological stereotypes and be the germ of ideological shakiness.

It is also very difficult for those who are interested to obtain additional information about world affairs. Of the world press, CC secretaries and departments and RC leading secretaries receive only the Soviet *Pravda*. Single copies of the newspapers of the communist parties of capitalist countries are received, but they go to the apparatchiks in the International Department who are responsible for such matters. As for the noncommunist press, only rarely is some world-renown daily newspaper received. Those interested in international affairs thus have to rely on the news monitoring reports of the press office, which the heads of CC departments receive daily. Other apparatchiks have access to them only after a week's delay.

The situation with regard to books is even worse. It isn't difficult for apparatchiks at central headquarters to receive books that have been published in Soviet bloc countries. There is, however, no interest in them. Noncommunist publications from the West are virtually inaccessible. CC secretaries and heads of departments can obtain some of them, since they stand at the top of the list of persons and institutions who receive publications coming in from the West and confiscated by State Security. State Security also issues a survey of confiscated books and periodicals. CC secretaries and heads of departments do not, however, take advantage of this privilege. They are not interested in the publications and do not know the languages they would need in order to read them. Lower-level apparatchiks can obtain these publications only through the head of their CC department and their secretary, to whom they have to show a work-related need for the book. Since they are afraid of the usual accusation "of heresy," they don't even dare to fill out an application.

The party apparatchik receives ideological education continually— in concentrated form at party school, otherwise in the course of ordinary work and through consultations, conferences, training, reading the press, and private conversations. His political thinking thus stays within clearly defined boundaries and is governed by rules learned through long experience. Everyone is subject to these rules whether or not he is aware of it. Adherence to them is a criterion for selection of those who work in the party apparat and is among the conditions for staying in it. It is also one of the principal ideological bonds tying apparatchiks to the thinking of the power group and the party aktiv.

The apparatchik's political thinking derives first and foremost from two factors: ideology and faith. Social reality and personal experience play only a limited role, since there is a limit to what a party apparatchik can think about and how much he can doubt. His thinking is most strongly shaped by ideological stereotypes, which he takes part in formulating and which are proclaimed by the power group as theoretical postulates. This state of affairs suits apparatchiks very nicely. They gladly accept this kind of thinking since it gives them a simple recipe for answers and solutions to all problems. They don't like it when the ideological stereotypes change and only reluctantly abandon the old and become accustomed to the new.

The second factor—faith, confidence—takes the form of a few firm, unshakable principles anchored deeply in the consciousness. First and foremost, there is unconditional confidence in the Soviet Union and its policies, the virtue of their own regime, in their own power group and its policy. Many apparatchiks occasionally have doubts about some particular decision of the power group. At the same time, however, they know that they cannot voice their doubts or allow them to grow into doubts about the regime and its overall political orientation.

The basic characteristics of political thinking are simplicity and unambiguousness in response to social problems. The party apparatchik has a "class perspective" on the world, which breaks down it into capitalist and socialist. All states and movements that do not subordinate themselves to the Soviet Union or support its policies are considered enemies of socialism. The capitalist world breaks down into the United States and the other capitalist countries, which the United States treats in the manner of an imperialist, colonial superpower. The capitalist states use considerable force to protect their regimes from the victorious advance of socialism in the world, especially in the Third World.

The apparatchik's perspective on domestic problems differs somewhat from his view of world affairs, with its boxlike categories. Although the point of departure here is conviction about the virtue of the regime, he cannot ignore reality as it actually is—full of inadequacies from top to bottom, from the difficulties of the everyday lives of citizens to the administrative activities of central institutions. He encounters these inadequacies in his everyday work, and the functionaries he comes in contact with remind him of them. He doesn't like to see them, doesn't like to hear about them, and doesn't like to talk about them, but he has to. He doesn't see their causes in the system, i.e., in a mistaken political orientation or in decisions of the party, but rather in faulty implementation of party policy by functionaries of extra-party institutions. Sometimes he also sees the causes in the activities of enemies of socialism. So he has a very simple way out—always consistently implement party resolutions and instructions and remove those who don't want to do so, who can't, or who even come out against the party line.

The simplicity, unambiguousness, and limitedness of political thinking produce a kind of self-confidence. The party apparatchik is convinced that the regime of actually existing socialism is the best form of social organization. He believes, or pretends to believe, in its coming victory in the whole world. He is convinced that the Soviet Union and his own party have the one true recipe for all problems of life on earth, and that they have a monopoly on truth. He automatically rejects all counterarguments and other perspectives as hostile, revisionist, and mistaken views. In short, the Soviet bloc is for him the center of the world, around which the earth revolves and which determines the course of world events.

Laziness is a characteristic of the mental activity of the party apparatchik in seeking ideas for the resolution of problems of his portfolio or in the invention of new forms of political work. Not much novelty is expected of him, and on top of this, he can't be sure that, in trying to implement novelties, he won't run into opposition from comrades who outrank him. He thus proceeds like an experienced routineer. He knows exactly where to get thoughts, ideas, and proposals. He knows how to deal with them, which are acceptable, and which won't survive at higher levels. He knows how to apply the commonly used work methods, following the well-worn tracks that party work is supposed to follow. And mainly, he knows that previous practices are good enough for him, that they are acceptable to "superiors and subordinates" and advantageous for him, since he has completely mastered them and can apply them without effort. And so, whenever he is given the task of assuring or organizing something, his mind is automatically equipped with a fixed, stereotyped response. It pops out like out of a drawer ready to use.

The motives that sustain party apparatchiks are ideological, power-political, and social in character. The effectivness of ideology has weakened significantly. Nonetheless, many continue to think that they are serving socialist ideals and feel like professional revolutionaries. For most of them, however, work in the party apparat soon becomes mere employment at the highest level. The bond of power, which continues to grow stronger, consists of the self-satisfaction of belonging to the most important power apparat and participating in the power that derives from it.

The strongest social motive is the fact that most functionaries have attained a higher standard of living through the party apparat than they would ever have otherwise had. In 1953 a pay scale for apparatchiks of the DC, RC, and CC apparats was issued, which has been only slightly modified over time. Pay level is determined on the basis of the function exercised, with variable supplements for education and length of service in the party apparat or section. Differences among the districts, regions, and the center are quite substantial, and salary differentials among CC secretaries, heads of CC departments, and auditors are even greater. In the central the salary of a secretary (15,000 crowns a month) is four to five times greater than that of an auditor, and the salary of a CC head of department or RC leading secretary (7,000–9,000 crowns a month) is two to three times greater.

The average salaries of party apparatchiks are lower than those for positions of corresponding level in the state and economic apparats, but they exceed the average salaries of the population on the whole. In 1967 the average salary of an apparatchik in the party apparat was 2,628 in the districts, 2,990 in the regions, and 3,453 at the central. The average worker's wage was 1,609; the salary of a technical engineer 2,288; and clerk, 1,451 crowns.

The following comparison is imprecise, since the figures for the average salary of an apparatchik contain the salary of a clerk as well as that of a party secretary, which is six or seven times higher. In 1967 only 4.3 percent of Czechoslovak working people had an income level of 2,500–3,000 crowns, and only 0.4 percent reached a level of 3,500 crowns. Apparatchiks thus belonged to the highest income category and its leading functionaries to the very highest. The proportions given have not changed substantially, and to the extent that they have changed it has been to the benefit of apparatchiks.

Sharp differences in privileges are part of the social bond. They are different for central headquarters personnel than in the districts, different for the CC secretary than for the office help. Belonging to the party apparat in itself opens doors and elicits friendliness and helpfulness from the bureaucracy. It is precisely this characteristic of the bureaucracy that is so difficult for the ordinary citizen to appreciate. Party apparatchiks have extensive connections and the protection that goes along with them. The fact that each of them manages some office, some segment of the economy or supply network, means that the apparat manages everything needed for life. Every party apparatchik arranges privileges for the others—e.g., obtaining goods in short supply and protection in administrative agencies, schools, and various other institutions.

The party apparat is divided up by territory and by the nature of its activities. Most important is the so-called operational part of the party secretariat. The second part consists of those party facilities that take part indirectly in the implementation of policy. The third consists of the party apparat in the armed forces. The fourth is made up of those state institutions that the party apparat controls directly and considers to be its indirect offshoot.

The operational part of the party apparat is a self-contained organization with central and lower-level units in the regions, districts, and factories. In central headquarters the apparat is treated as a whole. Its members regard the lower-level units more as their own subordinate agencies than as units of lower-level power groups. The lower-level units are doubly subordinated—to their own power groups and to the higher-level apparat, but the latter line of subordination is the more important, if not decisive. That is to say, the higher-level apparat's authority extends not only to the lower-level apparat but also to the power group that manages it.

This complete subordination to higher-level units is reinforced by the fact that, for all practical purposes, the party apparat controls the DC, RC, and CC secretaries. Every DC and RC secretary answers to his power groups and leading secretary, but mainly to the higher-level RC or CC secretary responsible for the same portfolio, who has the main say in nominating subordinate DC or RC secretaries to their positions. This subordination can be direct, but more frequently it is imposed through the head of department of the higher-level unit of the apparat.

The leading secretary (general secretary at the central level) also has a unique position in managing the apparat. He is the "super" secretary, since the whole apparat, with all its portfolios, stands at his disposal. He answers to his own power group, as well as the higher-level power group and leading (general) secretary, for the work of the entire apparat. The other secretaries are subordinate in their working relationships with him. He assigns them tasks, and they are responsible to him for their fulfillment. He can intervene directly in the activities of all departments and apparatchiks, out assign them tasks, and request information without consulting the secretary in charge. When the relationship of subordination between the leading secretary and another secretary is violated, or when there are pronounced disagreements between them, higher-level party institutions intervene and usually remove the insubordinate secretary.

Central headquarters places great emphasis on the subordination of lower-level units of the party apparat to higher levels. This is how it insures that there will be a unity of understanding, interpretation, and implementation of the decisions of its power group. It issues its own guidelines and checks up on their implementation. The functional unity of the apparat as a whole is assured through the use of tried and tested methods. Central headquarters transmits written guidelines of a general nature to the regions and districts by letter and teletype. For example, during the two-year period (October 1963–1965), the districts and regions received more than 300, roughly 1 every other day. Such guidelines can be sent only by a CC secretary. Instructions of an organizational character are sent frequently by every CC department to the corresponding departments in the regions. The transmission of guidelines on a personal basis is very important. CC instructors usually do this for the regions and regional instructors do it for the districts. For especially significant decisions to be implemented as countrywide campaigns, central headquarters sends political brigades made up of apparatchiks and other functionaries to the regions, and the regions send such brigades to the districts.

Conferences of secretaries are considered a very valuable means for maintaining the unity of the party apparat and the unity of interpretation of decisions and guidelines. Some regions hold regular conferences of DC leading secretaries and irregular conferences of secretaries holding particular portfolios. All conferences and the themes of the discussions that take place at them are approved by the RC secretariat. Conferences of district apparatchiks working in particular departments are authorized by a regional secretary. Conferences of RC leading secretaries called by the general secretary are no longer held. RC leading secretaries meet irregularly with the participation of members of the CC Presidium and Secretariat. These are big events about which the daily press publishes an official report. What is done at them, including the theses of speeches made, is approved by the CC Presidium. The CC Secretariat makes decisions regarding conferences of RC departmental secretaries and also discusses the theses of the speeches. Conferences of RC heads of departments are authorized by the CC secretary responsible for the department in question, and those of other apparatchiks by the responsible CC head of department. Only in rare cases—during periods of fundamental change in party policy—does the CC Presidium organize a countrywide conference of district leading secretaries.

Conferences of DC and RC secretaries are usually held to clarify and implement important party resolutions (e.g., when party policy regarding some domain of social life changes), for the preparation of political campaigns (e.g., for a CC resolution on education, the development of agriculture, or the economic plan; in preparation for agricultural work; for adminstration of the rank and file membership, for preparation of elections to organs of power), and for verification (e.g., as to how important resolutions and guidelines are being implemented). Conferences of apparatchiks (officials in individual portfolios deal with very concrete matters, e.g., the beginning of the school year, recruitment of subscribers to the party press, preparation of annual members' meetings, arrangements for various celebrations, socialist competition, the work of the trade unions) run according to stereotyped procedures. The convening secretary or head of department speaks about the political significance of the matters under discussion and their organizational implementation. Participants give reports on the state of affairs prevailing in the area under discussion. Great significance is attributed to the conferences. At their meetings the responsible RC and CC departments deal with what happened at them and mainly with information arising from the discussion that is relevant for their portfolios.

The Party Apparat
in the Districts and Regions

The party apparat's basic unit is at the district level. This is not, however, its lowest-level unit. The party apparats in large factories belong to it, most of them consisting of the full-time chairman of the all-factory committee, a secretary, and, depending on the size of the enterprise, up to three apparatchiks. Those factories in which the apparat is paid for out of party funds are approved by the CC Secretariat, but there are not many of them. Disproportionately more apparats are paid for out of the budgets of enterprises, and apparatchiks paid in this way do not show up in the published numbers of party apparatchiks. Decisions concerning the management of these apparats are made by the regions or by the districts themselves under whose authority they come. They are generally set up in factories with more than 1,200–1,500 apparatchiks, and the number of full-time chairmen is around 5,000.

The full-time chairman acts as the party's spokesman in the factory and is recognized as such. His position is reinforced by frequent contacts with the district party secretariat and control of the factory party organization, from which he obtains his own information about the situation in the workplace. He is a member of the top management of the factory by virtue of his position and takes part in all managerial consultations and conferences. He intervenes not only in commercial and economic activity but also in matters concerning production, management, and even technical affairs. He completely dominates cadre policy in the enterprise, since it is he who decides on appointments to all high-level positions (aside from the director) and even less important ones. He does this either on his own or through the party committee. He can even make decisions concerning the hiring of workers if he wants to. He controls the selection and activities of officials of mass organizations (trade unions, youth, physical education) and handles political-agitational work directly (specifically the factory press, radio, exhibitions, and decoration).

The district party apparat is considered the most important unit in bringing to life the resolutions and guidelines of the central headquarters. Since the sixties, around thirty-five people work in the party apparat of each district, two-thirds of them being political. At the head is the leading secretary and two or three DC secretaries who also manage the district party apparat. Each one administers a certain area of social activity with the help of a few officials coming under his portfolio. The permanent areas are intra-party work, mass organizations, and ideology. These include health, schools, and sports as well as party work in industry, the village, or agriculture. The leading secretary is also responsible for armed units (see the structure of the district party apparat in Appendix 1).

The district apparat assures implementation of the resolutions of its power group, and mainly those of higher power groups and their apparats. Preparation of documentary materials for its own power group is a subsidiary activity. For the most part district apparatchiks merely copy reports and decisions of regional organs or transmit reports prepared by extra-party institutions. The political aspect of their activity consists, first and foremost, of the fact that, as the last "transmission unit," they strongly influence the final form of the guidelines. Their interpretation and implementation bear the marks of the apparatchiks' political competence, life experiences, and tastes for power. They act as organization men not much interested in events that go beyond the boundaries of their districts and portfolios. They don't even read the daily press regularly. They are content with the information they get about party policy and domestic and foreign events at meetings and consultations, and this usually in the form of "assigned tasks." Of all party apparatchiks it is they who have the best knowledge of social reality and the difficulties of the daily life of the population. But it is also they who give the least thought to the clash between party policy and reality. They explain this clash exclusively in terms of "inadequate fulfillment of party resolutions."

The workday of the district secretariat and its apparatchiks is quite varied. It breaks down into a large number of tasks and problems of greater and lesser importance, which are dealt with each day. Aside from matters having to do with the implementation of the resolutions and guidelines, problems crop up in the daily life of the party, organizations, functionaries, and extra-party institutions. Regularly, on a weekly basis after the meeting of the DC presidium, a meeting is held of secretaries and their subordinate officials at which they are informed of their principal tasks. Irregularly, but almost weekly, a meeting takes place of some part of the district aktiv. Several times a week, an apparatchik will call a meeting of functionaries "from his extra-party institution," or take part in their post-meeting. He attends the meetings of "his" party organizations and visits the heads of institutions assigned to him, as well as the chairmen of organizations in the workplace, and discusses with them a wide range of matters having to do with their activities. Much of his time is taken up by internal party matters such as the organization of members' meetings and public meetings, party training, subscription to the press, and resolution of conflicts between members and between functionaries. Every day, dozens of communists and people without party affiliation come to the secretariat to settle routine organizational matters, get advice, make complaints, or request intervention. Unforeseen visits and taking care of the individual affairs of members and functionaries absorb most of the time of many apparatchiks.[3]

The relatively small number of party apparatchiks in the district means that they all know each other and come into almost daily contact. Although the boundaries of authority of their portfolios are clearly delimited, their portfolios are not isolated. Collaboration among apparatchiks of different portfolios is routine, indeed unavoidable. Apparatchiks from one portfolio may make reference to another portfolio at meetings of the organization, something that rarely happens at the regional level and even less so at central headquarters. Furthermore, the "service hierarchy" doesn't have nearly as great an influence as it does at the regional and central levels. Not only every party apparatchik but administrative staff member too has easy access to DC secretaries, even to the leading secretary. Although officials respect their service and functional subordination to DC secretaries, they deal with them more as partners than as superiors. Similarly, the relationships between party apparatchiks and functionaries of extra-party institutions are not complicated by hierarchy of service either. They meet often, in the most varied of circumstances, on party turf as well as in the workplace. However, their "official relations" are governed by carefully observed rules. For example, only the leading secretary has the right to deal officially with the chairman of the district national Committee, the commander of security, and the military administration. Only the DC secretary with the corresponding portfolio can deal with their deputies, etc. Likewise, correspondence with superior party institutions goes through the hands of the leading secretary. He also conducts, or at least approves, discussions with functionaries of higher institutions—and not only party institutions.

Relations among party apparatchiks in the district are not, however, free of antagonisms and conflicts. These result from differences and rivalries among portfolios as well as individual power ambitions. In many cases these antagonisms and conflicts persist over long periods of time and are sometimes quite intense.

Despite many bureaucratic features, the district secretariat is not like an office. The regional secretariat, in contrast, is an office. It serves as the intermediate link between central headquarters and the districts.

That is, it transmits the will and guidelines of central headquarters to the districts and supervises and checks up on lower levels of the party and power structure. Only rarely does it go beyond its passive role of transmitter and come up with its own initiatives. When it does, these initiatives are limited to means for implementation of decisions and instructions from central headquarters.

About 100–200 people work in the regional apparat, around two-thirds of them being political. Its structure is divided horizontally into secretaries, departments, sections, and instructors. Vertically, it is divided into departments for organizational-political affairs, ideological affairs, state organs, and economic departments for agriculture and national economic affairs.

The party apparat in the region is administered by the RC secretariat, i.e., the leading secretary and three or four RC secretaries, each responsible for one to three departments. The routine method of administration is by weekly meetings of heads of departments with their secretaries, which are held after meetings of the RC presidium and secretariat. These are followed by meetings of the individual departments, at which the main tasks for the coming week are laid out and assigned to individuals. Ordinary everyday matters and tasks that come up during the week are dealt with by an appropriate functionary upon consultation with the head of department; matters of greater consequence, upon agreement with a DC secretary. (See the structure of the regional party apparat in Appendix 2.)

The substance of the party apparat's work in the region fits its role as transmitter from central headquarters to the districts and back. A large part of the workday is taken up with meetings and discussions with officials of regional and district institutions, gathering information on the implementation of resolutions in the districts and the region, and preparing surveys and reports. Apparatchiks frequently travel to the districts ("to the field," as they say) in order to make sure the guidelines of central headquarters are being implemented and to get an idea of what is happening with them. Preparation of supporting materials for the RC presidium and secretariat is carried out in conjunction with specialists in extra-party institutions, and is among the most time-consuming element of the work of the regional apparat. Cadre proposals arising from the frequent transfers of functionaries, which have to be approved by regional organs, are handled similarly.

The operational aspect also predominates in the work of the regional secretariat, despite the fact that RC secretaries and central headquarters ask that these apparatchiks generalize somewhat from the information at their disposal, as well as that which they receive from the districts. However, few apparatchiks at the district and regional levels are capable of analyzing and generalizing. Those who follow events throughout the country and the world, and go beyond official press dispatches and internal party information, are rare exceptions. Most apparatchiks come to the region from a district apparat and remain at this level as obedient, routinized organizers and executors of guidelines. They are true "officials above politics." They are far from being political functionaries in the true sense of the word. They do not try to make their lives difficult or complicate their work by broadening their political knowledge beyond what is unavoidable to carry out their profession—that of party apparatchik.

Party apparatchiks in the region also know and very frequently associate with each other. Nevertheless, there is a differentiation by function and portfolio, and there exist three groups of apparatchiks that are more or less independently of each other. The first consists of secretaries and heads of departments, the second of heads of sections and officials, and the third of administrative and technical personnel. The differences among them are social (the first group, in addition to its own privileges, enjoys some that are accorded to central headquarters personnel, and their salaries are substantially higher than those of the others); ideological (the second and third groups have a better picture of reality); and power-political and organizational (the first group is considered to be the backbone and elite of the apparat, with the greatest of authority, and its members themselves feel this and behave accordingly).

To be sure, in public they all present themselves as unified and above politics, as agents of the supreme regional authority. Nevertheless, differences and conflicts among RC secretaries and departments frequently arise. Some derive from differences of opinion, but most derive from interdepartmental and power rivalries. Interdepartmental rivalries are especially sharply manifested in a critical attitude toward the extraordinarily strong power position and work methods of the organizational-political department and in undervaluation of the ideological department. Power rivalries take the form of efforts of individuals to achieve higher positions—from RC secretary to RC presidium, from head of department to RC secretary, from head of section to head of department, from official to head of section.

The region represents a conservative element in the party apparat system, a stabilizing element from the point of view of the central. It holds back calls from "below" for changes in party policy and work methods. This role is especially appreciated during times of domestic political crisis, when the tendency to maintain the existing state of affairs finds a broad and firm bastion of support here. The sources of the regional apparat's strong conservatism lie in the social status of the majority of its apparatchiks. They are aware that they have arrived at the apex of their careers and the power that goes along with it. It is an apex that exceeds even their capabilities. They see in every change the germ of their demise. They have grown accustomed to certain methods of work, mastered the routine of party work, and lack the capabilities and strength to abandon old ways and replace them with new ones. They are content to think at the level of the ideological stereotypes they receive from central headquarters and cannot and do not want to deviate from and weaken them. Stereotypes mean security and make it possible for them to know what is required of them, how to react to the speculations and evaluations of the political situation in central headquarters, and how to adapt to them effortlessly. The main source of their conservatism is thus a feeling of social, political, and ideological security, which the existing state of affairs gives them and which they themselves represent as the general need of the party.

The Central Party Apparat

The central party apparat consists of two components—the secretariat and the party machinery. From the point of view of political power, the Central Secretariat is the most important component of the entire executive apparat. This is the case because

1. It occupies the key position in the party apparat as a whole.
2. It is the apparat of the all-powerful central power group. It stands closest to that group's members, best knows their views, conceptions, and intentions. It usually formulates, interprets, implements, and assures the realization of the power group's resolutions and guidelines.
3. It acts and is recognized as the highest representative of the party; as cocreator, interpreter, and implementer of its policy; the defender of its interests; as "the highest agency—above politics."
4. It directly controls all units of the party apparat and all the apparats of extra-party institutions. Also bound up with this is its nearly unlimited capacity to intervene in all matters of social life and in the work of all institutions. It can intervene on instructions of the power group, of CC secretaries, or on initiatives from its own apparatchiks.
5. Its power is based on the privileged position of CC secretaries, who are the leading figures in the political life of the country; the power mechanism; and the Central Secretariat. This personal symbiosis of the most influential component of the power group and the administrative body of the party apparat reaches its apex

in the position of the general secretary—the leading representative of the party and the highest official of its apparat.

The Central Secretariat has been reorganized many times since 1948, but these reorganizations have only slightly affected the basic contours of its structure. The number of secretaries changes, and some departments and sections are created or abolished, but those units that constitute the skeleton of the organization remain stable. The precise structure is established by an organizational plan prepared by the departments and approved by the CC Secretariat and Presidium. This organizational plan designates the departments and their sections and officials, delimits precisely the substance of their work, and determines the domains and institutions for which they are responsible.

Horizontally, the CC secretaries are at the top and under them, the departments, which are broken down into sections, which in turn are made up of offices. Vertically, it is broken down by area of activity. (For the structure of the CC, see Appendix 3.)

The work of the Central Secretariat is formally directed by a CC secretary. However, he acts more or less as a mere coordinator of the activities of individual departments rather than as an initiator. Actual management of the everyday operation of the Secretariat is in the hands of the CC secretaries and heads of departments. They determine which issues are to be dealt with and indicate the kinds of solutions to be sought and the means for their realization. They have influence on many routine, less significant matters dealt with by their officials every day.

A CC secretary is responsible for one to three departments. The breakdown of responsibilities is proposed by the general secretary and approved by the CC Presidium. There are no binding principles for this. Portfolios are assigned or combined with no regard being taken of the qualifications of the CC secretary. In the process, secretaries endeavor to hold on to at least one department in which they are regarded as a specialist. One rule is maintained, however. The general secretary usually takes care of the State-Administrative and the Organizational-Political Departments. If he entrusts one of these to another secretary, that secretary has an advantage over the others.

The division of responsibilities gives rise to imbalances as well as conflicts among secretaries. Secretaries are not always content with the departments assigned to them, since they are not all regarded as equal in importance. There are conflicts over jurisdiction that are reflections of interdepartmental conflicts. It is, however, differences of opinion among CC secretaries on how to deal with various issues that have the greatest impact. And the critical reservations (often personally motivated) of one secretary regarding the work of another secretary and his department have an especially strong impact. The secretary's critical views carry over to his immediate subordinates—to apparatchiks in his office, and the leadership of his department. This takes the form of ironical remarks, intrigues, and slander.

A CC secretary's secretariat, or office, consists of two or three political and two administrative apparatchiks and a chauffeur. The political apparatchiks call themselves the secretary's auxiliaries, and each of them takes care of the affairs of one of the departments run by the secretary. He arranges contacts between the secretary and the department and the heads of all institutions coming under the authority of the department. He provides information about all important matters that turn up in his area and requests the department's views on various reports and proposals. He provides his own comments on all memoranda, information, and notifications coming from the department and institutions. Auxiliaries prepare comments on reports for meetings of the CC Secretariat and Presidium or obtain them from experts. Every day, they read the monitoring of news from the international press and draw attention to important items. They organize the preparatory work for speeches the secretary is to deliver. Speeches are usually drafted for secretaries (including the general secretary, with the exception of Gottwald and Zápotocký, who wrote their own speeches) by the appropriate CC department. The secretary usually outlines his ideas for the speech when work on it begins, and it is he who makes the final modifications. In between, his auxiliaries return the speech several times with various comments for revision.

The authority of an auxiliary in the Central Secretariat is significantly greater than his actual functions would suggest. This is due the fact that he sits in the antechamber of the CC secretary and is considered a kind of adviser to him. In reality, he plays the role of liaison between the secretary and the department and institutions. Only in exceptional cases—due to his specialized qualifications—does he play the role of adviser. The CC secretary, however, avoids acknowledging this position publicly.

The general secretary's secretariat enjoys a higher status, comparable to an independent department. It consists of two heterogeneous units—the technical section, including archives, and the general secretary's office. Its head enjoys a special and superior position with regard to the other heads of departments. This derives from his closeness to the general secretary, his responsibility of checking up on the other departments (in preparing reports for central party organs), and his function as recording secretary for the CC Presidium.

The work done by this office resembles that of the secretaries' offices. A significant difference is that it arranges contacts not only with those departments and institutions for which the general secretary is responsible but with all of them. Sometimes such contacts are made with the awareness of the CC secretary responsible for the portfolio, but mostly without it. After several years of efforts, despite Novotný's opposition, his office ceased being a merely organizational-technical unit and became more manifestly political. This political aspect is taken care of by two or three specialists in international and domestic politics.

The basic working unit and center of gravity of the Central Secretariat's operations is the department. The department acts as a relatively independent entity in its relations with other party and extra-party units. Most guidelines of the power group and instructions of secretaries are carried out by a department and in its name, and most discussions and consultations with officials of extra-party institutions take place within the department. These officials, as well as apparatchiks of lower-level units of the party apparat, turn directly to the department responsible for them. The independence of the department is so strong that apparatchiks who work for the Secretariat encounter each other mainly within the confines of their own departments. The apparatchiks of the entire CC Secretariat meet together as a body only once a year, at the general meeting of the CC Secretariat's party organization.

The departments break down into the political, the ideological, and the economic, and this basic classification has never been affected by any reorganization. Changes have taken place only within the framework of these three groups, and throughout all, some departments have been stable. The stable political departments are the political, the international, and the state-administrative. The political departments that have changed have been those dealing with mass organizations and elected state organs. Among the ideological departments, the stable ones have been those dealing with propaganda and agitation (called the ideological), as well as education and scholarly research. The ones that have changed have been those for culture and mass communications media, which are either independent or part of one of the two ideological departments. Among the economic departments, there have always been those for agriculture and for industry. The departments that have changed have been those dealing with living standards and for planning and finance, or economic departments with other names.

The departments are organized internally so that they cover all areas of social activity. There exists some unit or official in the Secretariat responsible for every central agency, institution, and mass organization. The CC Secretariat pays careful attention to this supervisory role.

When it gives approval for the establishment of a new interest organization, cultural institution, or periodical it also decides which CC department is to be responsible for overseeing it. When effective supervision of institutions and publications has not been provided for, the CC Secretariat prefers not to authorize them, or at least to think the matter over very carefully. The Ideological Department is especially vulnerable to criticism for not being competent enough to supervise the organizations that come under its supervision, mainly the mass communications media and publishing houses. Its leadership defends itself by pointing out that "it has a small staff, not large enough to look after everything."

A head of department has one to three deputies and an auxiliary who also serves as departmental secretary. Each deputy is responsible for the work of the section assigned to him. The head, the deputies, and the auxiliary constitute the leadership or, more precisely, the narrower leadership, which meets often as the need arises. It actually manages the work of the department. The regular weekly meetings of heads, deputies, and heads of sections are considered to be the broader leadership. (See the structure of the department in Appendix 4.)

The principal figure in the life of the department is its head. He is in contact with the CC secretary and presents reports to the Secretariat and, through the CC secretary, to the CC Presidium. And, conversely, these institutions consider him alone to be responsible for the activity of the department and those who work for it. He attends to all important matters himself, and the CC secretary will discuss all significant matters with the head, making no decision without knowing his position. Similarly, departmental apparatchiks ask his approval of the course of action they are taking in important matters. He issues guidelines for all of the more important discussions with officials of government departments that take place within the department and makes sure that he is informed about their results.

Meetings of all heads of departments are held on an irregular basis. They are called by the First Department, with the authorization of the CC secretary. They do not constitute an official body. Matters having to do with the work of the party apparat predominate on their agenda. Only rarely do they deal with internal party affairs, and when they do, it is in connection with preparations for especially large-scale political campaigns (party congresses, exchanges of party membership cards, parliamentary elections). Out of these meetings arise proposals and recommendations intended for CC secretaries, who then make decisions regarding their implementation.

A department is divided into sections—each being a kind of working cell. The sections are, it is true, allowed a certain amount of independence but only within the framework of the department. On the outside, they are seen as part of the department. (E.g., a CC secretary doesn't do business with the head of a section but only with the head of the department, who can bring along the head of a section if he so desires.)

Among the most important sections of the Organizational Political Department are those for instructors and for cadres, including high-level cadres, for mass organizations, and for information. In the State-Administration Department there are sections for the army, security, and justice. In the International Department there are sections for communist parties in socialist and capitalist countries and for international organizations. In the Ideological Department there are sections for propaganda, agitation, publishing, mass media, culture, for higher education and lower-level schools, and scholarly research. In the Economic Department there is a section for agricultural production; a section for the food industry; sections for planning, finance, transportation, and the postal service and communications, and sections for individual productive branches—e.g., fuels and energy and the machine industry.

A section is made up of several offices, each having a clearly delimited set of institutions it looks after and for whose activity it is responsible. All concerns of these institution are discussed in the department with the responsible official and head of section participating. To illustrate, I will give some examples from different sections. There are officials for the National Front, for trade unions, for agitation, for popular entertainment, for cultural activity, for agricultural and technical publishing houses, for the daily and weekly press, for radio, for television, for film, for party training (by individual levels), for technology, for universities, for scholarly institutes (especially for the economic, philosophical, and historical ones), for the church, for agriculurical cooperatives, for state farms, for precision machinery, for chemistry, for mines, for state trade, for trade involving cooperatives, for production cooperatives, for national committees, for parliament, for the Public Security (police), for civil defense, for the communist parties of Italy, France, the USSR, and Bulgaria, and for international interest organizations (see Appendix 5).

In addition to the departments and sections mentioned, there are also sectors that take care of the economic and technical aspects of the work of the Central Secretariat. Among the most important of these units are the typing pool for secret materials, where classified reports for the CC Presidium and Secretariat and materials are duplicated, and the "in house press," where information bulletins and minutes of CC meetings and other confidential materials are printed.

In the Economic Department, where the party finances and property are administered, there is an important section with a special accounting system and foreign currency reserves. Here, those financial resources are concentrated that support the party's international relations as well as aid to other parties and international communist institutions are concentrated.

From a formal point of view, all departments are equal in stature. In reality, however, there are visible differences among them. These derive primarily, though not exclusively, from differences in the power positions the departments have achieved, either in the party aparat or through control of extra-party institutions. The Organizational-Political (the First) Department maintains a privileged position. It actually controls and directs the internal life of the party and its lower-level units. It runs the Corps of Instructors, which maintains contact with the regions, making sure they realize guidelines and in this way acquiring information about the activity of the other CC departments. It also administers the informational system. Within this context, it communicates instructions from central headquarters to lower levels of the party and receives reports from them about matters that they determine. It then transmits these at its own discretion, and with certain intentions, to CC secretaries or heads of CC departments. Its monopoly over internal party life enables it to take positions on reports from all departments to the CC Presidium and Secretariat, which assign tasks to party institutions, and even to reject them. Finally, there is a cadre section in the First Department that is of special significance from the point of view of power since it contains cadre data files and a unit for high-level cadres. Consequently, the head of the department takes a stand on most of the cadre matters that are decided by the CC Presidium and Secretariat, including the assignment, promotion, and transfer of all party apparatchiks.

The State-Administrative (Eighth) Department enjoys a privileged position, though not as privileged as the First Department. This derives from the fact that it administers the apparats that are most important with regard to power—security and the army. The Eighth Department is cloaked in secrecy. Its apparatchiks behave secretively and are noted for their special, rather policelike assessment of political matters. Apparatchiks from other departments don't dare to ask comrades "in charge of the army and security" about their work for fear that this will look suspicious, as if they wanted to know too much. Differences in the status of the other departments are not as noticeable as those between the Eighth and the First and all the others.

The Central Secretariat appears to the public as an institution that is uniform in its views, united by political orientation and realization of the will of the power group. Within it, however, disputes and conflicts frequently occur. I have already discussed the relationships among CC secretaries; even more intense and more frequent are the disputes that arise among departments and their leading functionaries. There are two kinds of these. They can be one-time disputes arising out of differences of the moment, such as quarrels over jurisdiction, complaints that one department has submitted a report without the agreement of another department that is also affected, or the common daily skirmishes that all departments have with the First Department. Such disputes are rather easily resolved by agreement of the heads of the departments concerned or, in the worst cases, by the CC secretary.

The permanent conflicts, which can be called "the professional sickness," give rise to more serious consequences. Among departments and their apparatchiks there exist differing evaluations of social phenomena and often opposing conceptions of how to deal with problems. Even the substance and methods of work of the various departments cause differences. The political thinking of apparatchiks is influenced to a considerable extent by knowledge gained in their own sector, which they then extrapolate to other areas of social life. Every department has its group of functionaries from the extra-party institutions under its tutelage, from whom it obtains information, opinions, and proposals on how to deal with various matters, and they exercise an especially strong influence. Thus, for example, the opinions of police, soldiers, and procurators are reflected in the views of apparatchiks of the State-Administrative Department, and the opinions and wishes of district and regional functionaries influence the views of apparatchiks of the First Department.

The Ideological Department, which is responsible for the cultural and scholarly intelligentsia, schools, propaganda, and mass media, pays the highest price for this state of affairs. The activities of these institutions and others engaged in creative activities are the most frequent targets of criticism by all other departments. Their apparatchiks are totally incapable of understanding the peculiarity of the creative and educational work of the intelligentsia. They consider every artistic and political deviation from the conceptions of the apparatchiks or members of the power group as an unfriendly or a dangerous action and want to deal with it radically, by the means they use in their own portfolios. At party meetings of the Central Secretariat, calls can often be heard for harsh measures to be taken against the "disobedient" and ungrateful intelligentsia. Those who cry out especially loudly—and are even encouraged to do so by CC secretaries—are those who consider art, culture, and social science to be utterly useless. Moreover, the press, radio, television, film, and popular entertainment (singers) get special attention from party apparatchiks, since they are often exposed to these through television and consider themselves to be specialists in cultural matters. They condemn pictures and theatrical productions they don't understand and television programs in which they see something missing. Many of them are equipped with a political sixth sense. They can guess and predict potential dangers to the stability of the power monopoly, which the works condemned by them conceal.

Efforts of the Ideological Department to refute such attacks, and its lack of willingness to take severe measures against cultural and creative scholars and institutions, are considered incompetence, vacillation, liberalism, or surrender of party position. This atmosphere is also intensified by reports from security and voices from "the districts" (frequently ordered up by the First Department) concerning alleged negative responses to various cultural campaigns among workers, farmers, and functionaries.

The case of the Ideological Department is actually typical. There are similar, less extensive, and less intense latent conflicts among other departments as well. Most of these find expression in no more than verbal skirmishes in unofficial settings and conversations. They take the form of ironic remarks and grow into open conflict when a mood of criticism prevails throughout the department, and the CC secretary also publicly joins in it. Then personnel changes are carried out in the leadership of the criticized department.

There are also latent conflicts within departments, which often give rise to "secret" discussion among their apparatchiks. That is, it isn't unusual for the head of a department to have different opinions than the secretary or for the deputy head to differ with the head. Neither do the heads of sections always agree with the views of their superiors, and the same is true for officials. Many even express their views to higher-level colleagues, but not to their superiors. Outwardly, they support the views of their superiors, even when not entirely convinced they are right or even when they have been alerted to the problematic character of these views by functionaries in extra-party institutions.

Everyone enters the apparat with respect and admiration toward the "leading comrades." Only a few retain such an attitude. Most lose it gradually, express themselves critically with regard to the "comrades," and receive their decisions with lack of confidence and with reservations. This applies not only to the decisions of heads of sections but also to those of CC secretaries and the power group. Only unusually courageous individuals sometimes give vent to their dissenting views at meetings of the section and departmental leaderships. The others express their disagreement and criticism only among trusted colleagues. In the end, despite all reservations and disagreement, party apparatchiks are governed by an awareness of their party and service obligations to implement the decisions, guidelines, and instructions of superiors and the power group.

On the whole, the Central Secretariat remains the highest "office above politics." Its extensive powers make it a special office, both outwardly and internally. This outwardly most powerful office lives its own internal life. Because it confers excessive power on those who work in it, it places them above society and makes them into a kind of closed, self-contained unit with common interests, views, and life-style. Even the relationship of the Central Secretariat to the rest of the party is a relationship of superior to subordinate, of rulers and ruled. Although it is bound to the life of the party—as executor of the will of the power group—it still stands above the party and could also live without it as a self-contained office. It is so independent that it often regards the moods of lower-level units and party members as a nuisance.

It also has its own "social structure" in the sense that differences in the social standing and material advantages of those apparatchiks who work in it are maintained and protected. This differentiation creates castes and a strictly maintained hierarchy among them. At the highest level are the CC secretaries, with the heads of departments under them. The third group consists of their deputies and heads of sections, the fourth of officials who are political apparatchiks, and the fifth of administrative and technical staff members. The differences among the groups are not only in salary but also in scope of social advantages, such as health care, distribution of apartments, and use of service vehicles and recreational facilities. They are also manifest in the nature of their interests, in their mutual relationships, in their way of thinking, and in their understanding of social reality. The most pronounced boundary lines set apart the middle groups—between CC secretaries and all the others and between the fifth group and all the others. The higher the rank in the hierarchy, the greater is the isolation from the others and from real life.

The personal lives of apparatchiks in central headquarters are also evaluated by special standards. Family problems and personal vices (drunkenness), which are considered normal by the citizenry and even by functionaries, are considered "political" or "having a party character" in their cases. Violations are dealt with by the party committee and members' meetings or by CC secretaries and heads of departments.

The CC Secretariat has created and maintains its own world. It is a world with its own laws, moral criteria, and hierarchies; with its own views, deeply rooted dogmas, ideological stereotypes, and phraseology with its own atmosphere and climate of opinion. It has its own conflicts, opinions, and problems. Apparatchiks who work in it realize their interests and satisfy their appetites for power. This world is, however, completely different from its surroundings—the real world. It defies comparison with the everyday lives of ordinary citizens. Here, the voice of social reality sounds muffled and distant. There is no interest in sounds that clash with the mentality of most apparatchiks in the Secretariat. They are repressed and silenced. Most significant, perhaps, is the fact that these apparatchiks consider their world to mirror society as a whole; their opinions, interests, and wishes to reflect those of the party and citizenry.

Substance and Methods of Work

Daily Routine

The Central Secretariat, like every large office, has, over time, established its own rhythm of everyday life. This differs somewhat from one department to another and, for the individual, according to his position, initiative, and capabilities. There are obvious differences among apparatchiks. There are the competent, the less competent, and the incompetent. There are those who show initiative and look for work as well as those who would rather avoid things, do only what is unavoidable, and don't think up anything themselves. Their superiors don't entrust important work to the latter category, so these people have a lot of free time. They spend whole days, even weeks doing nothing of significance. Conversely, those few individuals in every department who are capable of writing reports, doing analyses, and writing speeches are assigned tasks that go beyond their portfolios.

There are several constants in the operation of the CC Secretariat: The CC Presidium meets on Tuesdays, the Secretariat on Wednesdays. On Wednesdays there is also a meeting of heads of departments and their CC secretaries. On Thursdays there is a meeting of the leaderships of the departments and heads of sections, followed immediately by meetings of the sections. The main reason for having regular meetings of the departments and sections is to distribute tasks deriving from the discussions of the CC Presidium and Secretariat.

All apparatchiks are informed on a weekly basis of the contents of reports and resolutions adopted by the power group. They are not, however, informed about the discussion leading up to their adoption. Only rarely are they given bits of information about some of the remarks made by members of the leadership. They also learn which reports will be made available to them. The information they receive about important reports and resolutions will include guidelines for their interpretation.

A typical day for apparatchiks in the Central Secretariat begins in the antechamber of the head of department, where a secretary sits. They arrive around 8:00 A.M. to get the news. Many debates about a wide variety of subjects take place here. The apparatchiks then go to their own offices and read the newspaper. Some do this until snacktime, going to the canteen at 9:30. Around this time, a secretary distributes the mail throughout the department. There isn't much; some people don't get any mail for a whole week. For the most part, the mail consists of citizen complaints or information from extra-party institutions. Only after snacktime do the apparatchiks get going, unless some unusual events have gotten them started earlier.

The everyday activity of party apparatchiks of all categories consists of passing on information, instructions, and decisions; of meetings and discussions; of taking minutes and making comments. On the whole, it is through this kind of routine, seemingly subservient work, that the party apparat fulfills two of its most important functions—implementing the policy and guidelines of the power group and supervising the activity of extra-party institutions and their functionaries.

Information, instructions, and decisions are transmitted in two ways: Either the apparatchik communicates with functionaries of extra-party institutions or his comrade in the region or he turns "to the CC Secretariat" on his own initiative. Such activities keep apparatchiks of all categories busy, especially the officials. Usually only members of the government or officials of comparable rank can approach a CC secretary or his office directly to request a decision on some concrete matter. Only in exceptional cases do those of lower rank do so. A CC secretary only rarely issues instructions, usually only when a CC Presidium or Secretariat resolution or instructions from the general secretary explicitly give him the task of informing functionaries or discussing some particular matter with them. In most other cases, he transmits instructions and information through his department or his auxiliaries. Heads of departments and their deputies answer many questions on the phone and in the course of visits from high officials of extra-party institutions, regional party committees, and apparatchiks from their own and occasionally other CC departments. Their answers are like decisions or guidelines. They personally transmit instructions only to high officials of extra-party institutions and apparatchiks of their own departments.

Most instructions and information, advice and decisions are obtained and provided by the head of the section. Either on his own initiative or on instructions from his superiors, he distributes individual tasks and instructions to "his functionaries" and requests information from them regarding various aspects of the activities of his institution. Much more frequently, however, functionaries come to him for advice and decisions on their own initiative. For example, the director of the press office may ask his section head when and in what form he should publish some proclamation. The editor in chief of a newspaper asks whether it is politically expedient to publish a certain article. The head of the press section issues an order that daily newspapers have to publish an article on a certain theme tomorrow. The editor in chief of a publishing house asks permission to publish a certain book that is "politically dubious." Some criticism of a television program expressed by the comrades at the highest level is passed on to those reponsible for television broadcasting. Officials from the Ministries of Agriculture and of Industry come with proposals for various measures to be taken in production. The heads of some large factories come with a request for assistance and intervention. Again, from the Ministry of Foreign Affairs, comes a request for some specific, concrete decisions. Some regional party apparatchik asks for intervention by a ministry, complains about functionaries of a mass organization at the central level, or wants advice on how to deal with some matter in the region. An apparatchik at central headquarters issues instructions to a region to find out why factory XY hasn't fulfilled its export quota, or why there has been some hitch in the purchase of agricultural products, in order to comply with a request by a high official of a ministry who is to visit him.

Meetings and discussions in which serious and controversial matters are on the agenda, and preparation for the most significant of decisions and political campaigns, are most frequently supervised by party apparatchiks of the highest categories—CC secretaries and heads of departments. Certain rules are followed: Every apparatchik can invite functionaries at his own and lower levels to meetings and discussions; a CC secretary can deal with functionaries up to the level of deputy premier in the government and the chairmen of large mass organizations; the head of a department can deal with with functionaries in positions related to his portfolio up to the level of minister. Deputy heads of departments and heads of sections can deal with officials up to the level of deputy minister, and party officials can deal with leading officials of extra-party institutions. Meetings with high officials take place in the office of the head of the section or department, or they are visited (except for ministers) in their own offices.

Meetings and discussions are held "on party turf," i.e., in the CC Secretariat. The leaderships of CC departments carefully prepare for meetings with ministers; more frequently, of course, they invite deputy ministers and secretaries of mass organizations. Some departments hold regular meetings with these deputies and secretaries to familiarize them with resolutions of party organs, or they invite them to meetings of their departments. Moreover, officials, heads of sections, and deputy heads of departments participate in working meetings of the extra-party institutions entrusted to them, e.g., collegia of ministers, leaderships of the secretariats of mass organizations, sections of ministries, scholarly boards of institutes. Only rarely do they conduct "official business" with high officials in the offices of their own institutions.

Some meetings are particularly important, mainly those that evaluate the activities of institutions and those held for the purpose of organizing snap political campaigns. Evaluative meetings are not held frequently or regularly. The impetus for them comes either from an official or head of the section responsible for the institution or from high officials of the institution or its party organization. Depending on the seriousness of the matters to be evaluated, the meetings may be held in the office of the official, head of section, head of department, or his deputy or, in exceptional cases, the office of the CC secretary. The degree of seriousness also determines the level of functionaries present. Meetings in an official's office usually deal with a few items of some important party resolution or specific sector of the activity of an institution—(e.g., how the trade union apparat has been implementing a resolution on cultural work among the youth; participation of some scholarly institute in atheistic propaganda; participation of certain newspapers or television and radio stations in some political campaign; how some section of a ministry has been promoting socialist competition in its enterprises, or supplies to the population of certain kinds of products). Participants include the top officials of the responsible section of the institution and members of the party organization.

Meetings in the office of a head of section or deputy head of a department deal with the overall activity of less significant institutions, (e.g., small mass organizations and central agencies), or with some broad area of the work of central agencies (publishing, cadre policy of a ministry, political work in the army) or large mass organizations (educational work of the union of youth or social policy of the trade unions). Participants include functionaries up to the level of deputy minister. Evaluative meetings held in the office of the head of department or secretary deal primarily with the overall activity of institutions or some broad segment of them. Participants include ministers and the responsible deputy premier.

Similarly, so-called superportfolio meetings are held by party apparatchiks at all levels, and at them the implementation of tasks in which several portfolios are participating is discussed—(e.g., economic propaganda, the progress of apartment house construction, commercial networks, the status of political campaigns). The initiative for such meetings comes from party apparatchiks when they find that portfolios are grossly neglecting their responsibilities in the implementation of tasks. Superportfolio meetings, in which leading functionaries of interested institutions participate, have the function of reminding the functionaries of their obligations "on party turf," and stimulating their activity by assignment of concrete tasks.

Evaluative meetings run a stereotyped course. A high-level functionary assesses the work of his institution. In response, a party apparatchik of equivalent rank states his position. A discussion then follows, which is often very heated. The discussion usually ends with agreement on measures to be taken with regard to the matter discussed. Two realities are characteristic of evaluative meetings:

1. Tasks are assigned to functionaries of extra-party institutions and their apparats mostly "behind the backs" of the responsible leaders of these institutions.
2. The meetings are among the effective forums for "party control" of extra-party institutions and their functionaries. Party apparatchiks value them especially as an important source of knowledge of "their" institutions.

Meetings for the organization of snap political campaigns are held soon after CC secretaries decide that a one-time, lightning campaign is to be conducted for several days against some manifestation of "unfriendly activity" (e.g., against Charter 77) [a citizens' initiative aimed at pressuring the authorities to abide by the country's own legal norms]. Or they launch a campaign of resolutions and pledges of support for some party decision or a press campaign on some international event. The order goes out from the CC secretaries to the heads of departments, and from them to the heads of sections, who inform their apparatchiks. These then call "urgent meetings" of functionaries of the extra-party institutions and assign them specific tasks.

Of special interest are those discussions in which party apparatchiks act as mediators. These happen often, and they usually take place in the office of a head of section or deputy head of department. It is very common that representatives of extra-party institutions want conflicts among their institutions resolved "on party turf," i.e., by the apparatchik responsible for the portfolio. These include not only conflicts among ministries, mass organizations, and agencies but also conflicts among large enterprises, between factories and ministries, between the planning office and economic units, between lower-level party and central economic organizations, between lower-level organs of power and ministries, etc. The contents of the discussions include a great variety of matters, such as complaints about unfilled orders by one enterprise against another, about investments that have been rejected, about the excessively high demands of a plan; differing opinions of ministries regarding implementation of government and party resolutions; conflicts about financial resources, about the distribution of buildings and equipment to individual portfolios; conflicts between the censorship office and the editors of newspapers, publishing houses, film studios, television; and disagreement of lower-level power institutions and central social organizations with decisions of central agencies or complaints about their work. The apparatchik will get advance approval from his superiors for the position he intends to take and impose, and he will very rarely allow himself to be influenced by counter arguments.

In exceptional cases, meetings of CC secretaries or heads of department with the entire leadership of a mass organization, institute, or minister's collegium are held. These usually come about for one of three reasons:

1. Conflicts among members of the leadership of an institution have become so acute that the activity of the institution is threatened.
2. Reservations, doubts, and disagreement about the correctness of some decision of the power group have emerged among members.
3. Dissatisfaction with the work of the institution.

These meetings are prepared for with special care by high officials of the responsible CC department. These officials work out for the CC secretary or head of department (who runs the meeting) analyses, positions and, if need be, proposals for personnel changes. If an institution of especially great significance is at issue (the leadership of a union, a collegium of the minister of the interior or defense), a meeting of all CC secretaries will precede the meeting.

On rare occasions there are also discussions between leading functionaries of extra-party institutions and the head of a section or department of the party apparat about differences on how to deal with matters under consideration or on methods for the implementation of party resolutions. Such discussions are requested by one of the parties to the dispute, and mutual agreement is reached in the discussions. The role of mediator is played by the highest-level party apparatchik— a head of department or CC secretary. The outcome of the discussions is not determined in advance. Usually, attempt is made to end the matter by agreement, in which the mediator tends to favor the position of the party apparatchik.

A party apparatchik has the obligation to inform his superior from time to time about extraordinary events and negative phenomena in the life and activity of "his" extra-party institution or to request approval of the measures he has decided to take. The *Zaznam*—as written information is officially called—goes to the head of the department, who either simply takes note of it and issues instructions to proceed further or passes it on to the CC secretary, who responds with his views.

CC secretaries and, to an even greater extent departments receive the widest variety of "materials" from extra-party institutions and other departments. These usually include evaluations of their own activities and analyses and proposals touching on nearly all areas of social life. Some come with requests for advice, others simply provide information about things the institution is preparing or intends to deal with. They are received by a deputy head of department, the head of a section, or sometimes by an official with instructions to prepare "comments on the material." Preparation of comments is considered a politically significant activity, and the abilities of a comment writer are judged by the volume of comments he produces. He tries to write as many as possible. He intently ferrets out "ideological inaccuracies and mistakes," deviations from the official policy line. Every department has its "king commentator," as they say, who writes whole treatises, and some apparatchiks even make their careers by writing comments.

Although the Central Secretariat is the highest authority above politics, the operational aspects of its activity predominate. By paying attention to the concrete details of everyday life it assures a unified interpretation of the decisions of the power group and checks up on their realization. Hundreds of routine specific instructions, suggestions, and position papers produced by the Central Secretariat and fused by a unified political orientation merge into one stream.

The apparatchiks get an overview of the work and problems of "their institutions" and their top functionaries, and a special relationship grows up among them. In official relations a functionary respects the superior position of an apparatchik, which derives from his affiliation with the Central Secretariat. This does not, however, automatically mean subordination. If a functionary disagrees with an apparatchik's views, or has different ideas about the matters under consideration, he defends and asserts his position, though he is aware that his career depends to a significant extent on how the party apparatchik assesses him. The functionary is also aware that, according to party regulations, the apparatchik writes a memo to his superior

about every one of his "stiff-necked disagreements." The party apparatchik, on the other hand, knows that these functionaries are his main
sources of suggestions on how to deal with matters within his portfolio,
of specialized expertise, of reports for superiors, and of information
about their institutions. In addition to this dependence on the specialist,
the social aspect plays a role too. No apparatchik can be sure that he
will be able to stay on in the Central Secretariat until he retires, so
he keeps in mind the possibility of being of use at some time in the
future in the extra-party institution for which he is responsible, when
the functionary who is, for the moment, subordinate to him, would
have an important say.

"Material for the Authority"

Work on reports for central organs stands out significantly in the
everyday routine of party apparatchiks. This is called "doing material
for the authority." The production of reports is considered the height
of political work, and long leaves its mark on the lives of the officials,
sections, and departments involved in it.

Preparation of speeches and resolutions for meetings of the Central
Committee are most highly valued. Several apparatchiks from one or
more departments take part in it, usually apparatchiks of higher rank.
The speeches and resolutions are revised several times after comments
by the CC secretary and leadership of the CC department, and so two
or more versions emerge. Then a group of routinized stylists gets to
work. They usually lock themselves up in the party hotel so as not
to be disturbed, and, under the supervision of the responsible CC
secretary, they put the "materials" into final form. From this point
on, the "materials" go through the approval procedures already discussed.

Reports for the CC Presidium and Secretariat are conceptual, operational, verificatory, informational, and cadre proposals. Conceptual
reports are considered the most important, the other types not being
appreciated nearly as much. Reports are called conceptual if they deal
with evaluation and change in policy line, analysis, and other tasks
in some areas of social life; if they determine the substance of political
actions, the trend of economic development on the whole as well as
in individual branches of the economy; conceptions of the activities
of mass organizations or cultural institutions, or positions for important
international meetings. Concretely, the conceptual reports include those
on the main trends of economic development, on the five-year and
annual plans, on the development of the machine and textile industries,
agricultural production, the construction of apartments, and health

care. There are also reports on the tasks of the mass media, on conceptions of publishing policy, on changes in higher education, on the tasks of the trade unions, on the work of the government, on positions and proposals for meetings of organs of COMECON, on the Warsaw Treaty Organization, etc.

Operational reports, in contrast, are specific and concrete in character, e.g., guidelines for the production of uranium, the condition of prisons, the balance of foreign trade, the state of preparedness of the people's militias, the state of textbook production. Verificatory reports can be characterized by the amount of statistical data they contain and are either continuing (e.g., on progress in cutting down on the state apparat, on the conduct of purchases of agricultural products) or final. The party apparat produces a lot of operational and verificatory reports, especially the Economic Department, which may even produce several a week. Their preparation does not take a great deal of time. For the most part, they are produced by extra-party institutions, and a party apparatchik modifies and adds to them. Many are submitted by the CC secretary in the same form in which he received them from extra-party institutions. He will append his own position to them, as prepared by the responsible CC department. Only in exceptional cases is the department capable of preparing a competent evaluation on its own. For the most part, it gets comments from members of its aktiv— functionaries of central agencies, the trade union central, or specialists from research institutes. Their views are then presented as the position of the department and the CC secretary.

The preparation of conceptual reports either flows directly from the plan of work of party organs, and then represents a component of the department's work plan, or it is forced by the urgency of problems or requested by the CC Presidium or a CC secretary. Not more than eight to ten conceptual reports a year fall to a department, still fewer to a small department. Preparation of conceptual reports is a complicated procedure. Within the department responsible for a report, a section and one or several officials deal with it, sometimes working on it full time for weeks or even months. Preparation often exceeds the capabilities of the official responsible, and the head of a section and his superior then take charge of it.

Work begins with the gathering of experiences, calculations, analyses, and statistical data. Sometimes meetings are called, or research is carried out in the regions and districts to acquire an overview of the current status of the matter under consideration. These actions are usually carried out by the responsible extra-party institution, its functionaries, or members of the central party aktiv. The official also requests from them an evaluation of previous experiences, proposals of conceptions for further development, and concrete measures on the problem. In this preparational phase, differences and conflicts often arise between the party apparatchik and functionaries of the extra-party institutions. They assess both the current state of affairs and its causes differently, as well as questions of how to proceed further.

In gathering supporting materials, an official thus prepares, or has prepared for him, a conception of the contents of the report, which he submits to his section. After corrections, it goes to head of the department and, if need be, to the CC secretary. After the conception has been approved, the period of sacred activity—the writing of the report—begins for the official or head of the section. He isolates himself in silence, has time for nothing else, and is excluded from the everyday life of the department so as not to be disturbed. Some ease their work load, or recognize that preparation of a high-quality report exceeds their capabilities, and have it written by functionaries of an extra-party institution.

As soon as the report is ready, the procedure is repeated. It is discussed by the section and the leadership of the department. It is corrected, abridged, and augmented and goes to the CC secretary, who gives his comments on it. These are the last modifications that are made within the department, and not infrequently they are of such a nature that they significantly change the original contents of the report, as well as proposals submitted by functionaries of extra-party institutions. Before the CC secretary approves the report by signing it, so it can be submitted to the CC Presidium in his name, he has to discuss it with the ministers, heads of institutions, and CC departments affected by it. In cases where they do not agree, their objections are attached to the report. This does not happen often, however, since the secretary tries to prevent it.

Conceptual reports follow certain rules of form and content. These are unwritten, but every apparatchik in the Central Secretariat soon gets to know them. First and foremost among them is the necessity of stressing, in the preface to the report, previous successes achieved by "the party's Marxist-Leninist policy" in the area under consideration. Criticism has to be cautious and represented as aimed at deficiencies of lower-level organs and ministries in the implementation of party policy. Proposed measures and changes cannot be presented as corrections of mistakes in party policy, but as the result of a new, higher level of development. The second rule is that the contents of the report, and especially its resolution, have to conform to the views and conceptions of the power group. They cannot conflict with these if the report is to have any chance of being approved. All who work on reports, from officials to CC secretaries, observe these rules without having to be reminded of them.

Formal rules for reports lay down the required format for them. They consist of four parts. The first is the cover (the so-called shirt). It contains the title of the report, the date, the serial number of the meeting of the leadership, a brief summary of the contents, the number of parts and pages, the number of copies printed, the serial number of the copy, and finally, which department prepared the report and who is to present it. The proposed resolution, the second part, has to specify by name who is responsible for each item of the resolution and the deadline for its implementation. The justificatory arguments, which constitute the third part, consist of an analysis of the status of the matter in question and justification for the proposed resolution. Not every report has a fourth part. This part contains draft letters, teletype messages, communications, and speeches to be used in informing lower-level party units, the public, and other communist parties about the matters dealt with in the report. If need be, it also contains plans for a campaign of agitation to popularize the resolution, including details about publication of the resolution and articles by members of the power group (i.e., when, where, and how they will be published).

As soon as the party organ approves the report, the second phase of its life begins. This phase has two parts: interpretation and propagation of the resolution and its implementation. If the report is an important one, it is officially interpreted for the public by a CC secretary. If it is less important, this is done by a lower-level functionary. As interpretation of the resolution filters down to lower-level party units, it increasingly takes on its own distinctive character. Propagation of important reports is done by means of meetings of functionaries as well as through the mass media. For less important reports, this is limited to informing functionaries within the responsible portfolio, and for decisions of a confidential character, it is limited to a specially selected group.

The report is implemented by the following initial steps. Functionaries receive a copy of a resolution intended for them from the Office of the General Secretary. The official and section that originated the report put together a plan for its implementation, which contains a list of meetings and conferences to be organized for familiarization with the report and a detailed breakdown of tasks for party and extra-party institutions. This means that heads of departments speak at conferences of CC instructors and editors of daily newspapers and provide information to the highest-level functionaries of extra-party institutions affected by the report. The deputy head of the department or a head of section takes part in meetings of ministers' collegia and secretariats of mass organizations and provides information to lower-level functionaries. The last are required to discuss the report within their respective institutions, and to work out their own plans for propagation and implementation of the resolution. Party apparatchiks or political brigades are sent out to the regions and districts with the task of explaining the significance of the resolution to the aktivs in those places and to ensure that they deal with it. The official makes reports to the head of the department on all these measures and on their realization.

After a certain time has elapsed, the official prepares a verificatory report on the implementation of the resolution. This is the third and last phase in the life of a conceptual report. The official obtains information from various offices and from lower-level units of the party apparat as to how the resolution has been dealt with and to what extent it has been fulfilled. If he finds in the process that the resolutions are not being adequately fulfilled, he may recommend that a conference of functionaries from the institutions concerned be called to remind them firmly of their obligation to fulfill the adopted resolution. Conferences called for the same purpose on instructions from the party organ that deals with verificatory reports on the implementation of resolutions are considered extremely serious, as proof of dissatisfaction at the highest levels of the party.

Party members and low-level functionaries have no interest at all in most of the resolutions of the central power group, and ordinary citizens are even less interested in them. Unless directly affected, they are not even aware of their existence. High-level functionaries—central, regional, and to some extent, district—are aware of the resolutions since implementation depends largely on them. They accept the resolutions as binding guidelines, since they take for granted that resolutions of the central cannot be opposed or their rightness doubted. And so, the saying commonly used by party apparatchiks, "Comrades, this is a resolution of the authority," has a spellbinding power over all functionaries. Many are affected this way since it has never occurred to them to doubt the rightness of party resolutions. With others, the magic formula about the interest of the party nips in the bud any courage to express any doubts or disagreement with a resolution. They would rather keep quiet, and if they are functionaries who are going to have to implement the resolution in their places of work, they look for ways to circumvent its problematic parts.

Conceptual and operational reports alike are joint products of the party apparat and functionaries of responsible extra-party institutions. Their genesis is often bound up with differences of opinion and conflicts between both groups and for the most part, the positions of the apparatchiks win out since the CC secretary stands behind them.

Cadre Work

Cadre policy takes first place among the activities of the party apparat as a whole, and of the Central Secretariat in particular. Its importance is theoretically justified and based on quotations from leading figures of the communist movement, like Stalin's well-known statement, "Cadres decide everything," or Gottwald's demand that cadre work constitute more than 50 percent of the work of the party apparat— these quotations have survived their authors as well as their falls from grace. And there is constant mention of the alleged Leninist principle that the prerequisite for realization of the leading role of the party (and thus its power monopoly) is that all leading and controlling positions in society be held by communists. The principle is inculcated into functionaries that the party's monopoly in cadre policy is among the most significant foundations and manifestations of their power, and that it is not shared with anyone.

According to party definition, cadre policy consists of the selection, training, assignment, and control of cadres. The power group has kept a careful watch over the implementation of cadre policy on the whole, but it pays special attention to the selection and assignment of cadres. It insists that all lower-level units of the party adhere to the guidelines in their cadre practices. It makes its apparat especially responsible for this, delegates substantial authority to the apparat in this domain, and gives it the task of following the "growth of cadres." Every party apparatchik does this within the domain of his responsibility. In fulfilling this responsibility, he does not go beyond those functionaries with whom he most often comes into contact, i.e., heads of institutions and two or three members of the party committee. It is to these people that he restricts his selection of persons for appointments to positions. Many other functionaries thus strive to get into this more or less closed circle, since cadre reserves for higher-level positions are recruited from it.

Cadre policy plays an important and many-faceted role in the hands of the power group and party apparat. It serves as one of the most important and ingenious instruments for the maintenance and solidification of their domination. That is to say, the power group assigns cadres to their positions and through them, dominates society. Positions are filled with obedient individuals, and care is taken that they be constantly reminded of their social dependence on the power group. Its power over the cadres grows out of this and is reinforced by constant control, a system of verification, and the threat of demotion and transfer. These factors give rise to existential insecurity in functionaries, who fear a loss of social prestige, and are the source of their obedience. In 1972, party institutions evaluated 350,000 functionaries at all levels and from all institutions. In two years the figure had reached 440,000, and by 1976, as many as 527,000. There was then a change from two-year to five-year evaluation intervals. Thus, destabilization of the existential security of functionaries becomes the stabilizing factor of power. Finally, there is another aspect of cadre policy that cannot be neglected. The authority to assign and control cadres strengthens feelings of power and self-confidence of lower-level power groups.

Cadre work is among the few areas of party life in which there are sharply delimited principles and authority for every unit. The basic organization concentrates on two sectors. Party rules stipulate that party organizations in production, transportation, and commercial enterprises are to play a role in the appointment of leading apparatchiks. Since this role is not clearly defined, the bureaus of many organizations stretch their mandate and express views on everyone except the workers, beginning with the foremen. The director or his deputy presents cadre proposals, and the bureau merely gives an opinion. It has no authority to make decisions. Instances of conflict between the director and the bureau are resolved by the higher-level party organization. The second area of the cadre work of all basic organizations involves issuing cadre opinions and evaluations of persons recommended for positions by higher-level party organs, or being represented in commissions for the evaluation of the leaders of their own factory. Cadre opinions are given by the basic organization only to its superior party organ and must be approved, at least by the bureau of the organization. This is done by the chairman's entrusting some member of the bureau or leader of the party group to prepare a draft opinion, which is discussed and modified by the bureau.

Party organizations in central offices and cultural and scholarly institutions do not have the authority to offer opinions on the appointment of high officials. Nevertheless, representatives of offices and institutions are required to come to agreement with the bureau of the organization on all more-significant cadre changes, and the superior party organ cannot discuss such matters without receiving the views of the basic organization.

The set of positions to which appointments must be decided upon by district, regional, and central organs is precisely laid out. These positions are set forth in the cadre procedures generally known as the cadre nomenklatura. They are prepared by the CC First Department on the basis of proposals from the districts, regions, and all CC departments; discussed by the CC Secretariat; and approved by the CC Presidium.

The nomenklatura emerged in the fall of 1948, during the period of the cadre offensive [extensive appointments of communists to high positions in various institutions following the establishment of communist rule]. It serves a dual purpose, setting forth precisely, for the leaderships of extra-party institutions, the positions it cannot fill without prior approval by the appropriate party organ and determining which positions they can fill, since many organs show an unusually broad interest in this area. This obligation also extends to the leaderships of institutions and to nominated individuals who are not communists.

In reality, the cadre nomenklatura is a list (book) of positions divided into three parts. The first contains those positions to which appointments are made by district party organs, the second defines this for the regional, and the third for the central. Internally, each part breaks down into positions approved by different organs at the level in question: positions approved by the district committee or its presidium; the same is done for the region, where there is also a RC secretariat; the section dealing with the central is divided into the domains of authority of the Central Committee, the Presidium, the CC Secretariat, CC secretaries, and CC departments. In the list, next to the positions to which appointments are made by a particular organ, those individuals who have only the right to express an opinion are also mentioned. For the most part, these are positions in institutions located in the district or region, for which appointments are approved by higher organs (e.g., the general director of a national enterprise that has its seat in the district, but factories throughout the region). Although their opinions are not binding, the party apparatchik still does not dare to submit a "controversial" nomination.

Since its emergence, the cadre nomenklatura system has undergone several changes. The body of approved functionaries has narrowed and expanded. Some positions have been transferred from the authority of one organ to that of another.

Around 115,000–130,000 positions come under the cadre nomenklatura of party organs. However, the number of persons is actually at least twice as large, since there are many positions held by more than a single individual in a given organization. For example, the nomenklatura includes the position of deputy to every minister, but every minister has three or even more of deputies.

Many basic organizations include other matters in their nomenklaturas, such as approval of trips abroad for apparatchiks, recommendations for studies, etc. And it is quite routine for heads of extra-party institutions to request approval from a party apparatchik, the bureaus, or just the chairmen of basic party organizations for a set of appointments that are not even in the cadre nomenklatura. In doing this, they protect themselves from the kind of possible future unpleasantness that can arise from appointments to positions. This is not something that happens only in isolated cases but is quite common.

Functionaries included in the cadre nomenklatura are "shielded or under protection." It is the organ to whose nomenklatura they belong that makes decisions concerning them in party—e.g. disciplinary—proceedings. Security cannot launch criminal proceedings against nomenklatura functionaries without the prior awareness or approval of the responsible party organ. For lower-level, less important officials, the DC or RC leading secretary or a CC secretary makes the determination, and does this on the basis of information from the district or regional command of security or the procurator. At the central level, it may also be the minister of the interior or his deputy. For high-level cadres, the party organ makes its decision on the basis of written reports from the responsible commander of security, procurator, or the ministers of the interior and justice.

The nomenklatura is strictly adhered to in making cadre changes and in making appointments to newly-created positions. Functionaries are rotated frequently for various reasons. The simplest, apart from retirement, is a politically motivated departure from a position, e.g. accompanied by expulsion from the party or as a party penalty. During a period of party purges, the party merry-go-round spins at full speed. Hundreds and thousands are relieved of their functions, and selection of their successors is based primarily on political reliability and obedience. The process of removing someone for reasons of incompetence or, as is commonly said, "because he didn't master the assignment," is somewhat more complicated. Frequently, the need arises to reinforce institutions from the cadre point of view (i.e. from a political and class point of view) or to fill newly created positions and also transfer some meritorious and worn-out functionary to a less demanding, but well-paid, position.

Suggestions for replacement of ministers and others at that level come from CC secretaries or the prime minister. Those for replacement of deputy ministers usually come from ministers and heads of CC departments. For other high officials of extra-party institutions, it is their superiors, and sometimes the apparatchik responsible for the portfolio, who make the suggestion. Similar procedures are followed in the regions and districts. Cadre changes are recommended and proposed by RC or DC secretaries, heads of departments, the RNC or DNC chairmen, and heads of extra-party institutions themselves, as well as by higher authorities, such as ministries, central headquarters, and regional offices. The impetus for cadre changes within the party apparat, in addition to requests for transfers from cadres themselves, comes from secretaries, heads of departments, and sections.

Procedures for the submission of cadre matters to party organs stipulate that along with a proposal for removal of a functionary, his replacement is nominated. This replacement is usually recommended by the initiator of the cadre change, and he submits several alternatives. The responsible party apparatchiks discuss and assess candidates before deciding on someone. Decisions about high officials are made at meetings of CC secretaries or by the secretary responsible for the portfolio and the general secretary. They also discuss the change with the functionary in question. The head of a department and the CC secretary come to agreement on the proposals for appointments that, following the cadre nomenklatura, are approved by the CC Secretariat and a CC secretary. Selection of those who come under the authority of a CC department is made by the department's leadership. In cases where no appropriate replacement can be found, they turn to the cadre section, the unit for high-level cadres (in the central), or the cadre files (in lower-level units of the apparat) to seek out proposals. That is, the section for high-level cadres has files on all functionaries and cadre reserves eligible for positions that, according to the nomenklatura, are approved by the Central Committee or its Presidium.

Reinforcement of cadres in institutions, the numerous cadre replacements resulting from the sudden dismissal of several officials from high positions, or appointments to positions in newly created units is accomplished by transferring people from other places of work, often from the party apparat, from cadre reserves, and from new graduates of party schools. All units of the party apparat, in the districts, regions, and the central, maintain cadre reserves. These are lists of persons eligible to accept positions within their respective organizations. Graduates of the lengthy course of study of the party university are utilized to fill positions in the central and the regions; graduates of regional schools to fill positions in the regions and districts.

As soon as a decision has been made for one of the individuals considered, preparation of the cadre proposal for the party organ begins. It is based on the nominee's cadre dossier stored in the cadre files. This dossier contains a questionnaire, a biography, cadre evaluations of the person in question by party institutions, and other party records (results of screening campaigns, party penalties). The dossier cannot be more than two years old, unless updated during this period. In addition to this, an official requests a so-called complex political-specialist's evaluation from the party organization in the nominee's place of work and, from the head of the institution, a justification for the departure of the individual and nomination of the new official.

The cadre proposal contains an assessment that mentions the political and specialized qualifications of the new appointee, the reasons for the departure of the official being replaced, and his subsequent placement. Before the head of the CC department submits the proposal to the CC secretary, the appropriate official has to speak with the official being replaced, as well as with his proposed replacement. The official includes a protocol of these discussions in the proposal. Cadre changes up to the level of deputy minister (i.e., those not contained in the nomenklatura of the CC plenum) are likewise officially negotiated with the bureau of the party organization in the institution affected (unofficially, this is done by the head of the institution himself before he submits the proposal to a party apparatchik). Any disagreement or comment has to be included in the proposal, though the CC Presidium or Secretariat usually doesn't pay much attention to it.

Members of party organs know only some of the nominees and can responsibly say something only about these. They make their decisions mainly on the basis of written information prepared by the party apparat. The districts have the lowest number of unknown individuals. There are far more in the regions, and in the central, they predominate overwhelmingly. Most cadre matters go through without difficulties or comments. Only sometimes do CC Presidium and Secretariat members discuss them, doubt the rightness of the proposal, or ask that it be removed from the agenda and modified. There is, however, no lack of cases in which cadre proposals are not approved.

The head of the institution affected finds out from the apparatchik who presented or prepared the proposal only whether or not it has been approved. He usually doesn't know the reasons for a proposal's being turned down and cannot, therefore, give them to the individual concerned.

The System of Information

The well-developed system of information in the party ensures a flow of information in both directions—from top to bottom and in the opposite direction. In both directions, this is mainly information from party sources, although it isn't limited to them. The flow of information from the central to lower-level components of the party organism is part of the preparation of political campaigns, primarily serves the party aktiv, and will be dealt with in the next chapter. At this point, I will concentrate on information flowing toward the center. This functions as an active element in the political decision making of the power group, since it plays a role in forming their notions of social reality and in providing them with reactions to their decisions. In the districts and regions, the power groups have almost no interest in information requested by the central, and aren't even made aware of it.

The heart of the informational system is the information section of the First Department. In the region, an official (or a section) performs this function, and in the district, it is done by an apparatchik whose principal responsibility is taking care of information. The information section at central headquarters processes the data it obtains for the power group and high officials of the party apparat. All of them receive the *Information Bulletin of the First Department*. CC secretaries also receive routine, everyday information, but some of it is reserved for the general secretary alone.

The informational system gathers a very wide range of information about what is happening in the internal life of the party (conduct of meetings, training, reactions within the party to decisions of CC organs). However, information about society as a whole predominates (reactions of the population to party and government decisions; reports on disturbances in the supply system, on the course of political campaigns such as elections or the First of May, the beginning of the school year, how agricultural work is proceeding and reactions to significant international events).

On an irregular basis, but at least once a week, the regions send reports to the central on routine events, about which the districts inform them. These are less-significant, haphazardly gathered views, mostly from local functionaries (on a par with "a lady told me . . ."). A selection of these is made for the CC secretaries, and only a fraction of them appear in the *Bulletin of the First Department*. These reports are sent from the region by the official in charge of information on his own, i.e., without their being signed by the RC leading secretary. Other reports must have his signature.

Great significance is attributed to information requested by the central. Instructions are given to the regions to submit by a certain deadline reports on political events or economic measures or to deliver periodic overviews of the course of agricultural work, the purchase of agricultural products, socialist competition, etc. The transmission of reports on political celebrations is considered a matter of routine. For example, reports on the celebration of the First of May have to include the number of places where festivities were held; the numbers of participants in the parade, at the speech, and on the sidewalks; the number of floats; the principal slogans; and the overall mood of the citizens. Most of the data in the district are determined by guessing, and numbers are exaggerated.

Information about reactions to party resolutions and instructions of the central, as well as their fulfillment, is considered especially important. Such communications are prepared on the basis of reports from the regions, reports from instructors of the central, written reports of speakers at members' and public meetings, protocols of meetings of district and regional party organs, and reports requested from extra-party institutions and, above all, mass organizations. They are put together into a complex overview, which takes up the most space in the First Department's *Bulletin.*

The picture provided by the information system of the reactions of citizens to decisions of the party and government does not do justice to the actual mosaic of views, and there are several reasons for this. With few exceptions, the data obtained come exclusively from party members and functionaries. Their views and opinions are so much influenced by party ideology that they already agree in advance with resolutions and positions of high-level party organs. Or they are the views of people who are disinterested in politics to the point where they cannot assess the significance of a set of measures. The reports usually give the opinion of communists or apparatchiks in factories and offices. In reality, the party apparatchik asks the chairman of the party or trade union organization, or some other functionary for his opinion and passes off this individual's opinion as that of the workers.

Most importantly, the information gets sifted. This process already begins in the districts, where anything that is too negative, expressing disagreement with measures or resolutions of the party and government, is modified or completely left out. It goes through another screen at the regional level. Apparatchiks at central headquarters know the limits of criticism acceptable to high officials and also know what kind of report they like i.e., the kind that expresses agreement with their policy. Information is thus compiled according to this criterion. They cannot, however, remain completely silent about all disagreement or criticism, so they take note of a few examples and represent them as isolated exceptions. If some complaints show up repeatedly in the information or come from a majority of regions (e.g., of a shortage of spare parts, problems in the supply of a certain kind of commodity), the CC secretary responsible for the portfolio asks his department to prepare a report and proposals for solution of the problem.

The deliberate influencing of high officials is likewise practiced in that the gathering of information is aimed at some specific area of activity, and indirectly at the institution that carries it out and the functionaries responsible for it. Almost every week, the information section receives the complaints of lower-level officials against some television or radio program, article, etc. Such voices, often encouraged from high places, are not corrected. It is possible to proceed in a similar manner against any high official and institution.

Public opinion, as expressed in resolutions of public meetings, has become an important source of information. At central headquarters, the number of resolutions is recorded, and a summary of them, including a few quotations, is prepared and given to members of the power group. They in turn take them as proof of the agreement of citizens with their policies, and as the true voice of the people. They present them in this form, not only to the public, but also among themselves, since they believe them. In reality, this is a public opinion created by them, and the technology of its production resembles that of the internal party discussion discussed earlier.

When the CC Presidium or Secretariat approves a major political campaign, it assigns the tasks of organizing meetings and sending resolutions, which expresses agreement with its decisions, and also to "launch a movement" of work commitments (e.g., for the party congress and various anniversaries). This practice became well established in the 1950s (a period known for resolutions demanding the death penalty for the victims of the political trials, thanking the party and government for lowering prices, or petition campaigns, e.g., in response to an appeal from the World Peace Organization, even including signatures of deceased citizens), and it is still in use. The regions and districts receive the appropriate instructions, and the machinery for the creation of public opinion is set in motion. Party apparatchiks in the districts summon or visit the chairmen of "their organizations" and assign them the task of sending resolutions. The chairmen quickly organize meetings, which are, for the most part, poorly attended, and have the prescribed resolution approved. Preparation of a pledge is more complicated. It is drawn up by an apparatchik in conjunction with the factory management and the chairman of the party organization and is usually proclaimed without the factory personnel being aware of it.

And thus, a few days after instructions have gone out from the central, the information system registers the first resolutions or pledges. Shortly after this, they appear in the press. High officials receive regular reports on the progress of campaigns. Since the seventies, public opinion formation has run up against obstacles—disinterest on the part of the workers resulting from unhappy experiences of the fifties. Nowadays, resolutions come mainly from agencies and from party and trade union officials in factories.

In addition to the *Information Bulletin of the First Department*, members of the power group, high officials in the central secretariat, and RC leading secretaries receive the *Bulletin* of the International Department, which contains news on international-political affairs. Only members of the central power group receive the secret (yellow) volume of news monitoring from the Press office. It contains specialized information from correspondents on the situation in one or another allied state or communist party.

The party apparat plays an important role in management of the information system of society. It makes sure that the will of the power group, as well as its own interests in this domain, is realized. The central power group establishes general limits of permitted knowledge, or more precisely, of prohibited knowledge. In the regions and districts, decisions are only made about publication of local news. Guidelines, authorizations, and prohibitions of this kind are issued by the responsible party apparatchiks. They are not concerned with protection of state secrets. They consider publication of information and unofficial opinions from a power point of view—depending on whether it weakens the regime, the authority of the party apparat, or their own positions vis-à-vis higher-ranking comrades. Party institutions have, over time, built up a mechanism of oversight and supervision that censors not only news and phenomena that are political in character but also scholarly publications, works of art, and educational and entertainment activities.

It is the CC secretary responsible for press affairs who, in consultation with the general secretary, makes decisions regarding publication of the most significant daily news items (e.g., a speech by the U.S. president, a domestic mine disaster, the events of 1981 in Poland). The director of the press office then receives authorization to release information into the category of news to which the mass media may refer. The mass media cannot report on events not referred to in the news from the press office. Editors in chief of daily newspapers and the heads of radio and television simultaneously receive instructions from the appropriate CC department telling them what news they have to make public, and how they are to comment on it. Similar procedures are followed for news of unquestionable publishability. The only difference is that the instructions stipulate the exact period and methods of publication. (This includes, e.g., news concerning Soviet views on foreign policy, decisions of the government, and CC speeches of communist politicians). In cases in which CC secretaries would like to suppress some news item but, for various reasons, cannot entirely keep quiet about it, they give instructions that it be broadcast only on the final television and radio news of the day, or that it be published in the last edition of a newspaper and this "in an obscure place."

Procedures for publication of new knowledge in the social sciences follow a kind of tacit agreement between scholarship and politics. Every scholar has the right, and obligation, to formulate his views without constraint, but it is up to the political organ to decide whether publication is politically expedient.

The power group and its apparats consider journalists, producers of culture, and social scientists as "their" subordinate employees and the institutions in which they work as their detachments. It issues instructions to them directly, i.e., informing their publishers and employers (e.g., the trade union leadership, the Academy of Sciences), and the heads of the mass media are in effect responsible for maintaining the "party line." They thus voluntarily become censors or, more accurately, self-censors.

The Central Publications Board [censorship office] also sees to it that the general guidelines are maintained and provides specific instructions regarding "prohibited knowledge." This office emerged in 1953 as a unit of the Ministry of the Interior (as part of security) and has been under the prime minister's office since the sixties. It has branch offices in the regions. State censorship is a party institution in the true sense of the word, an extension of a party apparat, which gives it guidance from the point of view of content. The Central Publications Board issues guidelines for its employees and *Daily Reports*, which are received by CC secretaries and the responsible CC department. The guidelines contain an enumeration of events and persons coming under the publication ban. Individual bans grew to such an extent that a file emerged of persons who cannot be spoken of and whose works are not allowed to be published. An analogous list of banned political events also emerged. The *Daily Reports* are filled with a list of interventions by the censorship office, i.e., of those "defective" thoughts and items of information whose publication it has prohibited.

Editors in chief of newspapers and publishing houses are responsible for compliance with the censors. If they do not agree, as is often the case, they have the right to appeal to the responsible party apparatchik. If they to not agree with his decision, any of the parties to the dispute can complain to the apparatchik's superior. In rare cases, the conflict goes as far as the CC secretary, who makes a final decision.

Organizational and Ideological Work

In the language of the party apparat, organizational work means an apparatchik's taking care of the party organization operating within his portfolio and the institutions subordinate to the party organization.

The power group sometimes proclaims the task of taking care of the party organization to be of utmost importance, even the principal mission of the apparat. It does this to emphasize the autonomy of extra-party institutions and to suppress or condemn the party apparat's natural tendency to direct and substitute itself for their governing organs. Apparatchiks pay no attention to the party organization, considering this to be the responsibility of the CC Political-Organizational Department. All appeals, efforts, and name changes have failed to alter the reality that the apparat and its functionaries primarily run, or "stand over" extra-party organizations, and have only minimal interest in the party organization.

Organizational work has not ceased to be a responsibility of the CC First Department, which, to a considerable extent, monopolizes this domain. It issues instructions and gathers information about the activities of party organizations. Apparatchiks in other CC and RC departments usually take part only in the annual members' meetings or conferences (in ministries) of their central institution. Only rarely do they go to meetings of the enterprise committee (i.e., the top party organization in central agencies). At most they meet with its chairman, but they have no overview whatsoever of the activity of lower-level units (basic organizations). At long, irregular intervals, the CC Secretariat (and, more regularly, the RC secretariats) receive reports on attendance of party apparatchiks at meetings of party organizations. The results are usually deplorable.

The power group, especially at the central level, likes very much to stress the great significance of ideological work in the life of the party, and it does so rather frequently. It sees it as a kind of cement for the party and society and expects it to convince citizens of the rightness of party policies. Both of these tasks are unrealistic and cannot be realized. In party terminology, one speaks of ideological work lagging behind the needs of the party, when it ought to be ahead of them. Among high-level communists, an exaggerated concern for ideological purity lives on as a legacy of the Comintern. Each and every minor, utterly insignificant deviation from their own interpretation of Marxism-Leninism is immediately noted and blown out of proportion, and a struggle against it is launched. Ideological struggles are among their political passions. Ideological zeal has always been a source of repeated conflicts between the power group and the party theoreticians as to where the center of theoretical work is supposed to lie. The power group emphatically rejects all attempts to make scholarly institutions the theoretical center. It has appropriated this function for itself and transferred its execution to the central party apparat. Nevertheless, it functions only as a censorship agency, not being equipped for real theoretical work. Furthermore, on the "theoretical front lines" it is requests for practical measures of party policy to be "worked out scientifically" that predominate.

The notion of "ideological work" is usually taken to mean propaganda and agitation carried out by party institutions, and party apparatchiks are constantly reminded of their obligation to make sure that such work is carried out in the areas for which they are responsible. In reality, the Ideological Department bears almost exclusive responsibility for ideological work. Despite the fact that its importance is stressed, and that substantial resources are invested in it, it remains the cinderella of the party apparat.

The most important element of propaganda is the system of party education going from the basic organizations all the way up to the central. Almost all communists and selected individuals in factories, communities, and districts who are not party members attend, or are supposed to attend, training units. They are trained by the numerous activ of propagandists and readers, consisting mainly of members of the intelligentsia—teachers and clerks. The regional and central corps of readers are responsible for preparing the training. The majority of the lower-level units do not meet at all, or meet very irregularly and merely go through the motions in their work. In the districts, efforts are made to check up on their activity and make them meet regularly, but these efforts are not successful. Data on numbers of meetings and on audience participation, which every training unit is supposed to record, are routinely inflated. It is estimated that about half the party membership takes part in training, and even this level of participation is irregular.

Party agitation is a matter having its own portfolio. It is taken care of by a section of the CC and RC ideological departments and by an official in the districts. At central headquarters, two apparatchiks look after the issuance of aids for opinion agitation, placards, slogans, wall posters, and two officials for personal agitation prepare booklets to help agitators. The interest in agitation of apparatchiks in other CC or RC departments does not go beyond criticism of its low level of effectiveness. The situation is similar in the districts. Although basic organizations are urged to build up permanent groups of agitators to carry out a systematic program of personal agitation among the fellow workers or fellow citizens assigned to them, this has little effect. Too few communists have either the desire or the courage to try to persuade citizens of the rightness of party policy.

Opinion agitation functions somewhat better than personal agitation. The central distributes placards, slogans, and wall posters to the districts, and the districts pass them on to the basic organizations. It often happens that materials lie around in basic organizations and even in district secretariats for a long time without being unpacked, or that they are even not used at all. There is thus a preference for sending them to local offices, which can be officially required to use them in time.

Party Finances and Administration

The expenditures required for the party's activities are considerable. They amount to around 600 million crowns annually (in 1967 they reached 528 million, and they exceeded 610 million the following year) and have been increasing every year. More than a third of all expenditures are absorbed by employee salaries. Expenditures for training, agitation, meetings, and organizational activities not including support of the youth organization make up about 20 percent of the budget (e.g., organization of district and regional conferences and party congresses costs more than 20 million crowns (see Appendix 6).

The party covers all expenditures out of its own resources. Its income exceeds its expenditures, and it has, over time, amassed large financial reserves.[4] The main source of the party's income is membership dues. (In the 1960s, they covered 80 percent of expenditures. This proportion then decreased somewhat, but continues to remain at more than two-thirds). It also receives profits from party enterprises—publishing houses and the press.

The party operates under a unified system of financial management, and all institutions are linked up to one central budget. Expenditures of basic organizations are covered by the district committee. The high-ups work out a financial plan, and the other organizations receive a kind of lump sum allotment. The district budget is part of the region's, and the region's is part of the central's.

The DC presidium deals with financial management or, more accurately, with the payment of membership dues on a monthly basis. Reports on this are prepared by the economic unit of the party apparat, which also sees to it that basic organizations regularly purchase their dues stamps. The principle is very simple: Each month, every basic organization reports the number of its members and has to purchase that number of dues stamps. Dues levels are established by a scale approved by the party congress. However, the majority of members pay lower dues.

The party has its ongoing system of administrative routines. It consists of various reports, the most important of which are those that register every member and those that give a picture of the organization in numbers. An applicant for party membership fills out a form, a kind of application, supported by two or three sponsors and approved by the committee and the members' meeting. The DC presidium, which regulates the admission of new members according to instructions from the central, makes the final decision—i.e., it does not approve the applications of some who are not working class, so as not to worsen the party's social makeup.

An application taken care of this way goes to the Central Secretariat, where a file card and membership card are filled out (first that of candidate, then of a member, whereby the same procedure is repeated). It goes back through the same channels. The member receives the membership card, one file card is kept by the district committee for its card file of members according to organization, a second stays in the card file of the Central Committee, and a third goes to the basic organization. If the member moves or changes occupations, the file card goes with him to the new organization, and the district also makes the change in its card file.

Every basic organization has its book of monthly reports, which it is required to fill in regularly and send to the district. The reports have headings for membership statistics, for changes during the preceding month, for numbers of meetings held—of the bureau, of the membership, and public meetings (and numbers present)—and for comments, complaints, and requests to higher-level institutions. The district secretariat meticulously records the information in the monthly reports and makes sure they are submitted. It prepares its own report with about the same information content (except for the comments and complaints), along with detailed statistics on the number of organizations and members in industry, in villages in schools. The region proceeds in the same manner. The regional summaries are processed in central headquarters by the First Department and transmitted twice annually to the CC Secretariat.

The accounts book of a basic organization contains its financial records, including the purchase and distribution of membership dues and other expenditures reimbursed by the district. Every organization that conducts party training submits an annual report on training units and the assignment of members to them. The propagandist keeps a kind of journal in which he records the member participation in training. The journal of a party group leader is, for the most part, a record of how well the members assigned to him are paying their dues subscribing to the party press. Commanders of the People's Militia also submit reports, which include the number of members of the unit and information on rallies and exercises conducted, on political training, etc.

Party Management

The party management administration looks after the education and training of functionaries and provides the technical and material prerequisites necessary for the party to function. It is an institution having ideological functions as well as performing technical, economic, and health services.

Institutions with an Ideological Function

Among the most important is the political university, administered by the Central Committee. The university employs about 350 people, of whom about 120 are teachers and professors. This university stands on a par with regular institutions of higher education and has the right to grant the title of doctor and scholarly and pedagogical ranks. Its purpose is to educate functionaries for the party, state apparat, armed forces, and mass organizations. It is a live-in institution, and all its students receive scholarships while studying there. The annual costs for one student amount to about 50,000 crowns (until 1968, expenditures for the university amounted to 27 million crowns annually and then declined somewhat). A party member with several years of experience in party work is eligible to study there. Each year, 160–170 functionaries complete a three-year course, receiving the title of RSDr and around 2,400 go through short courses.

The party university does not enjoy a good reputation in society, mainly among the intelligentsia. It is considered a school of inferior significance and quality. Even within the party there is a contradictory relationship to it. Functionaries see completion of the three-year course as a prerequisite for career advancement. The party leadership does not regard the party university as being like other institutions of higher education, only as an institution for training party functionaries. Although the leadership considers the faculty an important component of the party aktiv, which participates in the preparation of party documents, it doesn't have full confidence in its members. In its eyes, they remain wavering intellectuals, holders of views that are not always favorable to the party leadership and its policies. Due to the fact that the faculty members of the party university educate party cadres and can thus also influence the party's thinking, they are kept under constant supervision. At the school, one can always find people who alert the party leadership to discrepancies between what is taught and official ideology and policy. On the other hand, in a certain sense, the teachers belong to a privileged class among employees of universities and scholarly institutions. This status derives from their belonging to the party apparat and from their close collaboration with the Central Secretariat, which makes them very broadly informed as well as giving them access to confidential materials.

The CC Secretariat approves curriculum of the principal—i.e., the three-year—course of study. The Ideological Department then approves the programs for the short courses. The principal subjects are the history of the communist movement, the CPCz and CPSU, as well as Marxist political economy, economics, and philosophy. Only Marxist and communist literature and documents are studied at the school. As for non-Marxist literature, students become acquainted only with those excerpts that are criticized in lectures.

Students are nominated to attend the party university by the regional party committees. Some are sent by the army, security, and mass organizations. Nominations are gathered in central headquarters and approved by the CC Secretariat. The placement of graduates of the three-year course works in the opposite direction. The section for high-level cadres decides which ones get positions in the central and which return to their regions on the basis of evaluations and cadre assessments made on every student. In doing this, they proceed from the demands of the department for positions to be filled in central institutions, and not only in party institutions.

Almost all graduates of the party university improve on their previous social status and move up the ladder of their careers. A consequence of this is that although lower-level officials try to get into the university, high-level officials don't show much interest in it, fearing that they might have to return to another position at the same level. However, this happens only rarely.

The education of lower-level party officials, as well as of high officials of mass organizations and the state bureaucracy in the regions, districts, and factories, is taken care of by the party university in Bratislava and regional schools in Prague and Brno.

The CC Institute of Marxism-Leninism, formerly called the Institute for the History of Socialism, is considered to be an institution for research in the social sciences. It is directly responsible to the Central Secretariat, specifically to the CC Ideological Department. The central power group uses it to enforce its monopoly of the interpretation and teaching of party history. The institute thus functions as a "supreme agency" for the history of the communist movement and, simultaneously, serves as scholarly window-dressing for the regime. The communist leadership has never felt a need for this institution and never turns to it on its own initiative. For the most part, the leadership only approves the institute's proposals, and does so with distrust. Once a year, it discusses a report of the institute's activities and, on this occasion, criticizes it for not making enough of a contribution to the ideological education of functionaries. The institute also takes care of party museums and the shrines of meritorious communists. In Prague, there is a Gottwald and a Lenin Museum, in Bratislava, a Lenin Museum.

One component of the party's system of archives is located in the institute. It has control of the collections relating to the communist and workers' movement, and the leadership of the institute gives permission to do research in them. A second component of the archival system is the CC archives. They contain the most important documents of the postwar communist leadership. It has a historical and a "living" part. The historical section contains collections of meetings of central communist organs from 1945. It also contains the Gottwald collection and the collections of other high-level functionaries, CC departments, and CC secretaries and materials from meetings of party regional committees. The collection dealing with political trials is part of a special section containing the security files on the trials of prominent communist functionaries during the first half of the fifties. Great secrets lie buried in the so-called Švab archive, which contains the widest variety of data on communist and noncommunist functionaries from the period 1939–1951. The "living part" of the archives is made up primarily of materials having to do with actions of central communist organs during the preceding three years. It also contains papers of CC departments and secretaries for the same time period. The secret archives are a special component. These include general secretary's vault and the vault containing Slánský's [the general secretary from 1945–1951] so-called secret archive.

The communist party press represents a huge press monopoly and makes the power group the biggest press magnate in the state. The party's central press organ is *Rudé právo*, which has a daily circulation of over a million copies and a Sunday circulation of over a million and a half. The linkage between its editorial offices and the Central Secretariat is provided by the editor in chief, who is a member of the CC Secretariat, is in daily contact with the responsible CC secretary, and discusses with him those articles that are politically and ideologically most important. The substantive orientation of *Rudé právo* is determined by the CC Secretariat. It approves plans for the newspaper's principal articles and, in its resolutions, gives it instructions for its participation in political campaigns (as the CC Presidium also does). The cultural political weekly, *Tvorba*, has a similar, more or less autonomous status. The editorial offices of periodicals primarily intended for internal use within the party (*Život strany* and *Tribuna* for functionaries and *Nová mysl* for propagandists and readers) are integral components of the Central Secretariat.

Every party regional committee has its daily newspaper. Editorial responsibility for it falls to the responsible RC secretary, and these papers are also guided by the press section of the Central Secretariat. Plans for key articles in regional daily newspapers are approved by the RC presidium. In every district, there are newspapers published at least once a week, with most appearing several times weekly. They are published jointly by the communist leadership and national committee. The communist leadership determines the substantive aspects (and the editor is considered an employee of the party apparat), and the national committee takes care of the financial and material aspects of newspaper publishing. Large enterprises have their own periodicals, which appear regularly—at least once a month, but usually more frequently. They are published jointly by the management of an enterprise, the enterprise party committee, and the trade unions. The ideological contents are guided and supervised by the party committee.

The communist party has its own publishing house, which is directly responsible to the CC Ideological Department. The CC Secretariat discusses its plan at least once a year. It contains a list of titles of books it has decided to publish during the coming year and an evaluation of the past year from the points of view of ideological effectiveness and finances. (The publishing house yields several million crowns annually for the party budget.) Pamphlets for propagandists and the party aktiv, materials for agitation, and decisions of party organs for the use of lower-level functionaries are put out by *Rudé právo*'s publishing house.

Technical Services, Living Accommodations, and Health Management

Some technical services in the Central Secretariat are provided by the party service organization, which comes under the Secretariat's organizational system and is subject to its procedures. Chauffeurs and garages, cleaning and maintenance personnel belong to it. In the regional secretariats, they are in the organizational system of the economic department.

The party's publishing and printing enterprise, *Rudé Právo*, is an autonomous economic entity, with its own budget, and its profits flow into the party budget. The enterprise prints party materials, but the bulk of its work comes from extensive orders from nonparty publishing houses.

The Central Secretariat owns several buildings for the occasional quartering of foreign guests and members of the Presidium and Central Committee who live outside Prague while they are attending meetings. The main one is the Hotel Praha, which also provides food and refreshments for meetings and conferences held in rooms of the Central Secretariat itself, including meetings of the CC Presidium. (Secretaries and members of the CC Presidium—or, more accurately, their wives— have the right to order food through the Hotel Praha, and they take advantage of it.) A second building used for similar purposes is the so-called Barnabitky (a former monastery near Prague Castle); a third is the so-called Gottwald villa (also near Prague Castle). This villa was given to Gottwald when he was prime minister during the years 1946–1948 and has been at the disposal of the party Central Committee since 1957. The Central Secretariat also owns or has at its disposal several villas in order to quickly provide living quarters for secretaries or newly appointed heads of departments. They are maintained by the party service organization.

Foreign guests taken care of by the Central Secretariat are classified into those coming under the provisions of signed agreements dealing with the exchange of delegations among parties, those invited by the Czechoslovak party leadership or at the wish of their own party for vacations and cures, and functionaries of parties operating under conditions of illegality. There are differences in the way guests are taken care of. The amounts spent on guests and gifts for them are gradated according to the positions they hold. Gifts for top-level officials are usually approved on an individual basis, and quotas established for gifts to lower-level functionaries are determined by general guidelines. These gifts are not purchased but rather selected from the gift rooms where products of national enterprises given as gifts to the Central Committee are stored.

Apparatchiks in the Central Secretariat and high officials in the regions can benefit from the specialized medical care of the State Sanatorium (SANOPS) and have at their disposal a certain number of places in spas and sanitoriums. The Central Secretariat has set up a system of recreational facilities for its employees (which are inexpensive to stay at) with strictly differentiated usage. For CC secretaries there is the luxuriously furnished summer resort at Orlík, where everyone gets his own villa. Heads of CC departments have cottages in Hvozdy. Other apparatchiks use the recreational centers—a villa at Machová Lake and buildings on the Sazová River.

Indirect Components of the Party Apparatus

Some state institutions have special ties to the party apparat. They are a kind of "extended" party workplace and are subject to careful supervision by the responsible units of the party apparat. For the most part, these are institutions in the areas of ideology and culture. Among them are the editorial offices of all extra-party daily newspapers as well as the most significant weeklies, the radio and television, faculties of Marxism-Leninism at universities, some social scientific centers of the Academy of Sciences, and the Central Publications Board.

The party apparat considers these institutions as its extended arm and keeps a close watch on their activities and cadre placement. The responsible department or section expresses its views on appointments to all high- as well as low-level positions, makes decisions on all significant questions relating to their work (including some programs broadcast, the substance of articles published, etc.). It holds frequent conferences with them, or a party official takes part in their meetings almost on a regular basis. Conferences of the editors in chief of daily newspapers and important weekly periodicals are especially important. A secretary or head of a CC department carries out analyses of them, how they have related individual news items to important political campaigns, and establishes tasks to be carried out in the immediate future.

Apparatchiks responsible for the portfolio are invited by the heads of institutions or sent by their departments to so-called presentations of films and television programs. Decisions are made at such presentations regarding the release of programs to the public. All those present at such meetings proceed from the fact that the party apparatchik represents the party and assesses mainly the political inoffensiveness and expediency of the works presented. For similar reasons, apparatchiks figure among the commissions that approve film and television scripts, political exhibits, and placards or serve as referees for book manuscripts, and not only those that are political in character.

The party apparatchik informs the leadership of his department of all the measures he has recommended. In those cases in which he has reservations about the work presented, or is unsure of his decision, a CC secretary will receive his report, and sometimes the general secretary's office will too. Then there are negotiations with the leaderships of the film or television about changes. Things work similarly with books and exhibitions that are not recommended, even though it is rare for drastic interventions to occur in such cases, since party apparatchiks have already expressed themselves with regard to the publishing plans of every important publishing house and also on the scenarios of all exhibitions of political significance, whose conceptions are approved by some party organ.

The Party Apparatus in the Armed Forces

The Army

In September 1948, the CC Secretariat decided to establish party organizations in the army and approved the institution of the Army Command for Party Work. Since October 1, 1950, Soviet military procedures and organizational forms have been in effect, and these provided the framework within which the Main Political Administration (MPA) emerged. This is the highest party political organ in the army, and along with the party apparat, it represents the leading role of the party toward everyone except the minister. It is a kind of CC department paid out of the budget of the ministry.

The MPA apparat consists of the commanders unit (secretariat), the political-organizational and ideological departments, the departments for work with the youth organization, and the educational-cultural and the material-technical departments. It directs all the lower-level political administrations up to and including party organizations in units, party committees in the Ministry of Defense, and all army installations. It determines the substance of political-educational and cultural activities of all soldiers and officers and sees to it that they are carried out. The military press, publishing houses, radio broadcasts for soldiers, army films, and the Military-Historical Institute and Museum all come under the authority of the MPA. It issues its own publications and guides and educates propagandists.

The commander holds the key position—the Main Political Administration, in effect, serves him as an auxiliary institution—and the privileged position of his secretariat is based on this. Important functions are concentrated here, such as relations with ministries and with the administrations of the Ministry of Defense, most important those with military counterespionage (there is a liaison officer for counter-intelligence in the secretariat who prepares supporting materials for the commander), and decision making with regard to high-level cadres in the army (cadre proposals are prepared by the MPA cadre group and decided upon by the commander).

From the Main Political Administration downward, the party apparat breaks down into lower-level military units. There are political administrations responsible for the military districts of Prague and Trenčin, and their commanders control apparats structured like the MPA's apparat. There are political departments in divisions and other higher-level military units, as well as military academies, training institutions, and some military institutes. Here, several people work with the commander as auxiliaries (for organizational affairs, ideological and mass cultural activity, for work with youth organizations). Political groups exist in regiments and autonomous battalions and usually consist of the commander as well as the apparatchik in charge of organizational affairs, the head of the club, and the librarian. All heads of administrations, departments for political work, and political groups are simultaneously representatives of their commander for political matters.

The number of political apparatchiks in the army reached 6,400 officers in 1955. A decline then set in, and their number stabilized at 4,200–4,600 officers. In the mid 1960s, leading party committees emerged, and they assumed some of the responsibility of the political apparat in some high commands and military schools. There are leading committees at the Ministry of Defense, at the general staff, at the military academies, and in training institutions—that is, in noncombat units.

In short, all party-political work in the army is directed by the commander of the Main Political Administration. It is carried out according to guidelines of the CC State-Administrative Department, which is controlled by the general secretary. The commanders of army political administrations and military districts are subordinate to the commander of the MPA. The commanders of the political departments of divisions and brigades and, if need be, other high-level military units are in turn subordinate to them. The representatives responsible for political affairs in the brigades, in turn, come under the heads of the political departments, and it is they who run the party and youth organizations in the units. Both are broken down still further into lower-level organizations in battalions as well as in platoons if the need exists.

The activities of party organizations in army units are quite limited in scope compared to civilian organizations, and they have very little authority. They deal exclusively with political activities—agitation and propaganda—among soldiers and officers. They do not enforce the leading role of the party with regard to the military command. They cannot criticize the orders of a commander but are allowed to discuss the political means for their realization. They cannot criticize the actions of commanders either, but can alert the representative for political affairs to them. The representatives for political affairs can complain if they do not agree with some decision of their commanders. They even have an obligation to inform their superior—the head of the political department of higher-order units. He is of a higher rank than the commander who was the object of the complaint and has the authority to give him orders.

The same kind of machinery for the administration of political work operates within military units of the Ministry of the Interior, i.e., the border patrol and civil defense.

Security

The party apparat in security units is organized in a manner that is somewhat more complex than in the army, and its relationships of subordination are also more complex. At the central level, there exists a main party committee in security at the Ministry of the Interior. Party organizations in all security units, which are strictly separate from other organizations in the ministry, come under its authority. The bureau is elected at a conference, and its membership is approved by the CC Secretariat. The main committee is headed by a full-time chairman, who is in frequent contact with the State-Administrative Department, which is superior to him. The main committee has a modest party apparat of about five to six members, and it takes care of internal party affairs (party meetings, training, administration). The main committee also deals with cadre affairs coming under the authority of the minister, his deputy, and the head of the main administration.

The party organization of the intelligence service and State Security (political or secret police) has special status. In the intelligence service there is an autonomous committee and a small apparat. Its chairman deals only with the head of his CC department. The party organization in State Security also has its main committee, headed by a full-time chairman. A representative of the CC State-Administrative Department serves as a "special instructor" for this main committee. The same function is performed for the main committee of the Public Security Corps [regular police forces] by the head of the security section in the CC department. There are also instructors for party-political work and political administration in units of the border patrol and civil defense, as well as in SVAZARM [a paramilitary organization] and in units of the correctional services corps.

The party apparat can also be found in lower-level security units. There is a main committee in regional administrations of the national security, headed by a full-time chairman. The role of instructor is played by the head of the state-administrative department of the RC. At the district level, all unit organizations in security are administered by a corporate committee headed by a full-time chairman. The function of full-time chairman in the districts and regions, as well as in the central, is usually performed by a member of security. Personnel costs and material expenditures of the party apparat are covered out of the budget of the Ministry of the Interior.

The People's Militia

The communist party has its own armed units—the people's militias. They emerged in February 1948 and have undergone several more or less significant changes. Their development went through three roughly defined phases. In the first phase (from 1948 to 1952), attempts were made to establish people's militias in all plants, even small ones. People's militia units even cropped up in villages or groups of villages. After this there was a sharp reduction in the number of units. This was the second phase, during which they were established in large factories, ministries and other agencies. This form of organization has survived ever since. In the Czech lands, their membership numbers around 37,000, in Slovakia, around 8,000–8,500 thousand. The third phase dates from the second half of the fifties, when they were transformed into paramilitary units with extensive armament and military organization.

Only members and candidates of the communist party can belong to the people's militia. During the fifties, recruits were volunteers and were thoroughly screened. Nowadays, recruitment is carried out among young party members, and thus a large proportion of the militia's membership consists of office workers and foremen.

The people's militias, as the "party's armed first," are subordinate to and controlled exclusively by the power group. At least once a year the DC, RC, and CC presidia discuss reports on their condition and state of preparedness and approve the results of their exercises and maneuvers. The general secretary is commander in chief, and the DC and RC leading secretaries are commanders at the district and regional levels. The general staff of the people's militia (around fifteen members) operates within the system of the Central Secretariat and has the status of a CC department. It has sections for operational affairs, education, training, and material supplies. There are regional and district staffs. Three or four people work on a regional staff, and one or two on a district staff. In factories there is a unit commander and his political deputy. Only in large enterprises, in exceptional cases, is the commander released from his usual job. Otherwise, the commandership is usually linked to some position in the factory—e.g., the special tasks department. As a rule, the commander's political deputy is a member of the enterprise party committee.

The militia is paramilitary in character and organizational setup. Its units are organized in platoons and higher-order units, with their own uniforms and decorations. They conduct exercises with both light and heavy weapons, have their own telephone lines and radio links, and issue orders. They have their own mobilization plans, levels of alert, and motor pools to provide for the mobilization of members for surprise operations. Their regular combat exercises and also shooting practice take place on military terrains and are run by army instructors—professional officers. Costs associated with armaments and equipment are covered by the Ministry of Defense. Factories are responsible for taking care of the premises and for transportation to training exercises. They receive around 15–20 million crowns annually from the budget of the Central Committee.

The people's militia solemnly calls itself the iron fist of the working class, and its existence is justified to the public and mainly to its own membership in terms of defending factories against the class enemy and defending socialist power. It carries out this mission only on so-called critical days (e.g., on the anniversary of the Soviet occupation of Czechoslovakia) or on the eve of state festivities (First of May and the like). It also provides guard service to the factories.

The units' real mission consists of protection of the position of the power groups. They are not suited for anything else. The power groups make use of them when citizen unrest breaks out or is expected. They played such a role at President Eduard Beneš's funeral in September 1948, they took part in the liquidation of the "kulaks," they intervened during the currency reform of 1953, stood guard at Gottwald's funeral (1953), stood at full alert during the unrest in Hungary (1956), and were sent in against demonstrators in August 1969 (at the time of the first anniversary of the Soviet invasion of Czechoslovakia).

They have always been regarded as a politically dependable source of support for the party, as the most faithful and devoted element of the party membership and corps of functionaries. The party leadership has confidence in them and relies on them. Membership in the people's militia is evidence of dedication to the party and assures favored status in appointment to positions of responsibility. There is, however, another side to membership. Wavering belief, which is tolerated in ordinary members, is inexcusable for militia members. Any doubts about party policy in a period when the militias are sent into action or failure to report for duty or carry out orders is punished the first time by expulsion from the militia and the second time by party penalties up to and including expulsion from the party, with all the social consequences that entails.

In the early years of their existence the militias contained the greatest concentration of members and functionaries who unquestioningly supported the policies of the communist leadership. Within the party they represented the organization of the "die-hard" sectarians. They criticized district and factory functionaries for not being sufficiently "class-oriented," for indecisiveness, weakness, insufficient strictness, accusing them of protecting the enemy and the likes. Among the reasons for such attitudes was that they contained many communists who had not gotten high-level positions, and this was the way they gave vent to their dissatisfaction and envy. The militias constantly exert "a pressure from the left."

The people's militias thus fulfil a two-in-one task: They provide political support for the power group within the party and protect the party's power position in society. In all cases when they have appeared actively in public, they have gone against their comrades, the workers, or, as official propaganda refers to them, their allies, the peasants. Only in rare cases have they done anything to the "class enemy." In them, the communist leadership has created a diabolical instrument. They repress worker dissatisfaction and unrest.

Notes

1. E.g., in 1949, of 169 DC leading secretaries, 113 were workers, and 5 were farmers. In the years 1956–1957, of 295, 243 were workers, and 27 were farmers. In March 1949, 48.9 percent of the central apparat consisted of workers; by September 1950, it had already risen to 52.6 percent, and their numbers continued to increase. Table 3.1 indicates the social origins of the political apparatchiks on January 1, 1966, by percentage.

2. Although there were 294 apparatchiks working in the Central Secretariat in 1947, by March 1949, the number had risen to 528 (of them, 46.2 percent were political cadres), and by September 1950, there were 703 of them. In that period, there were 2,075 in the districts in the Czech lands and 1,306 apparatchiks in the regions with an average of 18 per district and 100 per region. In 1951, after Slánský's arrest, the apparat underwent a further reorganization, and its numbers increased. In 1956, there were 7,736 apparatchiks in it, of whom 784 worked in the central and 310 in the Slovak central. The following year, a ceiling of 5,839 people was established, which meant a decrease to 615 in the central. In the regions, the decrease amounted to 25 percent, in the districts, 8 percent.

3. The following record of the course of a workweek of a DC leading secretary comes from the first half of the fifties. Since then, some of the institutions in whose meetings he took part have disappeared. However, others have appeared, and the overall picture of a workweek has not changed substantially. The week of the DC leading secretary in Namenice and Lipou is shown in Table 3.2.

4. In the spring of 1968, 4 reserves amounted to 39.4 million crowns. The preceding year, they had been higher by 54 million, but the Central Committee had granted the youth organization a total of more than 134 million crowns.

TABLE 3.1
Social Origins of Political Apparatchiks
on January 1, 1966 (Percentages)

	Family Origin		Original Occupation	
	Worker	Farmer	Worker	Farmer
Central	72.8	7.4	61.4	0.4
Regional	77.6	12.6	70.0	1.1
District	78.6	11.8	75.2	1.1
Overall	77.6	11.7	72.8	1.0

TABLE 3.2
A DC Leading Secretary's Week

Monday	morning	Meeting of the Commission for the Construction of Agriculture
	afternoon	Meeting of the DC presidium, lasting from 15:00 to 22:00 hours
Tuesday	morning	Meeting of the coordinating group of four to check up on fulfillment of the plan in industry
	afternoon	People's Militia rally
	evening	Party meeting in the city
Wednesday	morning	DC secretariat meeting until noon
	afternoon	Meeting of instructors for basic agricultural production and purchase
	evening	Meeting of the district committee of National Front, of which he is chairman
Thursday	morning	Receives visitors
	afternoon	Meeting of the security commission; conference with security functionaries
Friday	morning	Conference of the church group of five
	afternoon	Meeting of the caucus of communist members of the DNC
Saturday		Greatest amount of activity at the secretariat, visits of functionaries from the communities and factories

4

The Party Aktiv

What Is the Aktiv?

The party apparat carries out decisions of the power group and conducts political campaigns. It also implements its own guidelines and instructions through the party aktiv. This is a body of over half a million functionaries, about two-thirds of whom hold positions that are insignificant from the point of view of power in party and mass organizations and the organs of power. These positions confer no power on those who hold them, and most of these people behave quite passively. The aktiv includes, e.g., most party propagandists, most heads of basic organizations, members of the elected organs of mass organizations (trade unions, youth and women's organizations), national committees, etc.). They represent a kind of intermediate group, between the passive mass of members and those who are active in the true sense of the word. The truly active group consists of those functionaries who, in one way or another, share in power—that is, high officials of party, state, economic, cultural, and all social institutions.

Communists are brought into the aktiv in two ways. One is for a party organization to appoint an already committed member or local official to a position coming under the cadre nomenklatura. This mode of selection from among the membership and low-level functionaries was used almost exclusively during the first ten years of the party's power monopoly. The other method is to entrust passive or "lukewarm" party members with "nomenklatura positions" due to their specialized qualifications. In most such cases—though not all—this move either entails involvement in the party aktiv or such involvement is expected.

The aktiv can thus be roughly defined as consisting of those positions under the cadre nomenklatura and the wielders of power in basic party organizations. We are thus looking at 220,000 people, i.e., around 1.5 percent of the total population and 13 percent of party membership. We arrive at the same figure by using the second criterion (in a certain sense, it is more accurate, since the cadre nomenklatura also includes noncommunists). This would mean determining the number of communists who moved up from the profession of "worker" to paid positions in various institutions. At the end of the sixties, 62.5 percent of communists, i.e., more than a million, were of working-class origin. However, 550,000 were workers by profession, and 216,000 were retired workers, that is, 774,000 in all. The remainder—more than 225,000—moved up to "higher level services," thanks to the party, and participate in the wielding of its power.

The party aktiv constitutes a self-contained social stratum, distinguished by some common characteristics. Among the main ones are

1. position in the power mechanism, i.e. the role of wielder of power and a relationship of mutual dependence with the power group;
2. sources of and motives for political dealings and the closely related political and social interests and political milieu in which the members of the aktiv function, including the limits, substance, and tendencies of their political thinking, ideological formulas and utilization of neologisms;
3. proprietary privileges of the most varied nature.

The aktiv plays an indispensable role within the party as its activity depends heavily on the capabilities, will, and determination of the aktiv. The power group regards the aktiv as the principal voice for the opinions and interests, not only of functionaries, but also of the party membership as a whole. Most important, however, is the aktiv's position in the power mechanism. It constitutes the regime's only clear base of social support. It participates in various ways in the formulation of policy orientations and guidelines, and mainly it represents a key component of the machinery that injects the decisions of the power groups and instructions of the party apparat into the life of society.

The power groups and their apparats are keenly aware of the key role played by the aktiv. Since they know that their power system would not work without it, they pay close attention to it. They delegate considerable authority to the aktiv, turn to it, and consult it. They do not skimp on expenditures for its education, and for training of its members to exercise higher-level functions. They also strive to keep it in a constant state of activity—even a state of alert. They grant it privileges in various ways, including not only social privileges (in particular, the majority enjoy financial advantages) but also privileged access to information about domestic and foreign affairs and about the aims of their own policies. In return they expect unconditional obedience and subordination from the aktiv. The power groups' relationship to the aktiv shows not the slightest dependency or hint of an attitude of requesting that it carry out their guidelines. To them, it is self-evident that functionaries have to carry out their instructions and that the apparat must insist on this. They all regard the obedience of functionaries as reciprocation for the social status the party has provided them.

I have already noted the three sources of the aktiv's motivation and obedience—an important prerequisite for the functioning of the communist power system. The first is ideological in character. Despite all the shocks experienced by the communist regime, and the disappointments it has caused, a large part of the aktiv continues to believe in the rightness, beneficence, or at least inevitability of party policy. Such attitudes relate more to concrete policy than to long-term programmatic goals. These functionaries are already so much a part of the existing regime that their thinking never strays outside the framework it has established. For many of them, the mere mention of their duty to fulfill tasks, wishes, interests and to serve their ends never fails to evoke extraterrestrial strength. And none of them ever asks what the party is. They see the party, not as an organization of people and institutions, but rather as a sacred concept, transcending reality and concrete individuals. They are trained in this spirit, and for them the party exists as an inviolable sanctity that makes no mistakes. Only the leadership and individuals can make mistakes.

The second motive is power-political. Most functionaries derive considerable self-satisfaction from participation in the exercise of power and in social and political self-assertion. The third is social in character. All these functionaries know that their social status and career depend heavily on the existing regime, on the one hand, and "on the service to the party," on the other. Whether consciously or not, their attitude of subordination bears the marks of many years of experiencing that obedience is part of the job. Obedience is "built into the job," since disobedience is punished and costs one's career.

The power groups and their apparats carefully follow currents of opinion among the ranks of the aktiv and are sensitive to any deviations from the party line. Naturally, there are differences of opinion within the aktiv, and to some extent they have to be tolerated. However, as soon as the boundary of what is allowed or tolerated is crossed, measures will follow. If the problem involves one or several disobedient functionaries, the appropriate power group intervenes whenever their actions threaten the authority of the power group. It is considered much more dangerous when the aktiv or some part of it shows insufficient conviction regarding the rightness of some resolutions, and insufficient enthusiasm in carrying them out. Any wavering on the part of the aktiv is thus particularly alarming—i.e., when it loses its faith in the basic orientation and principles of party policy and calls for reform. The party leadership and its apparat know that any wavering on the part of the aktiv weakens their power position and capability to govern, and that it is the germ of internal party crises. The situation is salvaged by partly granting the demands of the aktiv, promising improvements, and partly by simultaneously taking severe measures against those who have been most outspoken in expressing discontent.

The situation cannot, however, always be mastered. There may have been success in Czechoslovakia in 1956 and 1963, but not in 1967 and 1968, when differences of opinion within the aktiv developed into a split and part of the aktiv turned against the party leadership. In this latter case, weaknesses in the party's internal information system were paid for dearly. It had provided distorted information about the opinions of functionaries, and this state of affairs was rectified only later. (For example, it wasn't by chance that, beginning at the end of 1966, Novotný complained about the inadequacy of internal party information. He was concerned primarily with the opinions of functionaries.)

The party aktiv is actually an artificial construct, since it doesn't function as a single unit. It breaks down into district, regional, and central components. In this breakdown, the number of members, the professional and political level, and methods of work differ. The district units consist of 8–10 functionaries, the regional around 2,000, and the central between 5,000 and 6,000.

At every organizational level, the aktiv breaks down further into jurisdictions—ideological, economic, intra-party, and administrative. Within this framework of division, every department of the party apparat organizes its aktiv, which consists of "top officials" from all the institutions under its jurisdiction. Each official picks functionaries from within his sector. Quite frequently these functionaries and activists come from two departments (e.g., for science and also for propaganda, for agriculture and for schools). Within a department the aktiv is further broken down by section, e.g. into the aktiv of those working in the mass media; in scholarly institutions (and, in particular, historians, economists, etc.), universities, high schools; in culture, agricultural production, and justice, but also the courts, procuracies, branches of industry, trade, Public Security, and State Security. At the hub of each unit is a party apparatchik. Each has his own aktiv—a circle of functionaries with whom he consults and through whom he carries out his tasks. It usually consists of high officials of pertinent institutions, officials of their party organizations and of the Central Trade Union, and employees of scholarly institutes (since the sixties, it has become fashionable to link scholars with the aktiv).

Beyond this breakdown into jurisdictions is that part which can be
called the aktiv of high-level cadres, which is found at all levels and
consists of top officials. The head of the department chooses them for
his own portfolio, and they are approved by the responsible secretary.
At the central level, this is done by ministers and their deputies,
chairmen and general secretaries of large mass organizations and cultural institutions, and members of the presidium of the parliament.
In the regions, it is done by members of the council and high officials
of the RNC, parliamentary deputies, chairmen of large mass organizations, directors of enterprises, high officials of the security forces
and the justice administration. The situation is similar in the district,
where members of the central and regional committees of the party
are added to the process. The transjurisdictional aktiv is the core, or
the political, aktiv, and many functionaries consider it an honor, as
proof of their importance, if they are invited to its meetings. In the
central, region, and district, it is convened in periods of extraordinary
political events and in cases of especially important decisions, mostly
upon instructions from some central party institution.[1]

Work with the Aktiv

The party aktiv (not including the political aktiv) is an aktiv of
the party apparat, an extended arm of its departments, sections, and
officials. As resolutions instruct them to do, party apparatchiks are
always supposed "to work with the broad aktiv." In actual practice,
this means (1) using the aktiv in all phases of preparation and implementation of party decisions and other actions and (2) preparing
the aktiv to carry out its mission.

Individual components of the aktiv take part in the preparation of
decisions and political actions in different ways—directly and in a
mediating capacity. Direct participation is limited to a narrow segment
of the aktiv, predominantly in the central, less in the region, and still
less in the district. Individuals or groups of functionaries from extra-
party institutions either come on their own initiative or are asked for
suggestions on how to deal with issues or for analyses and recommendations, from which the majority of the most significant decisions
then emerge. Apart from this, there is a large group of "theoretical
people" represented in the central aktiv who prepare expert opinions
and variants of solutions to various problems and furnish advice to
party apparatchiks. Their views influence, even predetermine, decisions
of the power group. They even formulate many of these decisions
themselves. It is precisely this group of functionaries that is subject
to a severe self-censorship, attributable to their own experience and

to their lack of courage to go beyond the official limits of thinking. The party apparatchik who turns to them is well aware of this weakness. He thus often asks them to write and say what they really think, without paying attention to the official point of view on the matter under discussion. In making such a request, he assures them that their views, even if heretical, will not be used anywhere and that no one will be punished for them. Only individuals who are still inexperienced believe these promises, relax their self-censorship, and write even a fraction of what they really think.

The greater part of the aktiv participates indirectly in decision making in two ways. First, preliminary discussions of draft decisions within the aktiv of the responsible portfolio are common. When the party apparatchik has a clearer view of the substance of the proposed measures, he will call a meeting of the aktiv and ask for its views on his proposal. The discussion is often quite frank and heated, since on these occasions there is respect for the principle that before a decision has been reached, and within the confines of the party, free and uninhibited discussion is allowed.

The second kind of indirect participation takes the form of pressure exerted on the power group and on the apparat. Participants in aktiv meetings criticize, sometimes very sharply, various aspects of social life; the work and decisions of authorities, enterprises, institutions, and their functionaries; as well as party instructions. They point out short-comings and difficulties caused by others. They love to show great initiative in forcing solutions to more or less significant problems of the greatest variety, and they themselves make outspokenly radical proposals for solutions. The party apparat usually responds to their oft-voiced criticisms and tries to make improvements, since it fears the aktiv's discontent, seeing in it an indicator of potential unrest in society as a whole. Many decisions of the power groups and inter-ventions of their apparats are brought about in this way, or at least influenced by pressure from the aktiv. Yet, on the other hand, the apparat can itself instigate a request from functionaries for measures it has already decided to take. In the jargon of functionaries, this is called "preparing the political groundwork," or "calling for resolutions."

Politically significant decisions and campaigns are theoretically jus-tified and propagated. This is taken care of by the ideological segment of the aktiv. The communist intelligentsia in particular get very much involved in this, i.e., those who work in the party apparatus or in institutions administered directly by the party apparat (scholars, uni-versity instructors in the social sciences, journalists, propagandists). From time to time, groups with a critical attitude toward party policy emerge and point to the discrepancy between Marxist theory and political practice. Nevertheless, it is the obedient and the frightened, as well as the conscious supporters of the leadership and the power system among their ranks, who predominate.

They provide theoretical arguments, make up or disseminate ideological formulas to provide theoretical support for current policy, without taking account of its changes and failures. They can always find enough quotes from the classics, take them apart, and finally, make a theoretical conception out of them that supports the power group's policy of the moment. They are blind to reality, fleeing from it to theoretical heights. They speculate and carry on discussions about their today and, even more, their tomorrow from a cosmic perspective on society. Worst of all, however, is that they fail to go beyond useless discussion (e.g., concerning the nature of the current epoch and that of the Revolution, about the universal state), but they contribute actively to the formulation of ideological formulae and damnations.[2]

Most functionaries are involved in direct implementation of party decisions—i.e., with their interpretation, execution, and supervision of their implementation. In party terminology, the sum total of this activity is referred to as "politico-organizational implementation" and is carried out through two channels—through extra-party and through party institutions.

Along the first channel, functionaries of extra-party institutions carry out decisions and political campaigns in their places of work and make sure this is done in units subordinate to them—(the ministry, regional, district, and local national committee through the channel of the national committees; the Central Trade Union, regional, district, and works organizations—through the channel of the trade unions). Many take part as early as the stage of organization of political actions and campaigns. The party apparatchik asks "his" institutions for detailed proposals for the organizational implementation of the campaign "through their channel." A final plan is then prepared. After its approval by the party organ, the institutions turn the proposal into binding resolutions and guidelines with which the members of the aktiv are familiarized. At the meetings and conferences in which this takes place, functionaries express their ideas on how how to implement the decisions, as well as their reservations, doubts, and additions. The party apparatchik is supposed to keep higher levels informed about the voices of the aktiv. These higher levels react with an "expanded campaign of explanation" and, in exceptional cases, with corrections of their decisions or plans for campaigns in preparation.

Along party channels, functionaries see that resolutions and guidelines are carried out in party organizations, where they also keep track of how they are carried out by extra-party organizations. This part of the aktiv consists mainly of the chairmen and instructors of the basic organizations; members of the central, regional, and district corps of speakers; participants in political brigades providing assistance to regions and districts; and individuals who have been given special tasks to carry out in some party organization.

The chairmen of basic party organizations meet by jurisdiction— works, village, school, in offices, in an enterprise, etc. Their conferences are held almost regularly once a month by the DC secretary responsible for the jurisdiction. At these conferences, the activity of the organization is evaluated, political and organizational information is gathered and disseminated, and further tasks are assigned. An all-region meeting of chairmen of basic organizations is held only for especially important political campaigns (after party congresses, for changes in party policy, etc.). Meetings of instructors are also held regularly, mainly by jurisdiction. Here, apparatchiks of the district secretariat pick up information about the activities of basic organizations; the situation in communities, factories, and offices; and about their functionaries. They, in turn, familiarize the instructors with their tasks for the immediate future. The corps of speakers is called together occasionally, usually before a campaign of public meetings. The aim of the meeting is to "fill" the speakers with the contents of their speeches at the forthcoming public meetings.

Preparation of the aktiv to carry out its mission consists of systematic education, provision of information, familiarization with its current tasks, and organization of its activities. Education of functionaries is taken care of by the whole system of education, from the basic circles through the evening university of Marxism-Leninism in the districts to the party university. In addition to this, the district secretariat organizes lecture courses and seminars. For chairmen of basic organizations, annual short-term live-in training courses are conducted. Functionaries at the district and regional levels take long-term live-in courses at regional schools. High-level regional and central officials are trained in long-term courses at the party university. About twenty party officials a year study at the University of the Communist Party of the Soviet Union in Moscow. (By resolution of the CC Presidium, individuals who complete these courses must hold positions at least at the level of CC head of section.)

The information received by the aktiv through internal party channels goes well beyond the news that is publicly available. It may be about important domestic and international political events or be limited to detailed briefing for concrete tasks. The extent to which individuals receive information is strictly hierarchical. High officials find out about many resolutions that are considered secret. They get to know about them at conferences in the central and the region or through the blue bulletin, *Resolutions of Organs of the CPCz CC and the Government*, and many also have the news monitoring from the foreign press at their disposal. Other functionaries—mainly in the district and basic organizations—only rarely receive printed information. When they do, it consists of unpublished speeches made at Central Committee meetings and, in exceptional cases, some resolutions of its Presidium. Such information is designated as confidential and for internal party use. Most information is transmitted to these functionaries orally at meetings and conferences of the aktiv.

In organizational work with the aktiv, the party apparat makes use of these principal forms:

- *Personal relationships on an individual basis*: Every party auditor has working meetings with the members of his aktiv. These meetings take place irregularly, yet frequently. They are very important for mutual acquaintance and often result in the auditor and the aktiv growing closer.
- *Conferences with a small, selected group of party functionaries*: These are called for the purpose of transmitting information, consultations regarding problems resolved by the department, discussion of proposals and reports prepared for party organs, carrying out concrete tasks.
- *A meeting of the aktiv of one or several portfolios (departments)*: Such a meeting is called before every major political campaign (e.g., before elections to works councils, the launching of the school year, party education, reorganization of an industry or a business). The secretary or head of department responsible for the portfolio explains the political significance of and organizational arrangements for the campaign, and activists are acquainted with their specific tasks.
- *A large meeting of the aktiv*: For the most part, these are held in the districts, less in the regions, and rarely at the central level. Several hundred functionaries take part in them to "arm themselves ideologically" for the implementation of party decisions, for the explanation of some events, or for especially important political campaigns. They are called, for example, for presentation of information about the party's own congress, congresses of the Communist Party of the Soviet Union, important CC meetings, economic reform; before campaigns against "hostile ideologies"; to work on preparations for parliamentary elections, or when there are changes in policy line.

Let us look briefly at how the aktiv participates in political campaigns, using some concrete examples. I have chosen typical cases that contained all the principal and most commonly used methods of work with the aktiv. For every political action or campaign, first the central, then the regions and districts work out a plan of all actions to take place in the context of the campaign and, frequently, another plan setting forth the chronological phases into which the campaign is divided.

On July 1, 1953, a currency reform was carried out. It was prepared secretly, with the knowledge of only four members of the communist leadership and a commission of specialists working outside Czechoslovak territory. A narrow group of party apparatchiks—completely isolated in a hotel—prepared the plan for its political-organizational implementation. According to this plan, meetings of the party Central Committee and the government were called unexpectedly for May 30. There was only one item on the agenda sent out with the invitation: "organizational matters." In the afternoon of the same day, parliament and the central party aktiv met without an agenda having been distributed.

On May 17, the RC leading secretaries received sealed packages, which they were to open only on May 30 at noon. In the package were instructions to call a meeting of the regional committee aktiv for May 30 at 5 P.M., to arrange for a permanent session of the RC presidium and a state of alert of the party apparat. The DC leading secretaries also received packages to be opened on May 30 at 2 P.M. They contained instructions to convene the party aktiv on the evening of May 30, to arrange for party meetings in communities on May 31 (Sunday) and the factories on June 1, and to organize a state of alert of the party apparat and the people's militias and a continuous session of the DC presidium. Commanders of the people's militias in the regions and districts received special orders to call a state of alert for all members beginning on May 30 and to place twenty to sixty men in the district at the disposal of State Security. An order was enclosed to be read at all militia meetings. Security forces and the army were also on a state of alert.

In the morning of May 30, the CC passed a resolution dealing with the monetary reform. In the afternoon, the central aktiv was informed, and its members were sent out to the regions and districts. The communist leadership, meeting in permanent session, received a report during the night on repercussions of the currency exchange. On Sunday and Monday, meetings of party organizations were held at which party officials spoke, and central headquarters was informed as to how they went. The regions relayed news about the exchange of currency every hour. They reported unrest and strikes that occurred in their regions and received orders to put them down severely.

Elections to parliament and to all levels of national committees are prepared for over a long period of time. The district aktiv is extensively involved in preparations for elections; the regional aktiv substantially less. In the central, it is primarily the CC departments responsible for elections and their aktivs that take part in preparations. Preparations for elections include political, cadre, and organizational components and are broken down into several stages.

1. They begin with the setting of a date for the elections. This is usually agreed upon at a conference of CC secretaries, acting on a proposal from the responsible CC department, which consults with the leadership of the National Front and parliament. The general secretary presents the proposal to the CC Presidium along with the political plans for the preelection campaign. Finally, both are approved by the Central Committee. After this, the responsible CC department submits to the CC Presidium a list of members of the Central Elections Commission, principles for the selection of candidates, and a schedule for preparation of the elections. It submits to the CC Secretariat a plan for carrying out the propaganda and agitation aspects of the election, i.e., a plan for the preelection campaign.

The principles for candidate selection determine the social and political composition of the membership of the next parliament and national committees to be elected. The numbers are binding for lower-level party organs. The principles also include the placement of so-called central candidate-deputies, i.e., members of the power group, ministers, chairmen of mass organizations, and well-known personalities. Their nominations come from the appropriate CC departments and secretaries. The schedule gives the deadlines for organizational and administrative actions that have to be carried out by state organs under the supervision of party institutions—e.g., making up voter lists; setting up electoral commissions in the districts, regions, and localities; selecting and registering candidates; etc.

The plan for the preelection campaign consists of an elaboration of the main actions to be carried out by central party and extra-party institutions in preparation for the elections and of general tasks assigned to the districts and regions. Those members of the aktiv who are interested are familiarized with these documents at conferences—of RC secretaries at the central level and of DC secretaries at the regional level.

Procedures are similar for the regions and districts. The aktiv is informed about the significance of the elections, the party apparat prepares a schedule and a concrete plan for propaganda and agitation.

The chairmen and instructors of the basic party organizations are familiarized with them. The bureaus of the organizations produce plans containing dates for public meetings and get-togethers organized by the party and mass organizations in communities and factories.

2. Cadre affairs dominate the second phase. Party central headquarters issues confidential directives to lower-level units instructing them how to take care of the cadre aspects of the election. They include instructions about how to put together the electoral commissions and select candidates. A preponderance of communists in the electoral commissions must be assured, and the makeup of the national committees has to conform to guidelines concerning social and political composition. Proposals for the makeup of the commissions in the districts and regions are agreed upon by the DNC or RNC chairman and the DC or RC leading secretary. In communities this is done by the chairman and instructor of the party organization, after agreement with the chairman of the national committee, and is finally approved by the party bureau.

Nominations of members-to-be of the national committees in communities come from the chairman of the national committee, the party organization, and sometimes from members' meetings. Nominations for membership in the district and regional committees are made by DC or RC secretaries, party auditors, the chairman of the DNC or RNC, and frequently the basic party organizations (for DNC members) or DC secretaries (for RNC members). DC secretaries or the RC secretariat put the proposals in their final form. Before being submitted for approval to the presidium and district or regional committee, every nomination is discussed with the chairmen of the basic organizations of those communities and the chairmen of the DC presidia of those districts in which the future DNC and RNC members will be candidates. Nominations of paid, full-time elected officials of the national committees—i.e., for chairman and secretary in the community and members of the council of the national committee in large cities, districts, and regions—are confirmed by the superior party organ. This comes under its cadre nomenklatura.

Candidates for parliament for whose nomination the region is responsible are chosen by RC secretaries. In isolated cases, mainly where the selection of individuals from production is involved, they delegate this task to the DC presidium. The region's nominations have to be approved by the DC presidium of the district in which the future deputy's electoral district lies. The nomination is also approved by the regional and the Central Committees. This procedure is also followed for deputies of the noncommunist parties. The cadre selection procedure ends with the formal confirmation of the nominations by the organs of the National Front responsible for the territory in question. They proclaim them as their candidates.

3. The preelection campaign proceeds according to the plan dealing with the propaganda and agitation aspects of the election. Party institutions also keep a watch over the preparation of electoral platforms of future members of the national committees. Reports on the progress of all actions flow into the central from the districts and regions. The DC and RC presidia, as well as the CC Secretariat, deal with these on a regular basis. The reports give, for example, the number of meetings and public gatherings held, and participation in them, as well as citizen opinions expressed most frequently at them.

On the eve and on the day of the election, a state of alert is proclaimed for the party apparat, the ranks of functionaries, and the People's Militia. Beginning in the morning, the DC, RC, and CC presidia meet in permanent session. The regions find out how the central thinks the elections should turn out; the districts find out about the region's thinking and then try to tailor the results to conform to these expectations. Organizational and operational matters that have arisen during the election are handled by a commission of high-level apparatchiks (heads of departments).

Every two hours, the districts get reports from their liaisons about the course of the elections in the communities, data regarding the number of citizens who have already voted, and reports about the mood of the citizenry. The district transmits these reports to the region, and it in turn passes them on to the central. From there, instructions and information come to the regions. Central headquarters gives synopses of electoral participation in all regions, those that are late in reporting. It makes criticisms and asks the RC presidia to rectify the situation quickly. It provides information about both negative and positive experiences in other places on election day. From the sealing of the ballot boxes to the final evaluation, the districts report election results every hour. Information goes from the regions to central at like intervals.

From central headquarters come instructions on how to count the votes cast (i.e., which to treat as invalid, or as positive, and how the name of a candidate has to be crossed out in order to count the ballot as a vote against). There is also information about election results in other regions and comparison of these results with those anticipated for that region by central headquarters. Then, all kinds of adjustments and recounts are carried out to achieve the anticipated figures. It all ends with a proclamation by the CC Presidium representing the election results as confirmation of its policies. At the same time, so-called by-elections are called in those few election districts in which a candidate to the local or district national committee was not elected.

The third example of participation of the aktiv in party campaigns is its participation in the anniversary campaign. Every year, party organs approve political-organizational plans for celebration of the liberation of Czechoslovakia and the Russian October Revolution. The report contains slogans expressing the political aims of the celebration, names of speakers (agreed upon at a conference of CC secretaries) in both capital cities, and planned activities (i.e., demonstrations, festive meetings, articles by leading politicians). At the same time, reports are also prepared for the occasion of Press Day, Army Day, Gottwald's birthday, and similar, less significant anniversaries.

Large-scale celebrations take place on the most important occasions, like fifth and tenth anniversaries. On such occasions—e.g., the anniversary of the liberation of Czechoslovakia in 1945—an extensive report is presented, actually two of them. The political conceptions for the celebrations and for propaganda at home and abroad goes to the CC Presidium, and the CC Secretariat approves their political-organizational details. The report is produced by the Ideological Department. Its author requests from extra-party institutions lists of those actions they have decided to carry out within the framework of the celebrations. Their proposals appear in the report as binding tasks to be carried out "through the channel" of ministries, trade unions, cultural institutions, the press, and the party.

The report is received by the ideological departments of the regional committees, which prepare regional plans to provide for the political-organizational aspects of the celebrations with the aid of functionaries of extra-party institutions in the regions. What they do is more or less take over and modify the central plan. As soon as the plan has been approved by the RC presidium, it goes to the district where a party apparatchik breaks it down into its details, which are requested by functionaries of extra-party institutions. The district plan is quite concrete. It specifies what will be carried out "through the channel" of the national committees, schools, libraries, factory clubs, district press, factory newspapers, local radio, the speakers' corps, etc. After approval of the resolution by the DC presidium, the responsible secretary calls together all functionaries to whom the presidium has assigned tasks, in order to "instruct" them about these tasks.

For important anniversaries, work pledges and socialist competitions are organized. Any proposal for such an action will already contain a report and a plan for taking care of the organizational-political aspects of the celebrations. It also approves the orientation of socialist competitions, e.g., economizing in the use of materials or energy, surpassing norms of the economic plan, increasing work productivity, and the like. After the CC Presidium's decision, and having obtained the agreement of the Central Trade Union Organization, the responsible CC department chooses two or three enterprises and sends them a political brigade, which works out "a model pledge" along with enterprise and district functionaries. It is approved by the CC Secretariat and the Central Trade Union Organization and is published in the press along with their appeals. Political brigades then go out to the regions and districts in order to carry through the formulation of their own pledges in selected enterprises and to help in formulating them. The campaign ends with an oversight report for the CC Secretariat concerning the total number and value of the obligations which are represented as proof of the work activity and political activity of the working people.

The fourth example is aktiv participation in ideological campaigns. There are three types of these. One type results from criticism coming from the CC Ideological Department. Members of the power group often consider a low standard of ideological work of party institutions, a low level of citizen consciousness—especially of communists—as the root cause of certain kinds of "negative phenomena," of failure to realize resolutions. A rise in religiosity of citizens, for example, is attributed to the ineffectiveness of atheistic propaganda, a high turnover of worker-members is explained by lack of knowledge of the goals of economic policy, and the like. After such criticism, the leadership of the CC Ideological Department works out plans for a campaign of propaganda and agitation, which additional CC departments, and mainly extra-party institutions, join.

The second type of ideological campaign is instigated by an attack against some ideology. I have already mentioned snap, short-term campaigns. Apart from these, there are also long-term campaigns, e.g., a struggle against bourgeois ideology, against revisionism, nationalism, anticommunism, liberalism, etc. They usually occur after political crises of the regime or internal party crises that are explained as resulting from the influences of hostile ideologies upon the party. These campaigns are also organized by the CC Ideological Department. They are, however, distinguished by a high degree of involvement of members of the central power group and the party intelligentsia. A conference of CC secretaries decides which ism is the cause of the crisis, and thus to be the main target of the campaign. The CC Ideological Department then draws up plans for a large-scale campaign. It will include ideological conferences with meetings of the party aktiv in the central, the regions, and districts. A host of theoretical articles and special publications are put out, and not only by the party publishing house. There are also television and radio programs lecture series, and special themes are adopted into the curricula of party and trade union training institutions, into the party educational system, etc.

The third type of campaign serves as a kind of ideological preparation for an important political campaign—e.g., for the introduction of reforms in the economic management system or changes in policy orientation (after the Twentieth Congress of the CPSU, after Husák's accession to power in April 1969). The CC Presidium approves the subject of a political campaign as an important document (e.g., "Lessons of the Crisis Years 1968–1969"), and the Secretariat approves a plan for carrying out its propaganda-agitational aspects, prepared from the ideological point of view, in conjunction with the responsible CC department. The plan is stereotyped. It calls for large meetings of the aktiv at central headquarters, in the regions, and the districts, and tasks are assigned to extra-party institutions and the mass media. The campaign proceeds from central headquarters downward and ends with the members' meetings of party organizations, as well as of the trade union organizations if need be.

Among the sudden and irregular campaigns there have been, e.g., those connected with the events in Hungary in 1956, in Poland in 1976 and 1980, the wave of criticism in the CPCz in 1956, and Charter 77. The CC Presidium deals with them as the need arises, even holding special sessions when necessary. It discussed the revolts in Hungary and Poland at least once a week on the basis of reports put together from information received from Czechoslovak intelligence, embassies, and press agency and newspaper correspondents and from Soviet political authorities. It ordered that the party aktiv be informed of its point of view without delay. As soon as the instructions are received in the region, the "political aktiv" is immediately convoked, and speakers are sent out to meetings of the district aktiv in which the chairmen of the basic party organizations also participate. (If the instructions arrive during the night, the political service continuously on duty in every secretariat has to inform the secretary about them without delay and, at the same time, pass them on to the districts). For several hours—a day at most—the whole aktiv receives information and guidelines and gives the committees of the basic party organizations, as well as functionaries of extra-party institutions, information about them.

Summary

The most important activity of the power monopoly party is the creation and implementation of decisions and guidelines of the power group, from which the instructions of the apparat originate. For the

TABLE 4.1
Participation of Institutions in Creation and Implementation
of Decisions of the Power Groups

Phase	Decisions having a conceptual character	Decisions having an operational character	Oversight reports	Cadre proposals
1. Preparatory				
source of initiative	group apparat	apparat aktiv	group apparat	apparat aktiv
execution	apparat aktiv	apparat aktiv	apparat aktiv	apparat
2. Decision-making	group	group	group	group
3. Implementation				
interpretation	group apparat	apparat	--	apparat
publicity		aktiv	--	--
implementation	apparat	aktiv		aktiv
4. Oversight	group apparat aktiv	apparat aktiv	group apparat aktiv	apparat

most part, decisions take the form of reports and resolutions that are conceptual and operational in character, oversight reports, and cadre proposals. Their creation and realization, insofar as they stay within the purview of the party, go through four phases:

1. preparation
2. decision
3. implementation
4. oversight

In each phase, the participation of individual party institutions—the holders and executors of power—is different. This process is summarized in Table 4.1.

As should be evident from the above summary, the making and implementing of decisions—from the initiative that gives rise to them to their being put into practice—is a collective affair of all power elements of the party organism. The activity of the party apparat prevails in nearly all phases and is clearly conspicuous throughout the entire process. Only the second phase—decision making—is completely dominated by the power group. The party aktiv is represented—as the extended arm of the apparat—in most phases, most strongly in the implementation phase.

The three power elements do not always have the same views as to the solution of matters dealt with. They proceed from divergent experiences, and their proposals often do not agree. Nor are their interpretation and implementation of resolutions consistent. For the most part, these differences are not great. Nevertheless, they are manifested in party decisions and their implementation, in enforcing the unified will of the power group, as well as in the confrontation of the three power elements, which are even more differentiated internally.

Notes

1. During the events in Hungary in 1956, the regional and district "political aktiv," for example, met every second day in order to receive information and interpretation from central headquarters.

2. At the beginning of the sixties, during a period of economic crisis in Czechoslovakia, the communist leadership made use of a thesis worked out by a group of members of the party intelligentsia concerning the scientific-technical revolution. They made an ideological formula out of it, according to which the scientific-technical revolution in production, and the regulation of its consequences in social relations, were held to be the only way out of the crisis. All propaganda supported such a view, and functionaries put all their hopes in this notion of the scientific-technical revolution, and expected a miracle. The real causes of the crisis were completely different, lying in the structure of the economy, in organization, and the way it was administered.

5

External Influences

External factors frequently give rise to, influence, and predetermine decisions of the central power group. The country's membership in the Soviet bloc and its organizations—the Warsaw Pact and COMECON—and membership in the international communist movement, which is dominated by the Soviets, are especially strong influences.

Relations with communist parties of Soviet bloc countries take several forms. In addition to bilateral discussions between delegations, study delegations consisting of party apparatchiks are exchanged on the basis of agreements. Although these visits are formal in character, the level of international activity is assessed, even in Moscow, according to the number of them.

Ambassadors and high officials of Soviet bloc representative agencies play an important role. Ambassadors usually keep in touch with CC secretaries and heads of CC departments, and may, in exceptional cases, visit the general secretary. Other diplomats maintain relations with other high officials of the CC International Department. They pass on party information and the views of the leadership of their party on various issues, as well as complaints, requests, and proposals, and also receive such information from Czechoslovak sources. This is the way party intervention takes place when state and economic institutions cannot agree. (Such sources may include, for example, complaints that certain enterprises are not making deliveries according to contract or requests to increase exports of certain goods, or complaints about an unwillingness of trade representatives to incorporate items into a contract in the amounts requested.) In exceptional and urgent cases, reports and interventions are addressed to the general secretary or the party leadership. Ambassadors always transmit official letters of their party leaderships to the general secretary alone, who informs the CC Presidium about them. The answer goes back the same way, i.e., through the ambassador.

Diplomatic representatives of Soviet bloc countries also adhere to diplomatic protocol with regard to high officials of the party apparat. Every ambassador makes courtesy calls on CC secretaries and heads of departments when he takes up and leaves his post, as well as when a new CC secretary or head of department is appointed.

These visits are not restricted to formalities but often afford occasion for discussion "according to the party line" of the fulfillment of cultural and economic treaties concluded between the two states.

Most important is the relationship between the communist parties of Czechoslovakia and the Soviet Union, which can be characterized simply as subordination of Prague to Moscow. In the communist power system, this subordination goes beyond relationships between two parties and has significant influence in the life of society as a whole.

Subordination to Moscow is not and never has been a one-sided relationship, consisting solely of pressure from Moscow and fear of it. High- and low-level functionaries also subordinate themselves voluntarily, consciously, and purposefully. Their motives vary. Most low-level functionaries automatically accept Soviet views as correct without even reflecting on them since, among other things, these views are presented to them as right by their own leading comrades. Others regard agreement with Moscow as an integral part of the cadre profile of a functionary and as a necessary condition for career advancement. And there are always those who once had the kind of ideological and emotional bond to the USSR that prevailed during the 1950s, a bond that has been replaced by conviction that subordination to Moscow is a consequence of the integration of the Czechoslovak state into the Soviet power bloc.

Furthermore, high officials internalize subordination to Moscow as a firmly anchored ideological formula—the result of years of experience. For the old guard, which experienced the training and practice of the Comintern, this relationship has been a law of the communist movement. They have known that to violate it meant certain political damnation and liquidation. They didn't dare question even the most insignificant of Soviet policy moves, even among themselves. Only after Stalin's death did they venture to criticize some Soviet-inspired actions. The Comintern men were replaced, but the ideological formula remained, since their successors acquired their own, what might be called "old-new," experiences. These experience incline them as well to self-subordination. They know that subordination pays, and that disobedience is avenged and punished. They also know that Moscow doesn't forget, that its fingers have a long reach, and that not only their political careers but also their social fortunes depend on it. Furthermore, the relationships of subordination constantly reproduce themselves in new circumstances. Functionaries inherit them from their predecessors and bequeath them to their successors. This relay baton is taken up even by functionaries who have reservations about Soviet policy and take offense at the subordination itself, as well as at the forms it takes.

From 1948 to 1955, i.e., during the period of Moscow's distrust of high officials of the bloc states, subordination took on its crudest forms, amounting to total degradation of the sovereignty of national organs. It was carried out under strict instructions from Moscow, by means of a network of advisers and organs of international organizations dominated by the Soviets. Beginning in 1955, the number and importance of advisers decreased sharply, and direct instructions receded into the background. Khrushchev went over to sending various kinds of information and proposals to the general secretary in Prague and the organizing international conferences and bilateral discussions among party delegations and to increasing the importance of the organs of international organizations (COMECON and the Warsaw Pact). The rights of the other states were broadened, and although the leading role of the Soviet Union was maintained, it came to rely increasingly on its economic and power supremacy.

Over a period of ten years, the bond of rigid subordination and the crass forms it took during the Stalin era relaxed to such an extent that Czechoslovak high officials began to get the impression that they were free to make decisions on their own. Many members of the CC Presidium attributed this to merits of General Secretary Novotný. Either the ideological formula prevented them from understanding the decisive factor in the existing relationship, or they were afraid to understand it: The Soviet Union and its policies, past and present, could not be criticized and functionaries could not question their rightness. After the Soviet occupation of Czechoslovakia (August 1968), the bond of direct subordination to Moscow once again grew stronger. The presence of the Soviet army in the country has reinforced this bond, as has the so-called Prague Spring complex. Fear of a revival of the ideas of the Prague Spring encourages high officials to defend Soviet leadership. There has also been increased Soviet scrutiny of Czechoslovak affairs and intense competition among functionaries in Prague to maintain and increase Moscow's confidence.

The main forms of relations between both parties have become well established over the last thirty years. Through them flow information, recommendations, views, warnings, and instructions from Moscow and, in the other direction, inquiries, and requests for consultation, advice, evaluations, and assistance. These linkages take the form of meetings of organs and functionaries—official as well as unofficial. They include face-to-face as well as written exchanges and are arranged by the ambassadors and the party apparat.

As a matter of principle, neither members of the Soviet leadership nor the Soviet ambassador participates in meetings of the CC Presidium or other party organs. When, during a visit, the general secretary or members of the CC Presidium of the CPSU hold discussions with members of the Prague leadership, these are always called discussions, talks, or consultations. They are never billed as meetings of official bodies and are not archived as such either. The minutes of such meetings show that Czechoslovak participants try, by asking questions, to obtain advice and recommendations from their Soviet comrades. Or the Muscovites try to find out the views of their Prague comrades, so as to get an overview of the situation. They also make critical remarks about their policies.

Conferences of delegations representing the leaderships of both parties are a common and official form of relations. Most of these are formal in character and are limited to exchanges of information on the domestic political situation and views on international affairs. They are usually held according to plans prepared in advance, or at times when Moscow is changing its policies and is trying to obtain support from the other parties. The general secretary, who is the head of the delegation, has the CC Presidium approve the theses of his speech, and he informs it of the results of his discussions.

In extraordinary cases the CC presidia of both parties meet. The Soviet leadership usually calls the Czechoslovak leadership "on the carpet" when conflicts crop up among its members or when Moscow shows dissatisfaction with its political actions. Moscow acts as prosecutor and judge in cases of internal conflict. It acts very harshly, especially against those elements of the Prague leadership who are the targets of its reprimands. These are cases in which some functionaries have to be supported against others. Moscow may also send high-level functionaries to resolve conflicts in the leaderships of Soviet bloc parties. In especially serious cases, the general secretary himself goes. Such discussions are almost always very heated.

Impromptu meetings are also held in times of political crisis in one of the countries of the bloc (e.g., in 1956 in Hungary, 1968 in Czechoslovakia, 1980 in Poland). Moscow organizes such meetings as "conferences of parties of countries of the Soviet bloc" and uses them to exert pressure on the party under criticism.

Meetings of general secretaries are like state visits, with all incumbent honors, courtesies, and formalities. However, meetings in Moscow requested by the Czechoslovak general secretary, without a proper invitation and without the agreement of the CC Presidium, are quite different in character. The general secretary will request such a meeting when he needs to win Soviet support for his views against other members of the leadership (e.g., Novotný in 1967, Dubček in November 1968, Husák in 1978).

More recently Brezhnev introduced the practice of individual annual meetings with the general secretaries of Soviet bloc parties during vacations in the Crimea. Meetings had already been held in this resort area under Stalin and Khrushchev, but Brezhnev regularized them and gave them an official form, i.e., the press makes reference to them, and the views of the party leadership on their results are made public. Their significance, however, is no greater than that of ordinary meetings of general secretaries.

Members of the central power group are also invited personally to vacation in the USSR each year. If someone doesn't get an invitation, this is considered an expression of Moscow's mistrust or loss of confidence. The leaderships of other Soviet bloc countries also invite a certain number of high-level functionaries to vacation in their recreational facilities. Their selection is approved by the CC Secretariat.

Moscow also makes use of its supremacy in such international organizations as COMECON, the Warsaw Pact, the World Federation of Trade Unions, the International Youth Organization, students organizations, women's organizations, the organization of participants in the resistance, and the World Peace Council. At meetings of these organizations as well as at unofficial meetings of military personnel, COMECON officials, sport institutions, and mass organizations, Soviet comments, reprimands, critical remarks, allusions, and expressions of lack of understanding and surprise directed at Czechoslovak policies or the situation there can be heard. Whoever hears them writes a memorandum for the Central Secretariat of their party. These memos go as far as the general secretary's office and are regarded as Moscow's official point of view. The same goes for the views and remarks of Soviet functionaries who take part in various celebrations, cures, study delegations, and congresses of mass organizations in Czechoslovakia, as well as information obtained by high-level Czechoslovak officials during official visits in Moscow. The author of the memorandum for the Prague Secretariat assumes that the reprimands he has heard will also be included in the report the Soviet delegation submits to its own superiors.

After the departure of Soviet advisers the practice of consultations spread. The Prague leadership turns to Moscow officially with requests for advice, attitudes, and views regarding measures under preparation. The CC Presidium makes a decision on every case to be submitted in this way and sends a letter to the Soviet leadership. These are

consultations concerning economic matters, attitudes on important domestic measures, on international political measures, even measures of
lesser significance (e.g., the sale of weapons to this or that country,
rehabilitation of victims of political trials, or international relations
with socialist countries). Moscow's responses are treated as binding
guidelines. In 1954, the Soviet leadership started to send information
to Prague that was primarily in the realm of international politics—
e.g., on correspondence with U.S. President Eisenhower, regarding discussions with Tito or English Labourites, about disagreements with
China or Albania, about the contents of the indictment against L. P.
Beria, about the faction of V. M. Molotov and company, etc.

Telephone contacts are very frequent. The general secretary has a
direct line to his Soviet counterpart, and as I have already noted, he
monopolizes the relationship with the entire Soviet leadership. As far
as telephone contacts between employees of the Central Secretariat and
the corresponding offices in Moscow are concerned, only CC secretaries
are allowed to call, and this only with the permission of the general
secretary. Heads of CC departments may deal with matters having to
do with the Soviets only through the USSR section of the International
Department, which also transmits messages and requests to Moscow.

Most current information, messages, guidelines, proposals, and queries, as well as responses to them, flow through the section of the
International Department of both parties and the embassies of both
countries responsible for the other. The Czechoslovakia-Poland section
of the CPSU CC plays a significant role in the relations of both parties.
It follows domestic political affairs in Czechoslovakia carefully—the
activity of the party, the contents of the press, culture, scholarly activity,
in short, everything. It gets its information from reports of the Soviet
embassy in Prague and from party materials (members of the Czechoslovak communist leadership point out that the Soviet embassy knows
everything about their party). Other sources are the Soviet KGB, which
has an extensive espionage agency in Czechoslovakia, and liaison officers in the Ministry of the Interior, Soviet military officials in Czechoslovakia, and the Ministry of Foreign Affairs. The section prepares
reports on the situation in Czechoslovakia for high officials in Moscow
and takes part in the realization of Soviet interests in Czechoslovakia.

The Soviet section in the Prague Central Secretariat maintains relations with its counterpart in Moscow, the Soviet embassy, and the
Soviet section of the Prague Ministry of Foreign Affairs. The most
important aspect of its work from the political point of view is the
gathering of queries, requests, and mainly complaints, reprimands, and
criticisms that come in from Soviet institutions. It passes some of

these on to CC secretaries and heads of departments and takes care of others itself.

The Soviet embassy is more than a mere intermediary in relations between Moscow and Prague. Its ambassador transmits to the general secretary not only information from the Kremlin but mainly his own views and critical remarks, primarily concerning the domestic political situation and events in Czechoslovakia. And the ambassador also lets other members of the power group know his views at celebrations, receptions, and during "official visits." As far as I can tell from the few letters and minutes of the ambassador's interpretation I have read, they tend to be very sharp and are surprisingly full of details that the Prague leadership either doesn't know or doesn't ascribe any importance to. These comments are treated as the official Soviet position. They are taken care of, and sometimes a response to them is sent to Moscow.

Soviet embassy officials maintain relations with functionaries in the CC International Department. The embassy official in charge of relations with the party has the most intense relations. He keeps the leadership of the International Department informed of significant international and domestic political decisions of the USSR, and he requests and receives information from the International Department about the internal life of the party, the economy, culture, the Czechoslovak position on international affairs, etc. On the other hand, he is asked about the Soviet leadership's position on current international issues. Reservations expressed by Soviet embassy officials to high officials of the International Department or some other CC department are of particular political significance. These may be official as well as personal evaluations of various phenomena of Czechoslovak life that the Soviets view as negative, as threatening to the socialist regime and its ties of alliance. They draw attention to articles in the press, activities of cultural institutions—television, film, theater—to scholarly publications, the low level of enthusiasm of the population toward certain Soviet citizens, weak pro-Soviet propaganda, relations between Czechs and Slovaks, an increase in religiosity, or the behavior of Czechoslovak citizens in the Soviet Union. Records of all these conversations are made for the CC secretary. He decides what is to be done about them, which means, in most cases, that he has the comments investigated and the situation rectified.

Unofficial, personal, behind-the-scenes contacts constitute a special chapter in relations between the two parties. The KGB provides Moscow with information it has received from its collaborators about the situation in the Prague leadership and about individual functionaries. Furthermore, some Czechoslovak high officials send complaints through the Soviet embassy. According to an agreement between the two parties on transmission of correspondence, the Czechoslovak general secretary receives copies of them. This happened, for example, to Július Ďuriš, Barák, and Husák. Czechoslovak high officials also take advantage of official visits in Moscow to register complaints. For example, Ďuriš complained about Slánský in 1950; Novotný about Zápotocký in 1953 and, together with Barák, against Široký when they made arrangements in Moscow for Novotný to be elected president; and Biľak complained about Dubček in 1968-1969. According to Široký, Moscow likes to hear such complaints. Moreover, Moscow will even instigate campaigns against those they would like to get rid of. In 1954-56, Khrushchev led campaigns against Čepička and Zápotocký. In 1962, a KGB group tried to attack Novotný through Barák. In 1968-1969, there was a campaign against Josef Smrkovský, František Kriegel, Dubček, and others among their political friends. The men of the Kremlin are noted for the cavalier and shameless way they deal with those high officials of states belonging to their bloc who "have caught their eye." Stalin made sarcastic remarks about Zápotocký. Khrushchev also insulted him and behaved similarly toward Čepička. Brezhnev and his group made insulting remarks about Smrkovský and Kriegel.

Not all decisions made in Prague are preceded by Moscow's approval. There exists such a degree of synchronization of views between the leaderships of both parties that it isn't necessary for Moscow to control everything. High officials in Prague anticipate or sense Soviet attitudes and have learned to "hear the grass grow," i.e., to get a sense for what is new in Moscow and how this or that matter would be dealt with there. And Moscow also has ample means for realizing its interests easily after the fact in those cases in which Prague has already made a decision. It suffices for the Soviet officials to make a comment, indicate doubt, shrug their shoulders for a change to ensue in Prague. On balance, Moscow thus allows some limited scope within which Prague can exercise its own initiative. Nevertheless, the extent to which this is taken advantage of depends on the courage and interests of Czechoslovak politicians. Over a period of thirty years, this was attempted only for a short period of time during the second half of the sixties.

The Czechoslovak leadership discusses all of the more significant domestic political, economic, and cultural matters with Moscow—in particular, changes in policy line under preparation, basic problems relating to the party congress, tasks of the five-year plan, and sometimes internal party affairs, mainly party rules. If political changes give rise to conflicts, or even differences of opinion within the top leadership, the Soviets are asked to play the role of arbitrator—if they don't decide on their own initiative to take on this role.

All actions in the domain of foreign policy are coordinated with Moscow. Either Prague waits for the USSR to take a position on a given issue, or it asks for Moscow's views and adapts the Czechoslovak position accordingly. For the most part, international documents and points of view are made public only after they have been published in Moscow. Their importance—the extent to which the documents are published, their placement in the newspapers, the times of their broadcast on radio and television, and the way they are to be commented on—can be established according to this model. No significant international agreements are concluded without asking Moscow.

Almost all important military issues are decided by the Prague leadership on the basis of prior consent of the Warsaw Pact liaison officer in the Prague Ministry of Defence or the Soviet General Staff. This is true whether the issue involves the number of military personnel, weapons for the army, or the work and tasks of the arms industry.

In matters having to do with security and its activities, Moscow is usually consulted only in those cases in which international reaction to the security measures under preparation is anticipated. This is usually done by a telephone query from the general secretary to his Soviet counterpart. Relations in this area are somewhat more complicated. There is, at the Ministry of the Interior, a so-called liaison officer, a kind of remnant of the Soviet advisers of the fifties, who sends reports on the activities of Czechoslovak security to his headquarters. Reservations or disagreement with measures taken come from him.

In economic matters, Prague consults Moscow through party channels on its conception for long-term development. It asks Moscow for the views of Soviet experts and politicians regarding specific economic measures, such as the construction of large factories, arms production, trade with the West, and obtaining foreign credits. Moscow intervenes frequently in matters of arms production when Czechoslovakia hasn't met Soviet orders or when it asks for aid in the form of additional supplies of Soviet raw materials or in the granting of loans and more favorable repayment conditions. On such occasions, Soviet functionaries intervene with their analyses of the Czechoslovak economy and draw attention to incorrect decisions and various inadequacies in the management of the economy.

As for cultural affairs, I have already noted that the Soviet embassy in Prague follows the press, cultural programs, radio, television, and publishing. It alerts the appropriate Central Secretariat department to phenomena it views as negative, a CC secretary if need be, or very rarely, in especially serious cases, the general secretary.

During the first half of the fifties, Moscow intervened routinely in all appointments to the high-level party and state positions. Even now, the general secretary consults Moscow, not, however, as a hard and fast rule, but on his own initiative, as a preventative measure. In many cases this is more a query about Moscow's views than a request for prior approval, even though these views are treated as decisive. Such queries relate to all members of the power group and their state positions. For positions at the level of minister, the general secretary provides information about those individuals he wants to nominate. If some objection is heard in Moscow or at the Soviet embassy, the nomination is not put forward. Only for appointments in the Ministries of the Interior, Defense, and Foreign Affairs, the intelligence service, as chief of the general staff, or deputy minister of the interior for State Security is prior approval from the appropriate Soviet institution necessary. Insofar as the party apparat is concerned, information is provided on appointments of heads of CC departments and RC leading secretaries.

Above all, in cadre matters, Moscow has adequate means to bring about changes, even after an official has been appointed. It is usually sufficient for Moscow to hint at a lack of confidence. If this is not enough, criticism follows (e.g., in 1954 in the Čepička case and in 1968–1969 with Dubček and Smrkovský), or an official's Soviet counterpart will refuse to deal with him (as happened, e.g., to Ludvík Svoboda in 1949–1950, Slánský in 1957, Barák in 1961, and Dubček and Kriegel in 1968). Under such circumstances, his departure is inevitable. Only when even this does not suffice do Soviet officials publicly criticize officials they have decided to "remove," e.g., Smrkovský, Václav Prchlík, Josef Pavel, Kriegel, Jiří Hájek, and Dubček in 1968–1969.

Instead of a Conclusion

The communist party, as the nervous system of a power monopoly, is an organism made up of a chain of links of power and the powerless, containing hidden as well as publicly-expressed differences and conflicting interests and opinions. Nevertheless, the party operates in a way that assures its role as the most significant instrument for maintenance of the absolute domination of a small group of functionaries over society. Three bonds—ideological, social, and power interests—not only hold the party together, they are also the source of its activity, of its component parts contributing to the domination of society. The effectiveness of the ideological bond is limited and is continually growing weaker. The influence of the other two bonds is stronger. Particularly influential are the differentiated privileges bound up with party membership and the functions one exercises. All members, as well as low-level and passive functionaries, are protected from the persecution to which the majority of inhabitants is subjected. All functionaries who participate in the exercise of power and in decision making and who make up the core and backbone of the party are socially dependent on it—members of the smaller part "solely due to the fact" that they cannot practice their professions without the party's consent. However, the absolute majority consists of those who have attained and maintain their positions and the power that goes along with those positions thanks to the party alone. Their careers and social status are directly tied to the party and its power monopoly. It is they, first and foremost, who assure fulfillment of the party's power mission.

The party's internal life is guided by routines and long years of experience, generally called "the principles of construction of a party of the Leninist type." These principles determine the hierarchy of unconditional subordination of lower-level components and functionaries to their superiors and the tasks and authority of individual power institutions. To those without power falls the insignificant role of belonging to the democratic facade of this undemocratic organization.

During the period of the Prague Spring in 1968–1969, the communist party suddenly began to change. Members and functionaries called for democratization and thereby violated fundamentally what had, until then, been hard and fast principles. In addition to changes that occurred on their own momentum, intentional changes were also realized, which were most strongly expressed in the proposed new party statutes.

The point of departure for all changes carried out and proposed was the new position of the party in society and in the power system. It was to function as a genuine political factor, as the instigator of political decisions and maker of general political guidelines, rather than as an institution of centralized, directive management and decision making in all matters having to do with the state as an institution, "by which it makes decisions regarding every move of every member of society." From this there emerged a new power mechanism distinguished by many characteristics of political pluralism, in which the party had a position "that made possible control of power on the basis of partnership and opposition, competition of ideas and people." Extra-party institutions acquired a broad scope for self-realization in society, as well as in the power mechanism, and their autonomy and responsibility were increased.

The new social position of the party was manifest in several ways in its internal life. It opened itself up to control by the populace and began to implement effective control of higher-level organs and officials by lower levels and by the membership. Lively discussion started up in the party, election of organs by secret ballot was introduced, reports on meetings of central and regional party organs were published regularly. Not only did differences of opinion, previously not allowed in the party, become a natural phenomenon, but the proposed party rules made it possible for members to maintain views that differed from adopted resolutions and to call for revision of decisions on the basis of experience.

The rigid subordination of all functionaries to the power group and its apparat was also loosened. They were to be responsible in the exercise of their functions not only to "the party," but first and foremost to those citizens and the members of those institutions that had elected them. Functionaries were, in the exercise of their responsibilities, to be bound to those party decisions that support the constitution and the laws. The social dependency of members and functionaries on the party also decreased markedly as a result of changes in cadre policy. The cadre nomenklatura was abolished, and the range of positions requiring approval of party organs for appointment narrowed considerably. A reorganization of the party apparat was in preparation that would have made it deal primarily with the party's internal life and preparation of political decisions of party organs. It was to abandon its role of "shadow apparat," directing and replacing the apparats of extra-party institutions. It was to concentrate on preparing analyses of general problems of social life, to carry out sociological studies, and to obtain proposals for solutions to problems placed in perspective.

Efforts to transform the life of the party and break its old routines appeared not only at the central level but also in the districts and regions. Experiments were tried and efforts made to increase the authority of elected party organs and transform the apparat. In the central, a manual of procedures for the CC, an outline of tasks and activities of the CC and its organs, and other studies were produced. The process of regeneration of the party and attempts to transform it into a living organism came to a halt after the occupation of Czechoslovakia in August 1968, and ended definitively after the accession to power of the Husák leadership in April 1969. The party returned to its previous position in society (to its old methods of enforcing its leading role) and to old forms of internal party organization and life routines.

The Czechoslovak experiment again confirmed that change in the party is, in the final analysis, dependent on its social mission, i.e., the transformation of social reality. Internal party life and its routines are so conservative and deeply rooted and mainly so accommodating to the power group, that they prevent any attempt at change. The idea that a new generation of communists will "revolutionize the party" is not very realistic. More than 40 percent of all members entered the party in the seventies, but this new blood flows in old veins, and it flows in them obediently. The new people fall into a stream whose movement is brought about by old-new motives.

The new join the party either because they are recommended by the youth organization, because they come from a communist family, because they want to make a career, or because a committee picks them and entices or forces them to join. A candidate and beginning member has to "earn" his membership by holding a position in an extra-party institution. There he has to defend and carry out party policy in order to prove himself. Those who demonstrate this ability are classified into cadre reserves and nominated to high positions— in enterprises, in the districts—in order to carry out party policies there according to the wishes and instructions of the high authorities. Those who prove themselves especially well obtain paid functions in extra-party institutions, with some individuals going into the party apparat.

Each further step—to the region and the central, to the power apparat or some representative function—increases dependency on the party's policies of the day. Each "move upward" binds the functionary all the more firmly to the party—ideologically and socially. Furthermore, entry into the power structure automatically requires subordination to the routine and rhythm of its life. It determines the interests of individuals as well as their taste for power. On the way up, the member gradually turns into the functionary, who differs from the person seeking membership in his way of thinking, interests, and social status. Each new generation of members, in addition to quickly producing a multitude of passive members, always supplies enough obedient ones—carriers, wielders, and servants of power—to fill vacant positions in the power mechanism. And there are still many more waiting in reserve for the occasion to arise.

Appendixes

APPENDIX 1
Structure of the Party Apparat I: District Level

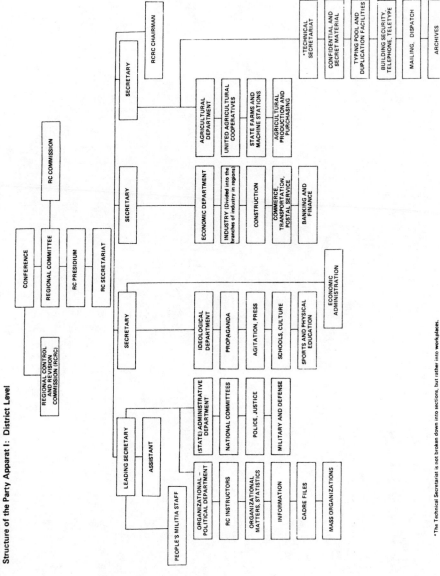

*The Technical Secretariat is not broken down into sections, but rather into workplaces.

APPENDIX 2
Structure of the Party Apparat II: Regional Level

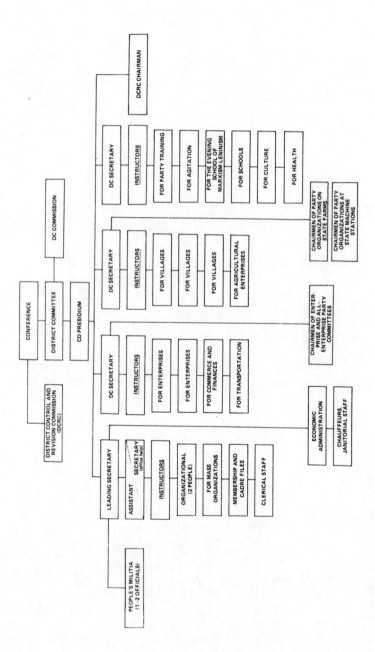

217

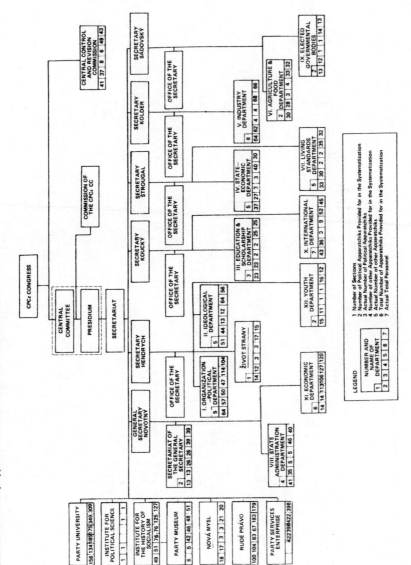

APPENDIX 3
Structure of the Party Apparat III: Central Committee (as of 31 December 1967)

APPENDIX 4
Structure of the CC Ideological Department (1965)

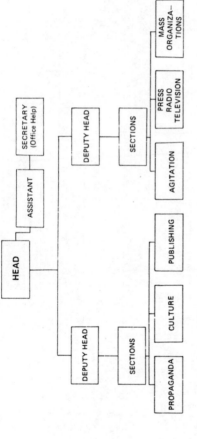

Structure of the State-Administrative Department (1965)

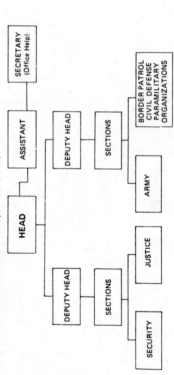

APPENDIX 5

SECTIONS OF THE IDEOLOGICAL DEPARTMENT (1965)

PROPAGANDA SECTION:

head of section

officials

    for party live-in schools
    for party education---lower levels
    for party education--higher
    for the University of Marxism-Leninism
    for political campaigns
    for international relations
    for economics
    for the party history and organization
    for philosophy and sociology
    for political science, state, and law
    for counterpropaganda
    for church-related questions
    readers

PRESS, RADIO, AND TELEVISION SECTION:

head of section (runs the press office)

officials

    for central daily newspapers
    for central weekly newspapers
    for the regional press
    for the local, enterprise, district press
    for the state radio
    for television

PUBLISHING SECTION

head of section (oversees party publishing houses)

officials

    for technical, scientific, pedagogical, and
        agricultural publishing houses
    for artistic publishing houses (belles
        lettres, children's literature, writers'
        union, graphic and plastic artists, etc.)
    for other areas of publishing (specialized
        literature, trade unions, sports, the
        army, non-communist parties)
    for regional publishing houses and printing
    enterprises

AGITATION SECTION:

head of section

officials

    for agitational work in industry and commerce
        (including enterprise radio stations,
        flyers)
    for agitational work in agriculture,
        communities and cities (community
        publications, radio)
    for opinion agitation
    for organization of celebrations, festivities,
        funerals of party high-officials
    for publication of printed matter for
        agitation, including wall-newspapers
    editor of the magazine Na pomoc agitator
    editorial assistant
    creative artist
    photographer

MASS ORGANIZATION SECTION:

head of section

officials

    for sport and physical education organizations
    for the women's organization
    for the union of Czechoslovak-Soviet
        friendship and for the organization of
        anti-fascist fighters

APPENDIX 6

Budget of CPCz Organs and Institutions in the Years 1967 and 1968

in thousands of Czechsoslovak Crowns (Kcs)

INCOME	1967	1968
Membership dues	318,759.6	351,133.5
Other receipts	25,342.2	30,064.5
Levies on party enterprises	39,500.0	44,500.0
Levies on regional party periodicals	23,482.9	22,675.9
Total income	407,064.7	448,373.9

EXPENDITURES		
Agitation, training, meetings	52,564.3	56,365.0
Salaries	212,729.6	246,929.6
Subsistence for those studying	27,845.5	12,566.5
International relations	22,612.1	19,405.3
Organizational expenses	94,108.8	118,269.1
Honoraria	732.3	1,107.8
Meals	8,934.0	8,713.0
Investments	60,113.3	82,506.9
Peoples' Militia	17,315.4	18,882.5
Subsidies to basic organizations	31,277.5	34,411.6
Total expenditures	528,232.8	599,157.0

For the first time in ten years the CPCz budget for the years 1967 and 1968 was in a deficit position due to exceptional special expenditures resulting from the internal crisis in the party. After 1970 the budget was again balanced.

About the Editor

Fred Eidlin is associate professor in the Department of Political Studies at the University of Guelph (Ontario, Canada). He studied at Dartmouth College, l'Institut d'Etudes Politiques de l'Université de Paris, Freie Universität Berlin, and Indiana University and received his doctorate in political science from the University of Toronto. From late 1968 to late 1969 he was a researcher specializing in Czechoslovak affairs at Radio Free Europe in Munich. He is the author of *The Logic of 'Normalization': The Soviet Intervention in Czechoslovakia of 21 August 1968 and the Czechoslovak Response,* as well as numerous papers and articles on Czechoslovak politics, problems in the study of Soviet-type regimes, and problems of social and political inquiry. He has edited *Constitutional Democracy: Essays in Comparative Politics* and the *Newsletter for Those Interested in the Philosophy of Karl Popper* and cotranslated Ota Sik's *For A Humane Economic Democracy.*

Index